TRENDS IN LEARNING RESEARCH

TRENDS IN LEARNING RESEARCH

SAMUEL N. HOGAN
EDITOR

CMC
Carroll College Library
Waukesha, WI 53186
Nova Science Publishers, Inc.
New York

NOTICE TO THE READER

The Publisher has taken reasonable care in the preparation of this book, but makes no expressed or implied warranty of any kind and assumes no responsibility for any errors or omissions. No liability is assumed for incidental or consequential damages in connection with or arising out of information contained in this book. The Publisher shall not be liable for any special, consequential, or exemplary damages resulting, in whole or in part, from the readers' use of, or reliance upon, this material.

This publication is designed to provide accurate and authoritative information with regard to the subject matter covered herein. It is sold with the clear understanding that the Publisher is not engaged in rendering legal or any other professional services. If legal or any other expert assistance is required, the services of a competent person should be sought. FROM A DECLARATION OF PARTICIPANTS JOINTLY ADOPTED BY A COMMITTEE OF THE AMERICAN BAR ASSOCIATION AND A COMMITTEE OF PUBLISHERS.

LIBRARY OF CONGRESS CATALOGING-IN-PUBLICATION DATA
Trends in learning research / Samuel N. Hogan, editor.
    p. cm.
Includes bibliographical references and index.
ISBN 1-59454-965-6
1. Learning, Psychology of. I. Hogan, Samuel N.
BF318.T74   2006
153.1'5--dc22   2005037263

Published by Nova Science Publishers, Inc. ✦ New York

CONTENTS

PREFACE

Learning as used here, refers to concerted activity that increases the capacity and willingness of individuals, groups, organizations and communities to acquire and productively apply new knowledge and skills, to grow and mature and to adapt successfully to changes and challenges. Such learning empowers individuals and organizations to make wise choices, solve problems and break new ground. In particular, it is sustainable, it is a lifelong, renewable process for people and for the institutions that serves people. Learning certainly includes academic studies and occupational training through high school and beyond but also encompasses the physical, cognitive, emotional and social development of children in the earliest years of their lives. This book presents new research in this explosive field.

The brain renin-angiotensin system (RAS) is best known for regulating blood pressure, body water balance, cyclicity of reproductive hormones/sexual behaviors, and pituitary gland hormones. These classic physiologies and behaviors appear to be mediated by the angiotensin II (AngII)/AT_1 receptor subtype system as described in chapter 1. A second angiotensin receptor subtype, AT_2, is maximally expressed during fetal development and is down-regulated in the adult. The AT_2 subtype opposes growth responses facilitated by the AT_1 receptor as well as growth factor receptors. Recent evidence suggests important contributions by a third angiotensin receptor subtype, AT_4, to non-classic RAS physiologies including the regulation of blood flow, modulation of exploratory behaviors, and facilitation of learning acquisition and memory consolidation. This angiotensin IV (AngIV)/AT_4 system appears to interact with brain matrix metalloproteinases to modify extracellular matrix molecules thus permitting the neural plasticity presumed to underlie memory consolidation, reconsolidation, and retrieval. Neural plasticity appears to be activated by facilitated activity, such as long-term potentiation, in several brain structures particularly entorhinal cortex, hippocampus, medial temporal lobe and prefrontal cortex. The contributions of the angiotensinergic and cholinergic systems to synaptic reconfiguration are discussed, however the specific details of this relationship have yet to be delineated.

Reading and writing are complex cognitive activities that are indispensable for adequate functioning in society. To enter the literate society of today students must know how to learn from reading and how to communicate while writing. Recent data indicates that a third of the student population manifest low levels of learning to comprehend and write. Such evidence emphasizes the need to develop effective learning environments that will promote student literacy. According to contemporary theory language plays a major role in education, not only as a subject in the curriculum but mainly as the medium through which meaning is shared and learning and teaching are carried out. Knowledge emerges from the interaction of voices therefore learning involves both individual interpretation and negotiation with others. Hence, discourse plays a crucial mediational role in learning as it allows for new understandings to be negotiated among participants. This implies that literacy is best acquired while learning in depth content that engages students in thoughtful reading, writing and discussion The reported studies in chapter 2 translate the above assertions into practice by applying a progressive instructional model designed to include opportunities for learning through negotiation. The instructional model integrates socio-cognitive learning principles and activities in a problem-based environment geared to teach literacy. The reported studies examine the efficacy of the instructional model in fostering reading comprehension and writing competence. The studies situated in junior high school language art classes compare between students engaged in guided inquiry within communities of discourse to students who were exposed to traditional methods of literacy instruction. Quantitative and qualitative methods of analysis are applied to trace the contextual features within the learning environment that promote literacy learning. Findings suggest that designing a learning environment in which students and teachers mediate and negotiate meaning while co-constructing their knowledge provides the context in which students develop cognitive tools for comprehension and generation of text.

Writing is a complex process requiring visual memory, attention, phonological and semantic operations and motor performance. For that reason, it can easily be disturbed by interfering with attention, memory, by interfering subvocalization, and so on as described in chapter 3. Using 23 female third-year students (23.4 ± 0.78 years old) from the University of Trieste, the authors investigated the production of errors in three experimental conditions (control, articulatory suppression and tapping). In the articulatory suppression condition, the participants produced significantly more linguistic impairments (such as agrammatism, unrelated substitutions, sentence omissions, and semantically deviant sentences), which are similar to linguistic impairments found in aphasia. On the tapping condition there were more perseverations, deletions, and substitutions, both of letters and of words. They then have considered 50 patients suffering from Alzheimer's Disease (CDR average' score=1.76±0.56): they evaluated their writing production, in the spontaneous, under dictation and on copy tasks. The authors collected the samples and analysed their production, with the same schema of mistake' classification score. They compared the results, and try to find a correlation with specific items of the AD population. These data suggest that writing is not an automatic skill. Only after many years of experience and practice of processing information (through cortical subcortical channels) can writing be considered an automatic skill. Limited experimental conditions can disrupt the writing system in normal subjects, probably interfering with the cortical subcortical loops, and link normality to pathology. In neurodegeneration, such as in Alzheimer' Disease, writing is precociously impaired and the disruption is early macroscopically evident.

In chapter 4, the authors make an overview of the literature on the learning styles, approaches to studying and the role of gender and handedness on second language (L2) learning and they report the findings from a three-fold research they undertook at the university of Thessaly in a sample of 452 undergraduate students. In the first part of the research they investigated the influence of gender, handedness and faculty choice on the performance of phonological, syntactical and semantic tasks in L2. In the second part they examined further how Greek students' approaches to studying in combination with gender, academic discipline and professional degree in English affect performance on verbal fluency tasks in English as a second language. In the third part of the research they investigated the relationship between Greek students' learning styles and performance in English phonological, syntactic and semantic tasks, in combination with their gender and discipline. The results showed that handedness alone did not influence the students' performance on L2 tasks. Gender was found to play an important role in the results with females performing better than males in both syntax and semantics. Approaches to studying alone or in combination with students' gender and professional degree in L2 influenced students' performance on syntactical L2 tasks, in which they used a deep or strategic approach, but not on phonological or semantic ones. Concerning learning styles, the study revealed that university students have a tendency to prefer a divergent learning style while performing phonological and semantic tasks and an accommodative learning style while performing syntactical tasks in L2. In conclusion, our research findings suggest that individual differences influence the way people learn and succeed in language study. However, more research is needed in the field in order to make individual differences practical in the classroom and enable the most learners possible to learn a foreign language in their preferred styles using their own approaches to studying.

In chapter 5, the authors focus on describing and applying a range of NLP theory, strategies and techniques in school and tertiary settings. The authors outline the principles behind, and give examples of several NLP teaching tools that promote the learning of primary, secondary, tertiary and teacher training groups. While occasional reference will be made to therapy and business environments, the majority of the content will focus on teaching, training and school counselling. Neuro-Linguistic Programming (NLP) techniques are based on an established set of theoretical principles that span the disciplines of psychology, linguistics, counselling, communication and hypnosis. However, while it is challenging to understand the basis on which these strategies and techniques rest, it is not essential to do so before trying out the techniques which have already been trialled successfully by others, as long as one stays within one's professional educational boundaries, and does not stray in to the field of therapy. While many teachers already apply some of these principles to teaching, and there has been a concerted attempt to design and deliver educational input, in a way that accounts for the different ways that individual students learn, there is still much that can be done to make teaching and learning more stimulating, challenging, and satisfying processes than they currently are.

The solving of ill-structured problems, commonly related to societal and educational questions, can be facilitated by a visual depiction of the variety of viewpoints relevant to the problem in hand, and the arguments used to support different solutions. Constructing argument diagrams is one way to visualise argumentation. Argument visualisation refers to graphical or other non-verbal means of making reasoning chains and conclusions explicit. In chapter 6, 7 male and 10 female Finnish secondary school students were assigned the task of constructing and elaborating an argument diagram on the issue of genetically modified organisms (GMO). The task proceeded in three successive phases using a network-based diagram tool. The students constructed their first diagram on the basis of their previous knowledge of GMO, modified it after having read three articles on the theme, and finalised the diagram after they had engaged in a dyadic chat debate on the same theme. The diagrams were analysed for shape and content. The students' final diagrams showed the largest number of argument boxes, the broadest and longest chains of argument, and the greatest number of topics relevant to the theme. The most evident change was observed after the students had read three articles on the topic. Thus the students deepened and broadened their knowledge on the theme during the course. It was concluded that by means of alternate phases of reading, discussion and reflection secondary school students' knowledge and thinking can be elaborated, thereby fostering their learning.

Coordination in sport skills is presently described by the ecological and the dynamical approaches. These approaches argue that coordination is an emergent property of constraints of an organism resulting from the interaction with environment. The constraints strain the movement, which is not the product of representation and computation to generate a motor program. Consequently, cognitive processes and human determinism are rejected, although learning of motor skill shows that the subject is active in his forming of change. Therefore, the concern of chapter 7 is to show that coordination of a gross motor skill such as playing tennis is also a consequence of the achievement of cognitive processes. The role of the cognitive style has been studied in coincidence-anticipation skills. The questioning of reflective–impulsive style indicated that style reflected a competence effect when the reflective children were the most efficient. As it has been shown through the results of a ball-hitting task and a ball-catching task, it is questioned about the coordination level of these motor skills and the effect of the experience of trained children. 35 nine-years-old boys were filmed and administered by the Matching Familiar Figures Test (MFFT). Children were classified into four groups using a double dichotomy of response latencies and errors on the MFFT (reflective, impulsive, fast-accurate and slow-inaccurate). Ethological categorization used to appraise the motor patterns of hitting a tennis ball with a mini racquet (split in two phases, one for orientating to the ball and the other for the stability during the contact with the ball) and of catching a ball with a trajectory, which felt close to the feet. Results showed that reflective boys are the most efficient and shaped the more mature motor patterns. On the set of performance, the comparison between the cognitive task and the two motor tasks shows correlation on response accuracy with the MFFT and the coordination levels on the two motor tasks. This finding is consistent with previous works showing that reflective–impulsive style reveals a competence skill particular to the reflective children, a very strong trend of these children that allows them to remain efficient whatever the situation by adjusting their response time to use the best solving strategy. The more efficient children in tennis show more mature motor patterns and score specifically on this task and are speeder than novices according to the speed-accuracy tradeoff concept. Among cognitive processes, we suggest that variation, selection, and activation-inhibition should be operative on motor pattern achievement. Coordination is not only an emergent process by mastering the degrees of freedom, as argued with the dynamical theories concerning Bernstein's work.

In: Trends in Learning Reserch
Editor: Samuel N. Hogan, pp. 1-39

ISBN 1-59454-965-6
© 2006 Nova Science Publishers, Inc.

Chapter 1

THE ROLE OF THE BRAIN ANGIOTENSIN SYSTEM IN LEARNING, MEMORY, AND NEURAL PLASTICITY

John W. Wright, Mikel L. Olson and Joseph W. Harding

Departments of Psychology, Veterinary and Comparative Anatomy, Pharmacology and Physiology, and Programs in Neuroscience and Biotechnology, Washington State University, Pullman Washington, United States 99164-4820

ABSTRACT

The brain renin-angiotensin system (RAS) is best known for regulating blood pressure, body water balance, cyclicity of reproductive hormones/sexual behaviors, and pituitary gland hormones. These classic physiologies and behaviors appear to be mediated by the angiotensin II (AngII)/AT_1 receptor subtype system. A second angiotensin receptor subtype, AT_2, is maximally expressed during fetal development and is down-regulated in the adult. The AT_2 subtype opposes growth responses facilitated by the AT_1 receptor as well as growth factor receptors. Recent evidence suggests important contributions by a third angiotensin receptor subtype, AT_4, to non-classic RAS physiologies including the regulation of blood flow, modulation of exploratory behaviors, and facilitation of learning acquisition and memory consolidation. This angiotensin IV (AngIV)/AT_4 system appears to interact with brain matrix metalloproteinases to modify extracellular matrix molecules thus permitting the neural plasticity presumed to underlie memory consolidation, reconsolidation, and retrieval. Neural plasticity appears to be activated by facilitated activity, such as long-term potentiation, in several brain structures particularly entorhinal cortex, hippocampus, medial temporal lobe and prefrontal cortex. The contributions of the angiotensinergic and cholinergic systems to synaptic reconfiguration are discussed, however the specific details of this relationship have yet to be delineated.

INTRODUCTION

Planarians, *Dugesia japonica*, are capable of learning a conditioned place preference with cocaine as a positive reinforcer (Kusayama and Watanabe, 2000). The round worm,

Caenorhabditis elegans, rapidly habituates to taps on its Petri dish (Rose et al., 2003). The medicinal leach, *Hirudo medicinalis*, displays habituation to repeated mild electrical stimulations applied to its posterior sucker, and sensitization to the brushing of its dorsal side skin (Zaccardi et al., 2001). The octopus, *Octopus bimaculoides*, can solve a spatial learning escape task in which only one of six clay pots is available as a lair with low water and high ambient light serving as noxious stimuli. Latency to find the available pot and pull the lid closed decreased over trials demonstrating that finding this safe location in the tank served as a negative reinforcer (Boal et al., 2000). The intact *Aplysia californica* can learn both classical and operant responses in an electrophysiological assisted preparation (Brembs et al., 2004). The pond snail, *Lymnaea stagnalis*, can be operantly conditioned to refrain from utilizing aerial respiration in favor of cutaneous absorptive respiration (Lukowiak et al., 2003). The sea lamprey, *Petromyzon marinus*, habituates to mechanical stimulation of the dorsal fin region of its body (Birnberger and Rovainen, 1971). Finally, the West Texas lizard, *Cnemidophorus inornatus*, demonstrates spatial learning in an open field (ambient temperature: 22°) that includes four flat rocks to rest on with only one heated (Day et al., 2001). Each of these species possesses the behavioral plasticity to solve a challenge to its optimal environmental conditions, and each is capable of solving the problem without the availability of brain structures such as hippocampus, amygdala, and neocortex as present in mammalian species.

As multicellular organisms evolved they acquired the ability to form extracellular matrix (ECM) thus permitting cell-to-cell and cell-to-matrix adherence. Many of these ECM molecules are thought to be involved in maintaining and changing the synaptic architecture presumed to underlie the processes of learning, memory, and neural plasticity. Interest in the neurobiology of learning and memory began with Tanzi (1893), Müller and Pilzecker (1900), and Cajal (1928), and continued with Hebb (1949) and Lashley (1950). Based on work by these earlier investigators, and those who followed, there has evolved the "Consolidation Theory" suggesting that important experiences initiate a sequence of neural events that eventually result in consolidation of the experience into a stable "memory trace" or "engram". This engram is thought to be initially fragile and easily disrupted, however, with time it becomes fixed in form and location such that the experience is stored and available for retrieval at a later time. The requisite steps involved in the formation and long-term storage of the engram are not well defined but would appear to begin with extracellular signals that ultimately impact nuclear function working through intracellular intermediates. Such cell signaling presumably initiates the specific gene expression necessary for synthesis of molecules important to reconfiguration of connections among neurons, and thus underlie the phenomena of neural plasticity and memory. Neural plasticity is predicated on changes in the efficacy of synaptic transmission that are activity driven. These changes can result in reconfiguration of synaptic connections leading to weakening or strengthening of such connections (Benington and Frank, 2003; Dityatev and Schachner, 2003; Frankland and Bontempi, 2005). Neural plasticity, as evidenced in memory, appears to undergo a continuous pattern of engram maintenance punctuated by updating and reconsolidation. Over recent years considerable research effort has focused on identifying those ECM, and related molecules, responsible for reconfiguring and storing these memory traces. A number of potentially important components have been discovered, and in turn, are forcing re-evaluation of the current theory of memory consolidation and retrieval.

Angiotensin peptides have been identified in the ganglia (brains) of the above species, and also in insects (reviewed in Salzet et al. 2001). However only in the crab, *Chasmagnathus granulatus*, have angiotensins been shown to enhance retention of habituatory responses to a shadow (danger) moving overhead (Delorenzi et al. 1997, 1999). In mammals the brain renin-angiotensin system (RAS) includes several effector ligands and receptor subtypes involved in a number of diverse functions ranging from the mediation of systemic blood pressure, sodium and body water balance, to cyclicity of reproductive hormones and accompanying sexual behaviors, and the release of pituitary gland hormones. These behaviors and physiologies appear to be controlled by the AT_1 receptor subtype (Allen et al., 2000; de Gasparo et al., 2000; Gard, 2002; McKinley et al., 2003; Thomas and Mendelsohn, 2003). A second subtype, the AT_2, has also been associated with the regulation of blood pressure, renal function, and vascular growth (de Gasparo and Siragy, 1999; de Gasparo et al., 2000; Speth et al., 1995). Less well documented is a third receptor subtype, the AT_4, that mediates cognitive processing especially learning and memory consolidation. Recent review articles have focused on this receptor subtype (Gard, 2002; Llorens-Cortes and Mendelsohn, 2002; Moeller et al., 1998; von Bohlen und Halbach, 2003; de Gasparo et al., 2000; Wright and Harding, 2004), however, the interaction of the AT_4 receptor with molecules known to contribute to neural plasticity, along with its influence upon the brain cholinergic system, has received very little attention.

The present chapter initially describes the biochemistry of the RAS followed by a description of the proposed role of extracellular matrix molecules in neural plasticity. Subsequent sections describe the contribution of the brain RAS to learning and memory and the interactions that appear to occur between the brain RAS and the brain cholinergic system. A final section considers several models of memory-associated neural plasticity.

BIOCHEMISTRY OF THE RENIN-ANGIOTENSIN SYSTEM (RAS)

Angiotensin II (AngII) has traditionally been considered the end-product of the RAS and the active ligand interacting with the angiotensin receptor subtypes AT_1 and AT_2. Accumulating evidence suggests that additional shorter chain angiotensins also serve as effecter peptides including desAsp[1]-AngII referred to as angiotensin III (AngIII) (Vauquelin et al., 2002; Wright and Harding, 1997), desAsp[1],desArg[2]-AngII referred to as AngIV (Albiston et al., 2003; de Gasparo et al., 2000; Thomas and Mendelsohn, 2003; Wright and Harding, 1994, 1997; Wright et al., 1995), and Ang (1-7) (Ferrario, 2003; Ferrario et al., 1997; Santos, 2000). The proposed functions mediated by AngIV acting via the AT_4 receptor subtype include influences on blood flow (Coleman et al, 1998; Kramár et al., 1997; Moeller et al., 1999; Slinker et al., 1999), kidney natriuresis (Hamilton et al., 2001; Handa et al., 1998), expression of plasminogen activator inhibitor (PAI-1) and endothelial cells (Kerin et al., 1995; Mehta et al., 2002), and epithelial cells of the kidney proximal tubule (Gesualdo et al., 1999), and memory facilitation (Albiston et al., 2003; Bohlen und Halbach, 2003; Wright et al., 2002a). Ang(1-7) stimulates the release of nitric oxide (NO) and vasodilator prostaglandins (Brosnihan and Ferrario, 1996; Li et al., 1997; Paula et al., 1995). Ang(1-7) stimulated release of NO appears to be primarily from vascular endothelial and smooth muscle cells (Jaiswal et al., 1992; Muthalif et al., 1998) and opposes AngII-induced vasoconstriction (Ueda et al., 2000). There is evidence that this ligand protects cardiac and endothelium functions, as well as coronary perfusion as demonstrated in a heart failure model (Loot et al., 2002). Ang(1-7) also facilitates baroreceptor reflex sensitivity and modulates circadian rhythm influences on heart rate and blood pressure (Campagnole-Santos et al., 1992; Silva-Barcellos et al., 2001).

Before we discuss the potential role of angiotensins in learning and memory processing, a description of the synthetic pathways of these ligands is presented.

1. Formation of Angiotensin Ligands

The precursor protein, angiotensinogen, serves as a substrate for a number of angiotensin peptides including angiotensin I (AngI), formed by the protease renin (EC 3.4.23.15) acting at the amino terminal of angiotensinogen (Figure 1). Angiotensin I is a substrate for angiotensin converting enzyme (ACE: EC 3.4.15.1), a zinc metalloproteinase that hydrolyzes the carboxyl terminal dipeptide His-Leu to form AngII (Johnston, 1990; Speth et al., 2003). Angiotensin II can be further converted to Ang (1-7) by carboxypeptidase P (Carb-P) cleavage of Phe (reviewed in Wright and Harding, 1997), or by ACE cleavage of the dipeptide Phe-His from Ang (1-9) (Vauquelin et al., 2002). Ang (1-7) can be further converted to Ang (2-7) by glutamyl aminopeptidase A (AP-A: EC 3.4.11.7, or A-like activity) acting at the Asp-Arg bond (Mentlein and Roos, 1996). AngII is also converted to the heptapeptide AngIII by AP-A cleavage of the Asp residue at the N-terminal (Chauvell, 1994; Rich et al., 1984; Wilk and Healy, 1993). Angiotensin III can be converted to Angiotensin IV via membrane alanyl aminopeptidase N (AP-N: EC3.4.11.2) cleavage of Arg at the N-terminal. In turn, AngIV can be further converted to Ang (3-7) via carboxypeptidase and propyl oligopeptidase (PO) cleavage of the Pro-Phe bond. Chymotrypsin and other endopeptidases further cleave Val, Tyr, and Ile residues accompanied by dipeptidyl carboxypeptidase. It cleaves the His-Pro bond reducing AngIV and Ang (3-7) to inactive peptide fragments and amino acid constituents (Johnston, 1990; Moeller et al., 1998; Saavedra, 1992; Speth et al., 2003; Unger et al., 1988).

Angiotensin I is considered biologically inactive, while AngII and AngIII are full agonists at the AT_1 and AT_2 receptor subtypes (reviewed in de Gasparo et al., 2000). AngIV binds with low affinity at the AT_1 and AT_2 receptor subtypes (Bennet and Snyder, 1976; Glossman et al., 1974; Harding et al., 1992; Swanson et al., 1992) but with high affinity and specificity at the AT_4 receptor subtype (Bernier et al., 1994; Harding et al., 1992; Jarvis et al., 1992, Swanson et al., 1992). A specific binding site for Ang (1-7) has been reported (Neves et al., 2003; Santos et al., 1994, 2000) but not fully elucidated.

2. AT_1, AT_2 and AT_4 Receptor Subtypes

The AT_1 receptor subtype is a G-protein-coupled receptor with signaling by phospholipase-C and calcium (de Gasparo et al., 2000). This signal transduction involves several plasma membrane mechanisms including phospholipase-C, phospholipase-A_2, and phospholipase-D-adenylate cyclase, plus L-type and T-type voltage sensitive calcium channels (de Gasparo et al., 2000; Sayeski et al., 1998). This AT_1 receptor (designated AT_{1A})

is additionally coupled to intracellular signaling cascades that regulate gene transcription in the expression of proteins that mediate cellular proliferation in growth and many target tissues. The AT_1 subtype is responsible for the classic functions of the brain RAS. Expression cloning was used to isolate the cDNA encoding this receptor protein (Murphy et al., 1991; Sasaki et al., 1991) and it was determined to be a 7-transmembrane domain protein of 359 amino acids with a mass of about 41 kDA (Sandberg et al., 1994). A second AT_1 subtype, AT_{1B}, was subsequently discovered and cloned in the rat (Iwai and Inagami, 1992; Kakar et al., 1992), mouse (Sadamura et al., 1992), and human (Konoshi et al., 1994). This AT_{1B} subtype is approximately 90-95 homologus with the amino acid sequence of the AT_{1A} subtype (Guo and Inagami, 1994; Speth et al., 1995).

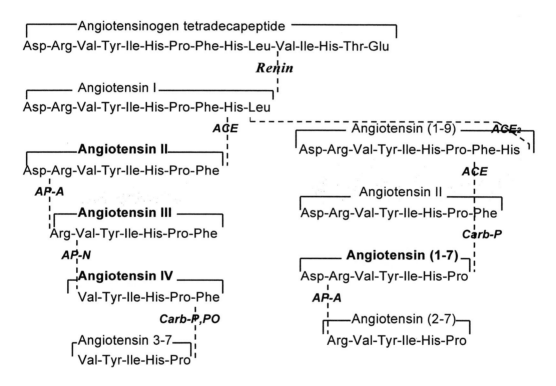

Figure 1. Peptide structures and enzymes involved in the conversion of the tetradecapeptide portion of angiotensinogen to angiotensin I through shorter fragments. Biologically active angiotensins include angiotensin II, III, IV, and angiotensin (1-7). Adapted from Wright and Harding (2004).

The AT_2 receptor subtype has also been cloned and sequenced using a rat fetus expression library (Bottari et al., 1991; Kambayashi et al., 1993). Again, this is a 7-transmembrane domain G-protein-coupled receptor, however it has only 32-34% amino acid sequence identity with the rat AT_1 receptor. The AT_2 receptor protein consists of a 363 amino acid sequence (40 kDA) with 99% agreement between rat and mouse, and 72% homology with human (de Gasparo et al., 2000). Although this AT_2 receptor subtype possesses structural features in common with members of the 7-transmembrane family of receptors, it displays few if any functional similarities with the group beyond being G-protein-coupled (Bottari et al., 1991; Kambayashi et al., 1993; Mukoyama et al., 1993). The AT_1 receptor subtype is primarily sensitive to AngII, but is also activated by AngIII. The AT_2 receptor subtype appears to be maximally sensitive to AngIII, but AngII also serves as a ligand.

The AT_4 receptor subtype was initially discovered using bovine adrenal membrane (Bernier et al., 1994; Harding et al., 1992; Jarvis et al., 1992; Swanson et al., 1992). These characterization studies indicated that the AT_4 receptor is distinct from the AT_1 and AT_2 sites given that ligands known to bind to these sites do not bind at the AT_4 site (Harding et al., 1992). [^{125}I]AngIV binds at the AT_4 site reversibly, saturably, and with high affinity and has been isolated in a variety of mammalian tissues including adrenal gland, bladder, colon, heart, kidney, prostate, brain and spinal cord. Binding to this site has been found to be insensitive to guanine nucleotides suggesting that the AT_4 receptor is not G-protein-linked. The AT_4 receptor subtype appears to be one subunit of a trimer of proteins with a molecular weight of between 160-190 kDA as determined by reduced SDS-polyacrylamide gel electrophoresis. The lack of linkage to G-proteins is supported in that GTPγS failed to alter [^{125}I]AngIV binding in rabbit heart (Hanesworth et al., 1993), guinea pig brain (Miller-Wing et al., 1993), and rat vascular smooth muscle (Hall et al., 1993). A single report by Dulin and colleagues (1995) indicated that GTPγS can inhibit AT_4 receptor binding in opossum kidney cells. However, taken together these findings all but preclude the linkage of the AT_4 receptor to G-proteins; however a definitive conclusion must await the cloning and sequencing of the AT_4 receptor.

3. Cerebral Distribution of Angiotensin Receptor Subtypes

High densities of the AT_1 subtype have been localized in the anterior pituitary gland, area postrema, lateral geniculate body, nucleus of the solitary tract, the anterior ventral 3rd ventricle region (including OVLT), paraventricular, supraoptic, and ventral medial nuclei, median eminence, and the preoptic region of the hypothalamus, subfornical organ, ventral tegmental area, and inferior olivary nucleus of the medulla (Table 1). The highest level of the AT_2 subtype are found in the amygdalla, medial geniculate body, hypoglossal nucleus, inferior olivary nucleus, lateral habenula, caudate-putamen, globus pallidus, locus coeruleus, thalamus, inferior colliculus, and ventral tegmental area.

Structures with the greatest densities of the AT_4 receptor subtype include anterior pituitary gland, caudate-putamen, globus pallidus, cerebellum and piriform cortices, lateral geniculate, habenula, hippocampus, inferior olivary nucleus, periaquaductal gray, superior colliculi, thalamus, and ventral tegmental area. Comparing the distributions of these subtypes the AT_4 site is expressed in reasonably high densities and uniquely in the cerebral cortex, piriform cortex, hippocampus, caudate-putamen, nucleus accumbens, medial habenula, periaquaductal gray, nucleus basalis of Meynert, ventral tegmental area, and cerebellum. Several of these brain areas are intrinsically involved in learning and memory processing.

Table 1. Predominant brain distributions of the three angiotensin receptor subtypes identified in mammalian brains.

Subtype	AT_1	AT_2	AT_4
Structures:			
amygdala	√	√√	√
anterior pituitary	√√	√√	
area postrema	√√		
caudate putamen	√	√√	√√
cerebellum	√	√	√√
cerebral cortex	√√		
dentate gyrus	√		
geniculate, lateral	√√	√√	
geniculate, medial	√√	√	
globus pallidus	√√	√√	
habenula	√	√√	√√
hippocampus	√√		
hypoglossal nucleus	√√		
inferior colliculus	√√	√	
inferior olivary nucleus	√√	√√	√√
lateral olfactory tract	√	√	
locus coeruleus	√	√√	√
mammillary body	√		
medial preoptic nucleus	√		
median eminence	√√		
nucleus accumbens	√		
nucleus basalis of Meynert	√		
nucleus of lateral olfactory tract	√		
nucleus of solitary tract	√√		
organum vasculosum of thelateral terminalis	√√		
paraventricular nucleus	√√		
periaqueductal gray	√√		
piriform cortex	√	√√	
preoptic nucleus	√√	√	
red nucleus	√		
septum	√	√	√
subfornical organ	√√		
substantia nigra	√		
superior colliculus	√	√√	
suprachiasmatic nucleus	√		
supraoptic nucleus	√√		
thalamus	√√	√√	
ventromedial nucleus	√		
ventral tegmental area	√√	√√	
zona incerta	√		

Adapted from Gard (2002), Wright & Harding (1997), Wright et al. (1995)

MATRIX METALLOPROTEINASES (MMPS)

The matrix metalloproteinases are a family of proteolytic enzymes important to the restructuring of ECM molecules (Birkedal-Hansen, 1995; Kahari and Saarialho-Kere, 1997; Stamenkovic, 2003). To date over 20 MMPs have been identified (Table 2). All MMPs appear to require activation by serine proteinases, specifically plasmin and/or other MMPs. A propeptide must be cleaved off in order to reveal the catalytic domain. Various MMPs have been implicated in the physiological processes of angiogenesis, blastocyst implantation, ovulation, and wound healing (reviewed in Ennis and Matrisian, 1994; Yong et al., 1998).

MMPs are involved in the pathophysiology of CNS diseases such as Alzheimer's disease (Gottschall and Deb, 1996; Yoshiyama et al., 2000) multiple sclerosis (Lee and Benveniste, 1999; Opdenakker et al., 2003; Rosenberg, 2002a,b; Sellibjerg and Sorenson, 2003; Sobel, 1998; Vos et al., 2003; Yong et al., 1998) and atherosclerosis (Kunz, 2002). MMPs are also involved in tumor metastasis and cell invasion (Berkendal-Hansen et al., 1993; Goldbrunner et al., 1998; Handsley and Edwards, 2005; Kaczmarek et al., 2002; Sounni and Noel, 2005).

Extracellular matrix degradation by MMPs is carefully controlled and accomplished by three mechanisms: 1) regulation of gene transcription; 2) regulation of pro-enzyme activation; and 3) via the presence of tissue inhibitors of metalloproteinases (TIMPs). Most MMPs are nonconstituitively expressed, however gene transcription may occur via growth factor stimulation, oncogene products, phorbol esters, as well as cell-to-cell and cell-to-ECM interactions. These stimuli often provoke various transcription factors including members of the c-Fos and c-Jun proto-oncogene families, resulting in the formation of homo- and hetero-dymeric forms of AP-1 transcription factors. Such activation of MMP genes requires the combined effects of AP-1 protein and other transcription factors (reviewed in Kaczmarek et al., 2002; Mann and Spinale, 1998).

It is also possible for MMPs to activate other MMPs. For example, MMP-2, MMP-3 and membrane type MMPs (MT-MMPs) activate MMP-1 and MMP-9, while MT-MMPs can be activated by inhibitory pro-peptide removal, specifically accomplished by furin, also a serine protease (Yong et al., 1998). These characteristics of MMPs make them very attractive candidates concerning their potential contributions to the phenomena of memory consolidation, reconsolidation, and retrieval.

Tissue inhibitors of metalloproteinases 1-4 (TIMP-1-4; Table 2) form a family of secreted glycoproteins (Maskos and Bode, 2003; Skiles et al., 2004; Woessner and Nagase, 2000). MMP proteolytic activities can be inhibited by TIMPs that form tight non-covalent complexes with them (Bode et al., 1999; Jeng et al., 2001). Imbalance between the normal levels of MMP activity promotes remodeling, and inhibition of their actions by TIMPS may result in pathology (Lukes et al., 1999). These imbalances have been seen in arthritis, atherosclerosis, Alzheimer's disease, cancer, Guillain-Bere syndrome, ischemia, infarctions, and other disease states (reviewed in Jeng et al., 2001; Kaczmarek et al., 2002; Lambert et al., 2004; Lukes et al., 1999; Rivera and Khrestchatisky, 2000).

Table 2. Matrix metalloproteinases, tissue inhibitors of metalloproteinases, and their preferred substrates

Group	Members	Abbreviation	m.w. (kDa)	Substrate
Collagenases	Fibroblast collagenase	MMP-1	54	fibrillar collagens
	Neutrophil collagenase	MMP-8	53	fibrillar collagens
	Collagenase-3	MMP-13	54	fibrillar collagens
	Collagenase-4	χCol 4	57	collagens
Gelatinases	Gelatinase A	MMP-2	73.8	gelatin, elastin fibronectin, types IV-VI collagens
	Gelatinase B	MMP-9	78	gelatin, elastin, fibronectin, types I,IV & V collagens
Membrane-type	Membrane-type 1-MMP	MMP-14	63	pro-MMP-2, collagens, gelatin, elastin, casein, fibronectin, vitronectin, aggrecan
	Membrane-type 2-MMP	MMP-15	64	pro-MMP-2, collagens, gelatin, fibronectin, laminin, nidogen, tenascin
	Membrane-type 3-MMP	MMP-16	64	pro-MMP-2, collagens, gelatin
	Membrane-type 4-MMP	MMP-17	72	pro-MMP-2, collagens, gelatin
Stromelysins	Stromelysin-1	MMP-3	54	fibronectin, collagens, laminin, non-fibrillar
	Stromelysin-2	MMP-10	55	fibronectin, collagens, laminin, non-fibrillar collagens
	Stromelysin-3	MMP-11	55	gelatin, fibrillar collagens, α 1 proteinase inhibitor (serpin)
	Macrophage metalloelastase	MMP-12	54	elastin
	Matrilysin	MMP-7	30	fibronectin, collagens, laminin, non-fibrillar collagens, aggrecan, casein, decorin, insulin
Others	Enamelysin	MMP-20	54	amelogenin
	Xenopus collagenase	MMP-18	55	unknown
	?	MMP-19	?	aggrecan, gelatin, tenascin C
		XMMP	?	unknown
TIMPs		TIMP-1	28	all MMPs except MT1-MMP
		TIMP-2	21	all MMPs
		TIMP-3	24	all MMPs
		TIMP-4	22	all MMPs

Adapted from Kahari & Saarialho-Kere (1999), Murphy et al. (1999); Rivera & Khrestchatisky (2000); Wright & Harding (2004); Wright et al. (2002b); Yong et al. (1998).

In the adult normal unstimulated brain expression of MMPs is exceedingly low (Yong et al., 2001). Of the ten specific MMPs measured in mouse brain only MMP-2, MMP-9, MMP-11, MMP-12, and MMP-14 were expressed at measurable levels (Pagenstecher et al., 1997; Vecil et al., 2000). The hippocampus and cerebellum have been implicated as having potentially the greatest expression of MMPs. MMP-24 mRNA and protein have been detected in mouse and rat hippocampus and dentate gyrus (Jaworski, 2000a; Hayashita-Kinoh et al., 2001; Sekine-Aizawa et al., 2001). Backstrom and colleagues (1996) reported MMP-9 mRNA and protein in pyramidal neurons of the human hippocampus and dentate gyrus. Szklarczyk et al. (2002) have concluded that hippocampal MMP-2 expression appears to be of glial origin, while MMP-9 expression is primarily of neuron origin. Vaillant et al. (1999) have reported reasonably high levels of MMP-2 and lower levels of MMP-9 in adult rat cerebellum, especially in Purkinje and granular neurons. They also reported high levels of MMP-3 and MMP-9 in the cerebellum of 15 day old rats during a time when a high rate of synaptogenesis would be expected.

Nedivi and colleagues (1993) were the first to report increased dentate gyrus levels of TIMP-1 mRNA following seizures. Subsequently, elevated TIMP-1 mRNA in protein were measured in the hippocampus with seizure (Jaworski et al., 1999; Rivera et al., 1997). Kainate-induced seizures also elevated MMP-9 mRNA expression in protein within a few hours (Szklarczyk et al., 2002). Enhanced MMP-9 mRNA expression was seen in both the dendritic layers and neuronal cell bodies primarily within the dentate gyrus. These results were interpreted to suggest that MMP-9 expression is involved in activity-dependent remodeling, perhaps via influencing synaptic connections.

It has been suggested that synaptic site local mRNA translation at activated synapses may be very important to the process of neural plasticity, a process presumed to underline memory consolidation (Job and Eberwine, 2001; Steward and Schuman, 2001). Local protein synthesis at activated synapses could provide specificity regarding memory formation (Frey and Morris, 1998; Martin et al., 2000). However, the precise mechanism(s) underlying such specificity has yet to be identified.

CONTRIBUTIONS OF THE BRAIN RAS TO LEARNING AND MEMORY

1. Angiotensins and Long-Term Potentiation (LTP)

In this section we review available information concerning brain angiotensins' role in learning and memory. Several laboratories have investigated the influence of AngII and AngIV on long-term potentiation (LTP) a presumed "building block" of memory formation (Bliss and Collingridge 1993; Lisman, 1989; Martin et al., 2000; Teyler, 1987). In the early 1970's Matt Wayner's group reported that the intravenous infusion of AngII produced both increased and decreased discharge rates in dentate gyrus neurons (Wayner et al., 1973). In the early 1980's it was initially reported that microiontophoretic application of AngII excited hippocampal neurons (Haas et al., 1982). However, Wayner and colleagues (Armstrong et al., 1996; Denny et al., 1991; Wayner et al., 1993a,b, 1995) subsequently reported that AngII, delivered just above the CA$_1$ field of the hippocampus in intact urethane anesthetized rats, inhibited LTP in perforant path-stimulated dentate granule cells. This AngII-induced inhibition could be blocked with the nonspecific AT_1 and AT_2 receptor antagonist saralasin, or the specific AT_1 receptor antagonist Losartan (DuP753); while the AT_2 specific receptor antagonist PD123319 failed to block this AngII inhibition of LTP (Wayner et al., 1993b). Wayner's laboratory further established that both ethanol (by gavage), and diazepam (intraperitoneal injections), inhibited LTP in a dose-dependent fashion, and this inhibition could be blocked by saralasin delivered into the dorsal hippocampus (Wayner et al., 1993a,b). Angiotensin III was found to be 40-50-fold less potent than AngII in inhibiting LTP (Denny et al., 1991). These investigators also reported that AngII injection into the dentate gyrus of alert rats impaired retention of a conditioned passive avoidance response (Lee et al., 1995). This AngII-induced impairment could be significantly attenuated by pretreatment with Losartan. Thus, it appears that a neural pathway within the hippocampus must express LTP in order for a newly acquired conditioned response to be retained. Taken together these results suggest that ethanol and diazepam-induced inhibition of LTP may be AngII dependent, and this process may be mediated by the AT_1 receptor subtype. These findings also offer a possible mechanism for the memory dysfunction associated with alcohol and benzodiazepine-induced blackouts (Wayner et al., 1993a, 1994).

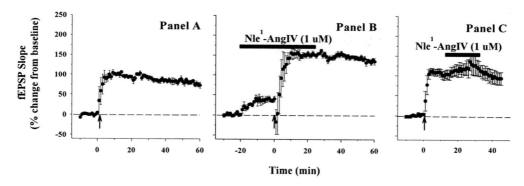

Figure 2. Angiotensin IV agonist, Nle[1]-AngIV, enhances LTP in the dentate gyrus and CA_1 dendritic area in the hippocampus. Graph illustrates field EPSP slopes as a function of time during infusions of 1 µM Nle[1]-AngIV in the CA_1 region (Panel B) and dentate gyrus (Panel C). Control slice traces during 60 min post-tetanization are included for comparison (Panel A). The arrows indicate theta wave tetanization. Adapted from Wright et al. (2002a).

The potential contribution of AngIV to LTP has recently been investigated by Kramár and colleagues. Pretreatment with the AT_4 receptor agonist, Nle[1],AngIV significantly facilitated LTP in the dentate gyrus and CA_1 field of the hippocampal slice preparation (Kramár et al.., 1999, 2001; Figure 2). Pretreatment with the AT_4 receptor antagonist, Divalinal-AngIV, blocked this Nle[1],AngIV-induced facilitation of LTP. In support of these results Ikeda et al. (1998) have reported a similar AngIV-induced facilitation of LTP in the intact urethane anesthetized rat. AngIV was infused into the dorsal hippocampus during induction of LTP which was recorded from perforant path-stimulated dentate granule cells. This AngIV facilitation of LTP appears to be mediated by the activation of voltage-dependent calcium channels (VDCCs). Blockade of L-type Ca^{2+} channels with nimodipine significantly reduced NMDA-independent LTP in the CA_1 region of the hippocampal slice preparation

(Davis et al., submitted for publication). This dependence of AngIV facilitation of LTP on VDCC fits well with Tim Teyler's hypothesis (Teyler 1999; Teyler et al., 2001) that the activation of VDCC-LTP is required for the preservation of memories beyond a few hours. Further, these results suggest that AngII and AngIV have opposing influences upon LTP, and are in agreement with results from other preparations. For example, AngII stimulates vasoconstriction in vascular beds, while AngIV induces vasodilation (Kramár et al., 1997, 1998). This appears to hold for AngII and AngIV stimulation of kidney cortical blood flow (Coleman et al.., 1998). Further, AngII and AngIV appear to produce opposite effects upon field potentials recorded from the lateral nucleus of the amygdala (Von Bohlen und Halback and Albrecht, 1998).

2. Angiotensin II, Learning and Memory

Also in the early 1970's Barbara Rolls and colleagues (1972) placed rats on a progressive ratio schedule-bar press response for food and water, and found that the motivational levels of rats were approximately equal following 24 hours of water deprivation and when not deprived but prepared with an injection of AngII into the preoptic area of the hypothalamus. Graeff et al. (1973) trained water-deprived rats to press a bar for water, and then injected AngII into the septal area and measured equivalent bar pressing when rats were satiated. These results suggest that AngII injections can simulate the motivational characteristics present while water-deprived. At about the same time it was reported that intracerebroventricular (icv)-infused AngII interfered with performance of a variable interval operant task in rabbits (Melo and Graeff, 1975). Similarly, icv renin infused 1 minute prior to the initiation of acquisition training on a passive avoidance task in rats interfered with memory recall of that task 1 and 2 days later (Köller et al., 1979). Angiotensin II was assumed to be disruptive of memory recall given that this performance deficit was attenuated by icv infusion of the ACE inhibitor Captopril. It was also reported that AngII injected into the dorsal neostriatum, 5 minutes following passive avoidance conditioning, interfered with the recall of the conditioned response 24 hours later (Morgan and Routtenberg, 1977). Along these lines, De Noble et al. (1991) reported that icv infused renin disrupted performance of a passive avoidance task in a dose-dependent fashion, i.e. as dosage increased the level of retention decreased. The co-application of an AT_1 receptor antagonist (EXP3312 or EXP3880), and the ACE inhibitor Captopril, attenuated this renin-induced deficit. Since co-application of an AT_2 receptor antagonist (PD123,177) failed to influence this performance deficit produced by renin, it was concluded that the AT_1 receptor subtype mediated this deficit. Lee and colleagues (1995) reported that bilateral injection of AngII into the dentate gyrus impaired retention of an inhibitory shock avoidance response. This impairment could be prevented by pretreatment with systemic Losartan (an AT_1 receptor antagonist). Similarly, treatment with icv AngII, or immobilization stress following training on the plus maze or step-down passive avoidance task, produced impaired retention in rats (Raghavendra et al., 1999). Since these deficits could be attenuated by Losartan, the authors concluded that the AT_1 receptor subtype mediated these effects.

Given the above findings it is reasonable to assume that compounds designed to decrease AT_1 receptor activation should facilitate cognitive processing. Such cognitive enhancement has been reported in patients placed on ACE inhibitors (Gard, 2002). A similar facilitation of memory has been reported in mice systemically treated with Captopril or Losartan, as related to a step-up active avoidance task (Raghavendra et al., 2001). Facilitation of a passive avoidance task has also been reported in Dahl salt-sensitive rats placed on a low dose of Cilazapril (ACE inhibitor) for 18 months (Hirawa et al., 1999). This improvement was correlated with an increase in hippocampal CA_1 neurons and capillary densities. The authors concluded that improved memory recall by treated rats was likely due to the increased hippocampal blood flow afforded via the increased capillary densities.

Shepherd et al. (1996) have reasoned that if ACE inhibitors produce mood elevating and cognitive enhancing effects in hypertensive patients (Croog et al., 1986; Deiken, 1986; Zubenko and Nixon, 1984), and such effects are mediated by the AT_1 (and/or AT_2) receptor subtype as suggested by Barnes et al. (1990; 1991), then treatment with Losartan or PD123177 should produce similar effects. Shepherd and colleagues utilized rats tested on two paradigms of working short-term memory, the operant delayed matching-to-sample task, and the spatial reinforced alternation task in the T-maze. Losartan and PD123177 were subcutaneously administered 30 minutes before testing either alone or with scopolamine. Treatment with scopolamine had previously been shown to impair performance on both of these tasks (Stanhope et al., 1994, 1995). Results indicated that neither Losartan nor PD123177 influenced acquisition of these tasks, nor did they inhibit the impairment in performance induced by scopolamine.

In contrast with the above findings, central injections of AngII and Ang(3-7) have been reported by some laboratories to improve acquisition and recall. Baranowska et al. (1983) icv injected AngII (1 and 2 µg) 15 minutes prior to active avoidance conditioning trials in rats. A buzzer served as a conditioned stimulus and foot shock as the unconditioned stimulus. AngII facilitated acquisition of the response but did not influence extinction. A low dose of icv infused AngII (0.5 µg) inhibited the acquisition of this conditioned response. Pretreatment with the AT_1 receptor antagonists saralasin or sarile ([Sar^1, Ile^8]AngII) failed to block these AngII effects. These results were interpreted to suggest that AngII may exert a bimodal action upon learning, that is, an inhibitory influence at low doses and a facilitory effect at high doses. Subsequent reports from this laboratory indicated that icv delivered AngII, Ang(3-7) and AngIV (1 nmol ≈ 1 µg), 15 minutes prior to retention testing, facilitated the recall of a passive avoidance conditioned response (Braszko and Wisniewski, 1988; Braszko et al., 1987, 1998). These treatments also facilitated the acquisition of a shuttlebox active avoidance task (Braszko et al., 1987, 1988; Georgiev et al., 1988). Further, such treatments facilitated T-maze performance when delivered immediately following acquisition training. However, if AngII and AngIV were administered 15 minutes prior to testing for recall of T-maze performance, no facilitation of performance was noted (Braszko et al., 1987, 1988). Along these lines, microinjection of AngII into the CA_1 hippcampal field has been shown to facilitate acquisition of an active avoidance (shuttle box) task in rats (Belcheva et al., 2000). Kulakowska and colleagues (1996) extended this work to an object recognition task in which AngII facilitation could be blocked by pretreatment with Losartan. These results suggest that the AT_1 receptor subtype mediated this AngII-induced improvement in object recognition. Surprisingly, Braszko (2002) has recently reported that icv AngII-induced facilitation of passive avoidance conditioning, conditioned avoidance responding, and open field locomotor behavior could be blocked by combined pretreatment with Losartan plus an AT_2 receptor antagonists (PD123319), but not by each alone. Further, Braszko and colleagues (2003) have attempted to explain these variable AngII effects on acquisition by measuring changes in motor and anxiety responses to icv infusion of AngII. They found significant increases in anxiety as measured using an elevated "plus" maze, and impaired motor coordination as measured with the "chimney" test. Pretreatment with either Losartan or PD123319 counteracted the AngII-induced heightened anxiety effects, but only Losartan offset the impaired motor coordination effects.

Recently Kerr and colleagues (2004) prepared rats with bilateral chronic intrahippocampal guide cannulas permitting the infusion of compound directly into the CA_1 field. The infusion of AngII immediately following, or 30 min after training, on a one trial step-down passive avoidance task, produced a dose-dependent amnesic effect. This amnesic effect could be blocked by pretreatment with the AT_2 receptor antagonist, PD123319, but not by Losartan. Neither PD123319 or Losartan alone impaired retention. The authors concluded that AngII appears to block memory consolidation of passive avoidance memory via a mechanism associated with the AT_2 receptor subtype.

3. Angiotensin IV, Learning and Memory

The vast majority of the above studies utilized native angiotensins rather than analogs that are resistant to conversion to shorter chain peptides. Thus, it is very likely that these results are due to a combination of effects resulting from the conversion of AngII to AngIII and perhaps to Ang(1-7), (2-7), (3-7), and AngIV.

In line with the above caution, the frequently noted failure of AT_1 and AT_2 receptor antagonists to influence performance on cognitive tasks, or block subsequent AngII facilitation of a conditioned response, may indicate that AngII is converted to AngIII, and then to AngIV (or an AngIV-like compound), and it is this ligand that acts at the AT_4 receptor subtype to improve cognitive performance. Our laboratory has discovered that the icv infusion of AngIV leads to c-Fos expression in the hippocampus and piriform cortices, while similar injection of AngII failed to induce c-Fos-like immunoreactivity in these structures, but did activate c-Fos expression in circumventricular organs (Roberts et al., 1995) and the hypothalamus (Zhu and Herbert, 1996). Pretreatment with Losartan prevented this AngII-induced c-Fos immunoreactivity, while pretreatment with the AT_4 receptor antagonist, Divalinal-AngIV, blocked AngIV-induced c-Fos expression (Roberts et al., 1995). There were no crossover effects exhibited by these antagonists. Along these lines, Braszko and colleagues (1988, 1991) reported that icv injected AngII and AngIV were equivalent at facilitating exploratory behavior in rats tested in an open field, improved recall of passive avoidance conditioning, and the acquisition of active avoidance conditioning. Our laboratory confirmed and extended these findings in that icv infused AngIV improved the recall of a passive avoidance response in a dose-dependent fashion, with the most prominent facilitation at the highest dose (1 nmol) employed (Wright et al., 1993, 1995). We also found that icv treatment with Divalinal-AngIV, disrupted recall of this response (Wright et al., 1995). Along these lines osmotic pump icv delivery of Divalinal-AngIV during 6 days of training significantly impaired acquisition of the Morris water maze task of spatial memory (Wright et al., 1999). Our laboratory has also determined that icv injected metabolically resistant analogs of AngIV can be utilized to facilitate acquisition of successful search patterns in the circular water maze task as compared with control animals treated with artificial cerebrospinal fluid, or a pentapeptide that does not bind at the AT_4 receptor subtype (Stubley-Weatherly et al.,

1996; Wright et al., 1999). A similar facilitation of acquisition by AngIV analogs (eg. Nle[1]-AngIV) has been observed in scopolamine treated rats (Pederson et al., 1998, 2001), and perforant path damaged rats (Wright et al., 1999). In addition, Fred Mendelsohn's laboratory has reported LVV-hemorphin 7 (LVV-H7) to bind at the AngIV receptor subtype which they have identified as insulin-regulated aminopeptidase (IRAP). LVV-H7 also facilitates cognitive processing (reviewed in Chai et al., 2004).

THE BRAIN CHOLINERGIC SYTEM

The central cholinergic system is clearly an important modulatory neurotransmitter system involved in learning and memory. This assertion is based in part on the observation that in neurodegenerative diseases such as Alzheimer's disease, there is a selective loss of cholinergic neurons in the brain (Arendt et al., 1985; Bartus et al., 1982; Muir, 1997). Further, the integrity of cholinergic neurons is correlated with cognitive ability in elderly humans (Mufson et al., 2002; Perry et al., 1987). While various loci of acetylcholine-transmitting neurons are found throughout the mesencephalic and diencephalic regions of the mammalian brain, those regions particularly involved in learning and memory function appear to be prominently situated in two forebrain areas. The nucleus basalis magnocellularis (NBM) is a major source of cholinergic innervation to the neocortex (especially prefrontal) and amygdala, while the medial septum/diagonal band (MS/DB) region provides cholinergic efferents to the hippocampus via the fimbria-fornix pathway (Mesulam et al., 1983; Nicoll, 1985; Woolf, 1984).

The involvement of the NBM and MS/DB in learning and memory is supported by research findings from three experimental approaches: 1) the micro-injection of acetylcholine (ACh) receptor ligands into these structures to determine their influence on learning and memory; 2) the measurement of ACh release in these structures following pharmacological manipulation; and 3) the measurement of ACh release in unperturbed animals during task acquisition (reviewed in Gold, 2003; Sarter and Parikh, 2005).

The cholinergic system interacts with several neurotransmitter systems including dopamine, noradrenaline, serotonin, GABA, opioids, galanine, substance P, and AngII (reviewed in Bacciottine et al., 2001; Decker and McGaugh, 1991; Gulpinar and Wegen, 2004). The interaction between the cholinergic and angiotensinergic systems has received relatively little attention. However, Lee and colleagues (2003a) prepared guinea pigs with unilateral knife-cut lesions of the fimbria-fornix pathway and then evaluated the tissue for changes in acetylcholinesterase, and AngIV binding via in vitro AT_4 receptor autoradiography. This lesion produced a significant decrease in acetylcholinesterase staining in the ipsilateral hippocampus along with small decreases in [125I]AngIV binding in both the CA_2 and CA_3 hippocampal fields. The authors concluded that much of the hippocampal AT_4 receptor binding is post-synaptic in the guinea pig brain. These results are in agreement with the finding that AngIV facilitates potassium-evoked ACh release in both rat (Lee et al., 2001) and guinea pig hippocampal slices (reviewed in Lee et al., 2003b).

There are further suggestions of an interaction between the brain cholinergic and angiotensinergic systems. Specifically, Isbil-Buyukloskun et al. (2001) have reported that icv AngII-induced elevations in blood pressure and heart rate could be blocked by icv pretreatment with either atropine or mecamylamine. Further, Hajdu et al., (2000) icv infused the somatostatin analog octreotide, and noted a dose-dependent robust drinking response and elevated blood pressure. These responses could be significantly attenuated with icv infused Captopril, Losartan, or atropine. With respect to learning and memory, Yonkov and Georgiev (1990) examined the influence of a cholinergic agonist oxotremorine, and the muscarinic receptor antagonist scopolamine, on icv AngII-induced facilitation of active avoidance and passive avoidance conditioning tasks in rats. Combined treatment with oxotremorine and AngII facilitated memory retrieval of these tasks, while scopolamine interfered with AngII-induced memory facilitation. On the other hand, Raghavendra et al. (1998) have reported that intraperitoneal Losartan enhanced retention of passive avoidance conditioning in mice. Treatment with Losartan also attenuated deficits in recall induced by scopolamine. The authors concluded that Losartan-induced facilitation of memory was due to elevated release of ACh.

The interaction of nicotine and AngII regarding their influence on LTP has also been investigated. Wayner and colleagues (1996) reported that AngII inhibition of LTP in the dentate gyrus could be blocked by pretreatment with Losartan (Wayner et al., 1993, 1996). Pretreatment with nicotine prevented this AngII inhibition of LTP, while nicotine alone had no influence on LTP. These results suggest that: 1) AngII has a negative effect on LTP (and presumably memory retrieval; see Lee et al., 1995); 2) nicotine acting via the cholinergic nicotinic receptor appears to influence the AT_1 receptor system.

Recently our laboratory has reported that icv treatment with the nicotinic cholinergic receptor antagonist, mecamylamine, disrupted acquisition of the Morris water maze task. Intracerebroventricular application of Nle^1-AngIV (an AT_4 receptor agonist) could overcome this deficit in spatial learning (Olson et al., 2004; Figure 3). However, Nle^1-AngIV did not compensate for impaired acquisition resulting from the combined application of scopolamine plus mecamylamine. These results suggest that Nle^1-AngIV-induced compensation via the AT_4 receptor subtype system may be dependent upon the brain cholinergic system. This notion is supported by the observation that AngIV and LVV-H7-induced the release of acetylcholine from rat hippocampal slices in a dose-dependent fashion (Lee et al., 2001). This release of ACh could be blocked by Divalinal-AngIV. Recently, Lee and colleagues (2004) have reported both native AngIV and LVV-H7 facilitated spatial learning in a Barnes circular maze in which the animal must locate one escape tunnel among eight possible locations.

Taken together these results suggest an important interaction among the $AngII/AT_1$ and $AngIV/AT_4$ receptor systems in combination with the brain cholinergic system. Although it remains to be determined whether angiotensins directly modify ECM molecules important in neural plasticity, preliminary results indicate this to be the case (Harding, unpublished observations).

MODELS OF MEMORY-ASSOCIATED NEURAL PLASTICITY

The behavioral sciences have a history of subdividing memory and conditioning into several classifications including the major categories of explicit and implicit memories (Figure 4). Under explicit memory is included episodic (events) and semantic (factual and biographical information). Implicit memory includes motor learning, non-associative and associative learning. Although this approach is useful from a teaching perspective, it is unlikely that separate molecular processes occur with each of these classifications. Rather, a single basic series of biochemical cascades probably underlies the establishment of all memory traces and these cascades are adapted to accommodate diverse environmental circumstances. This section begins by describing an emerging model of how memories appear to be consolidated. This is followed by a discussion of the reconsolidation theory of memory. Next, the potential roles of tPA, MMPs, and TIMPs in these processes are described. Finally, a theoretical model is proposed that attempts to integrate contributions by the AngIV/AT$_4$ and cholinergic systems to synaptic plasticity.

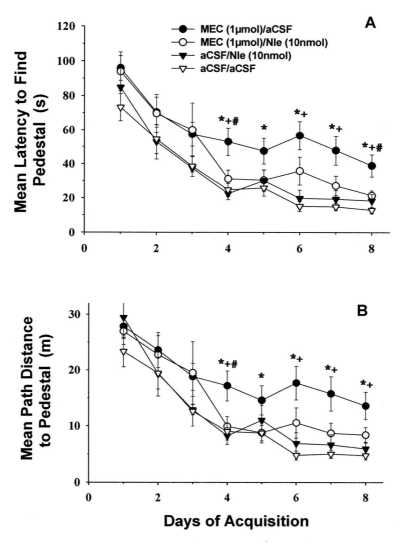

Figure 3. Mean (+ SEM) latencies (A) and swim distances (B) to find the pedestal for each group following icv injections of 1 μmol mec/aCSF, 1 μmol mec/10 pmol Nle1-AngIV, aCSF/10 pmol Nle1-Ang IV, or aCSF/aCSF. The μmol group was compared against aCSF/aCSF (*), aCSF/10 pmol Nle1-Ang IV (+), and 1 μmol mec/10 pmol Nle1-Ang IV (#) on days 4-8 using one-way ANOVAs and Dunnett tests (P < 0.05). From Olson et al. (2004).

Types of Memory

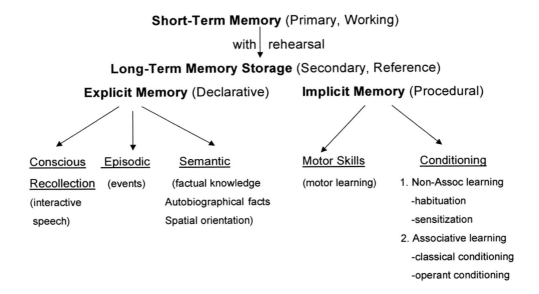

Short-Term Memory (Primary, Working)

with ↓ rehearsal

Long-Term Memory Storage (Secondary, Reference)

Explicit Memory (Declarative)   **Implicit Memory** (Procedural)

Conscious	Episodic	Semantic	Motor Skills	Conditioning
Recollection	(events)	(factual knowledge	(motor learning)	1. Non-Assoc learning
(interactive		Autobiographical facts		-habituation
speech)		Spatial orientation)		-sensitization
				2. Associative learning
				-classical conditioning
				-operant conditioning

Figure 4. Short-term memory can result in long-term memory consolidation with rehearsal. The major categories of long-term memory storage are explicit and implicit memories and their subcategories.

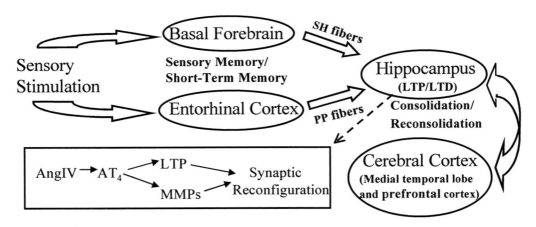

Figure 5. A pathway model of how sensory stimulation may activate sensory and short-term memories in basal forebrain and entorhinal cortex structures resulting in the formation of long-term potentiation/depression and memory consolidation in the hippocampus. Septo-hippocampal and perforant pathway fibers appear to be of major importance concerning information flow into the hippocampus. The AngIV/AT$_4$ receptor system may facilitate memory consolidation in the hippocampus by at least two mechanisms. Activation of this system facilitates hippocampal LTP and promotes the activation of MMPs that may facilitate new plasticity by initiating reconfiguration of the ECM. There is reason to suggest that consolidated memories located in the medial temporal lobe and prefrontal cortex can be reactivated in the hippocampus, modified and reconsolidated, thus providing an efficient and rapid mechanism for updating existing memories. Adapted from Wright and Harding (2004).

1. Memory Consolidation Theory

The theory of memory consolidation proposes that the consolidated trace is initially fragile and easily disrupted, but over time can be converted into a stable long-term memory (McGaugh, 1966). Recently this process has been divided into synaptic consolidation presumed to be complete in just a few hours (Squire and Kandell, 1999; Dudai, 2004), and system consolidation that may take days, weeks, or years to complete (Dudai, 2004; Franklin and Bontempi, 2005). There is considerable evidence to support roles for LTP and long-term depression (LTD) in synaptic consolidation (Figure 5) that may involve changes in spine protein synthesis, shape, and numbers resulting in synaptic reconfiguration (Kelleher et al., 2004). There is also a growing body of evidence in support of systems consolidation that suggest shifts in storage location of the consolidated memory from the hippocampus and/or amydala through association cortex and finally resting in the prefrontal cortex and medial temporal lobe (Miyashita, 2004; Franklin and Bontempi, 2005).

At this point the memory trace has been assumed to be "permanent" and long lasting. However, this assumption has been challenged by reconsolidation theory that was originally posited some years ago (Lewis, 1979; Misanin et al., 1968; Rubin and Franks, 1969; Rubin, 1976).

2. Memory Reconsolidation Theory

There is considerable evidence that the permanence of long-term memory can be disrupted with memory retrieval/reactivation (Nader, 2003). The retrieval process is hypothesized to return the trace to a labile state permitting modification and updating. There appears to be many similarities between the initial consolidation process and the reconsolidation process including: 1) both can be blocked by anisomycin (a generalized protein synthesis inhibitor); 2) both appear to require activation of CREB and Zif 268 (reviewed in Lee et al, 2004). On the other hand Taubenfeld and colleagues (2001), using a more refined approach, have shown that expression of the transcription factor CCAAT enhances binding enhancer binding protein β (C/EBP β) in the CA_1 field of the hippocampus is essential for consolidation of passive avoidance memory, but not during reconsolidation. There is also recent evidence that consolidation requires brain-derived neurotrophic factor (BDNF), while reconsolidation is dependent upon activation of Zif 268 (reviewed in Lee et al., 2004).

3. tPA, MMPs, and TIMPs

There is a wealth of data from animal spatial learning experiments to indicate a role for the hippocampus in spatial learning and memory. This hypothesis is also supported by the observation that hippocampal damage results in a compromised ability to solve tasks that demand recognition of spatial cues and strategies (Morris et al., 1990; Olton et al., 1978; Sutherland and McDonald, 1990). Much of the sensory input to the hippocampus appears to be via the septo-hippocampal (SH) pathway that originates in the basal forebrain (Muir, 1997), and the perforant pathway (PP) that arises in the entorhinal cortex (Hjorth-Simonsen and Jeune, 1972; Klug et al., 1998; Skelton and McNamara, 1992; Figure 5). Once the hippocampus is activated it appears that neural plasticity occurs in the form of LTP and LTD along with concomitant changes in synaptic morphology in the dentate gyrus and subfields of the hippocampus (reviewed in Benington and Frank, 2003; Wright et al., 2002a). There is considerably less information concerning the possible ECM modifications that may occur and mediate memory consolidation.

Very little research attention has been given to the topic of learning-induced changes in the ECM as related to memory consolidation. It seems logical to assume that an increase in neural activity induced by input from the SH and PP pathways may represent an experience that the animal must retain in order to gain a future behavioral advantage over competitors. This presumably results in a cascade of gene expression and protein synthesis that is necessary in order to affect the neural structural changes, synaptic modification, and/or synaptogenesis, presumed to mediate long-term memory storage (Bailey et al., 1996; Bartsch et al., 1995; Bear and Malenka, 1994). Thus it is necessary to identify the target genes that are activated by learning-induced experiences and whose production is necessary to the process of neural plasticity and remodeling. To date there are only a few identified potential candidates that are capable of initiating such a series of events. The first is tPA, the serine protease responsible for the conversion of plasminogen to plasmin that in turn activates some MMPs. Support for tPA's role in memory consolidation comes from the following observations: 1) tPA knockout mice exhibit impaired maintenance of hippocampal LTP and impaired learning (Calabresi et al., 2000; Frey et al., 1996; Huang et al., 1996a); 2) tPA mRNA expression is increased during LTP (Qian et al., 1993); 3) cerebellar tPA protein is increased with motor learning (Seeds et al., 1995); 4) disruption of corticostriatal LTP has been reported in tPA deficient mice (Centonze et al., 2002a). There is also the observation that AngII acting via the AT_1 receptor subtype, and AngIV acting via the AT_4 receptor subtype, are serving opposing functions. This notion has been offered by Vaughn (2002) from research completed using coronary artery endothelial cells and coronary vessels. Specifically, it has been shown in apolipoprotein E-deficient mice that AngII promotes the elevation of uPA mRNA expression (Wang et al., 2001) that would be expected to facilitate the formation of plasmin and ultimately the activation of MMPs designed to break down ECM proteins. On the other hand, AngIV stimulates the expression of PAI-1 mRNA via activation of the AT_4 receptor (Kerins et al., 1995; Gesualdo et al., 1999; Mehta et al., 2002). Such activation would be expected to interfere with the formation of plasmin and ultimately inhibit the activation of MMPs, thus preserving ECM proteins. These preliminary findings support the tentative hypothesis that with the introduction of an animal into a new environment an elevation in the release of brain AngII is necessary in order to facilitate tPA mRNA expression during LTP, and to stimulate the initial breakdown of ECM proteins that are maintaining *status quo* regarding synaptic configuration. Along with the expression and maintenance of hippocampal LTP is the opportunity for synaptic reconfiguration via changes in terminal numbers and connections. These processes could be accomplished within a few minutes if solution to the task is rapidly acquired permitting time for AngII to be converted to AngIII and then to AngIV. At this point AngIV activation of the AT_4 receptor would promote PAI-1 expression designed to interfere with further plasmin production and ultimately return the newly configured ECM back to a quiescent state. Although there are several potential problems with this model, not the least of which is the time delays necessary for increases in mRNA expression in synthesis of proteins, at present it seems plausible and a testable notion.

A second candidate downstream from tPA and plasmin are MMPs. There are well over twenty MMPs thus far identified (Table 2) but only a subset of these appear to be important concerning brain neural plasticity. Pagenstecher et al., (1997) and Vecil et al., (2000) measured low levels of expression for MMP-2, MMP-9, MMP-11, MMP-12 and MMP-14 in the mouse brain. Sekine-Aizawa et al., (2001) reported that MMP-24 (also referred to as MT5 MMP) accounted for approximately 60% of the total MMPs lacking a fibronectin-like domain in the rat brain. Other MMPs include MMP-14 (23%), MMP-15 (13%), MMP-3 (1.3%), and MMP-8 (0.7%). Vaillant et al., (1999) measured reasonably high levels of MMP-2, MMP-3, and MMP-9 in Purkinje cerebellar neurons in the adult rat along with MMP-3 and MMP-9 in granular cerebellar neurons. Fifteen-day-old rats have been shown to express high levels of cerebellar MMP-3 and MMP-9 simultaneous with the occurrence of a very high rate of synaptogenesis. A second structure that has received attention is the hippocampus. MMP-2 and MMP-9 mRNA expression and protein have been reported for the origin of MMP-2 primarily from glial cells and MMP-9 from neurons (Szklarczyk et al., 2002). Reasonably low levels of MMP-24 mRNA and protein have also been reported associated with pyramidal particle neurons, thalamic neurons, and in the olfactory bulb (Jaworski, 2000a; Sekine-Aizawa et al., 2001).

The final candidate is TIMPs. TIMP levels are potentially important to the process of neural plasticity because they regulate the proteolytic activity of MMPs by forming tight noncovalent complexes with MMPs thus deactivating them (Bode et al., 1999; Jeng et al., 2001). There is evidence that TIMPs are also capable of binding to latent forms of MMPs (Kleiner and Stetler-Stevenson, 1993). TIMP-2 mRNA has been identified in many parts of the brain. TIMP-4 mRNA is especially abundant in the cerebellum, followed by TIMP-1. TIMP-3 is present at high levels in choroid plexus (Fager and Jaworski, 2000; Jaworski, 2000b). Cerebellar TIMP-1, TIMP-2, and TIMP-3 appear to be expressed by granular neurons (Vaillant et al., 1999). Following proteolytic injury ECM remodeling normally occurs, along with elevations in TIMPs presumably to inhibit further action by MMPs. There is considerable evidence to suggest that pathology can accompany an imbalance between appropriate levels of MMPs to facilitate remodeling, and their inhibition by TIMPs (Lukes et al., 1999; Stamenkovic, 2003). The disease states that appear to accompany chronic activation of MMPs due to such an imbalance include cancer, arthritis, athrosclerosis, diabetes mellitus, multiple sclerosis, Alzheimer's disease, Guillain-Barre syndrome, ischemia, renal disease, infections and others (Eikmans et al., 2003; Engbring and Kleinman, 2003; Heeneman et al., 2003; Jeng et al., 2001; Lukes et al.., 1999; Rivera and Khrestchatisky, 2000; Tsilibray, 2003). Therefore, the maintenance of an appropriate balance among these glycoproteins is imperative.

The long established notion that memories are permanent once consolidated is presently being challenged in the form of the reconsolidation theory (Nadel and Land, 2000). The proposition that long-term memories can be reconfigured, updated, and restored is appealing both from an ongoing neural plasticity perspective and concerning efficiency of effort. Hippocampal reprocessing or "synaptic re-enter reinforcement" (Wittenberg et al., 2002) does appear to be involved in the updating of established memories (Nader, 2003). Given that both the hippocampus and neocortex are important to long-term storage of memories and the hippocampus is primarily responsible for reprocessing and updating established memories, there appears to be the necessity for frequent exchanges of information from neocortex to hippocampus and back again. Support for such a process is offered by the observation that hippocampectomy renders both animal models and humans severely impaired with respect to either forming new memories or modifying established explicit (declarative), spatial, and contextual memories (Alberini, 2005; Bayley et al., 2003; Frankland and Bontempi, 2005; Manns et al., 2003; McEwen, 2001). The two neocortical structures most frequently implicated concerning declarative memory formation and storage are the medial temporal lobe (reviewed in Powell and Duncan, 2005; Power et al., 2003; Squire et al., 2004) and the prefrontal cortex (reviewed in Frankland and Bontempi, 2005; Otani, 2002). Therefore, a continuing exchange of information would be anticipated between the hippocampus and at least these two structures of the neocortex when updating of existing memory traces is required (Simons and Spiers, 2003). Further if hippocampus is the primary structure responsible for reprocessing and updating memory traces, then it should follow that one or more of the potential markers of neural plasticity, i.e. tPA, MMPs, TIMPs should be activated in the hippocampus during reconsolidation of previous traces. This reactivation of the hippocampus should occur coincident with reintroduction back to a previously salient location, or the revisiting of an important previous experience, given that some additional information or modification of the memory is necessary. Such predictions remain to be tested.

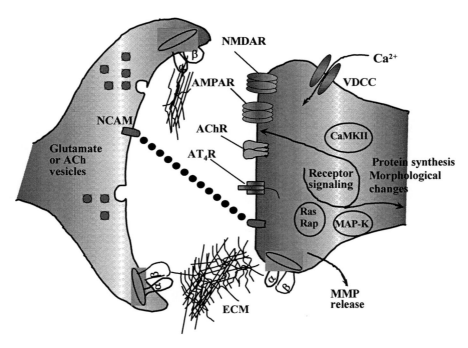

Figure 6. Hypothetical model depicting the possible relationship among ECM molecules, and several receptor systems in the control of neural plasticity. Cell surface receptors such as integrins (α, β subunits) and NCAMs interact with receptor tyrosine kinases (not shown) at pre and post-synaptic appositions thus influencing receptor and cytoskeletal functioning. Glutamate release activates AMPA and NMDA receptors ultimately facilitating Ca^{2+} entry into the cell. Tenascin-C is also thought to interact with VDCC to further facilitate Ca $^{2+}$ entry. Reconfiguration of ECM molecules appears to be, at least in part, triggered by Ca $^{2+}$ signaling. Cellular signaling may also occur through Ras and Rap. Activation of the AT_4 receptor has been shown to initiate Ca $^{2+}$ entry and activate MMPs thus providing another stimulus for ECM rearrangement. The relationship among VDCCs, AMPA, MNDA, AT_4, and cholinergic receptors is in need of further investigation. Adapted from Dityatev and Schachner (2003), Kaczmarek et al. (2002), Wright and Harding (2004).

A model that illustrates these presumed steps necessary for memory consolidation is offered in Figure 6. This hypothetical model presents possible relationships among ECM and MMP molecules and several receptor systems in the control of neural plasticity. Cell surface receptors such as integrins (α and β subunits shown) and NCAMs interact with receptor tyrosine kinases (not shown) at pre- and postsynaptic appositions to influence receptor and cytoskeletal functions. Glutamate release activates AMPA and NMDA receptors ultimately facilitating calcium entry into the cell. As described earlier, there is recent evidence suggesting that activation of the AT_4 receptor subtype results in calcium entry via VDCCs. Reconfiguration of ECM molecules appears to be triggered by calcium signaling. Cellular signaling may also occur via Ras and Rap. Activation of cholinergic receptors by acetylcholine is involved in memory consolidation, however recent evidence, as discussed earlier, strongly suggest that pharmacological blockade of the cholinergic receptors and resulting inhibition of learning and memory can be overcome by the concomitant activation of AT_4 receptors. Thus, the brain AngIV/AT_4 receptor system appears to provide a parallel pathway for the initiation of ECM rearrangement and neural plasticity.

CONCLUSION

This chapter summarized available reports concerning the role of the brain angiotensinergic and cholinergic systems and memory consolidation, with particular emphasis upon those extracellular matrix molecules presumed to mediate neural plasticity. In this regard several pieces of information are particularly relevant: 1) AT_4 receptor agonists facilitate LTP that in turn elevates entrodendritic calcium that initiates changes in protein kinases in cytoskeletal proteins important in synaptic reconfiguration. 2) LTP also facilitates increased tPA levels that act upon plasminogen to form plasmin that serves to convert MMPs from their pro to active forms (including MMP-1, MMP-3, and MMP-9). 3) The degradation of existing ECM molecules appears to be a prerequisite to synaptic reconfiguration. 4) Increases in hippocampal NCAMs correlate with successful behavioral conditioning; icv infusions of antibodies against NCAMs interfere with successful conditioning. Future research attention must focus upon specific molecular changes that mediate synaptic remodeling and the temporal patterns, location(s), duration, and reconfiguration of consolidated and reconsolidated memories.

ACKNOWLEDGMENTS

The work from our laboratory presented in this chapter was supported by NIH grant R01-HL64245-03, NSF grant IBN-0091337, the Edward E. and Lucille I. Lainge Endowment for Alzheimer's Disease Research, and funds provided for medical and biological research by the State of Washington Initiative Measure No. 171. We thank Mrs. Ruth Day for secretarial assistance provided during the course of writing this manuscript.

REFERENCES

Alberini, C.M. (2005). Mechanisms of memory stabilization: Are consolidation and reconsolidation similar or distinct processes? *Trends in Neuroscience 28*, 51-56.

Albiston, A.L., Mustafa, T., McDowall, S.G., Mendelsohn, F.A., Lee, J., and Chai, S.Y. (2003). AT(4) receptor is insulin-regulated membrane aminopeptidase: potential mechanisms of memory enhancement. *Trends in Endocrinology and Metabolism, 14*, 72-77.

Allen, A.M., Oldfield, B.J., Giles, M.E., Paxinos, G., McKinley, M.J., and Mendelsohn, F.A. (2000). Localization of angiotensin receptors in the nervous system. In R. Quirion, A. Bjorklund, and T. Hodfelt (Eds.), *Handbook of Chemical Neuroanatomy*. Amsterdam: Elsevier, pp. 79-124.

Arendt, T., Bigl, V., Tennstedt, A. and Arendt, A. (1985). Neuronal loss in different parts of the nucleus basalis is related to neuritic plaque formation in cortical target areas in Alzheimer's disease. *Journal of Neuroscience Research 73*, 593-602.

Armstrong, D.L., Garcia, E.A., Ma, T., Quinones, B., and Wayner, M.J. (1996). Angiotensin II blockade of long-term potentiation at the perforant path-granule cell synapse in vitro. *Peptides, 17*, 689-693.

Bacciottini, L., Passani, M.B., Mannaioni, P.F., and Blandina, P. (2001). Interactions between histaminergic and cholinergic systems in learning and memory. *Behavioural Brain Research, 124*, 183-194.

Backstrom, J.R., Giselle, P.L., Cullen, M.J., and Tőkés, Z.A. (1996). Matrix metalloproteinase-9 (MMP-9) is synthesized in neurons of the human hippocampus and is capable of degrading the amyloid-β peptide (1-40). *Journal of Neuroscience 16*, 7910-7919.

Bailey, C.H., Bartsch, D., and Kandel, E.R. (1996). Toward a molecular definition of long-term memory storage. *Proceedings of the National Academy of Sciences, USA, 93*, 13445-13452.

Baranowska, D., Braszko, J.J., and Wisniewski, K. (1983). Effect of angiotensin II and vasopressin on acquisition and extinction of conditioned avoidance in rats. *Psychopharmacology, 81*, 247-251.

Barnes, N.M., Champaneria, S., Costall, B., Kelly, M.E., Murphy, D.A., and Naylor, R.J. (1990). Cognitive enhancing actions of DuP753 detected in a mouse habituation paradigm. *NeuroReport 1,* 239-242.

Barnes, N.M., Costall, B., Kelly, M.E., Murphy, D.A., and Naylor, R.J. (1991). Cognitive enhancing actions of PD123177 detected in a mouse habituation paradigm. *NeuroReport, 2,* 351-353.

Bartsch, D.G.M., Skehel, P.A., Karl, K.A., Herder, S., Chen, M., Bailey, C.H.,and Kandel., E.R. (1995). Aplysia CREB2 represses long-term facilitation into long-term functional and structural change. *Cell, 83,* 979-992.

Bartus, R.T., Dean, R.L., Beer, B. and Lippa, A.S. (1982). The cholinergic hypothesis of geriatric memory dysfunction. *Science 217,* 408-414.

Bayley, P.J., Hopkins, R.O., and Squire, L.R. (2003). Successful recollection of remote autobiographical memories by amnesic patients with medial temporal lobe lesions. *Neuron, 38,* 135-144.

Bear, M.F., and Malenka, R.C. (1994). Synaptic plasticity: LTP and LTD. *Current Opinions in Neurobiology, 4,* 389-399.

Belcheva, I., Ternianov, A., and Georgiev, V. (2000). Lateralized learning and memory effects of angiotensin II microinjected into the rat CA_1 hippocampal area. *Peptides, 21,* 407-411.

Benington, J.H., and Frank, M.G. (2003). Cellular and molecular connections between sleep and synaptic plasticity. *Progress in Neurobiology, 69,* 71-101.

Bennett, Jr. J.P., and Snyder, S.H. (1976). Angiotensin II binding to mammalian brain membranes. *Journal of Biological Chemistry, 251,* 7423-7430.

Bernier, S.G., Fournier, A., and Guillemette, G. (1994). A specific binding site recognizing a fragment of angiotensin II in bovine adrenal cortex membranes. *European Journal of Pharmacology, 271,* 55-63.

Birkedal-Hansen, H. (1995). Proteolytic remodeling of extracellular matrix. *Current Opinions in Cell Biology, 7,* 728-735.

Birkedal-Hansen, H., Moore, W.G., and Bodden, M.K. (1993). Matrix metalloproteinases: a review. *Critical Reviews in Oral Biological Medicine, 4,* 197-250.

Birnberger, K.L. and Rovainen, C.M. (1971). *Journal of Neurophysiology, 34,* 983-989.

Bliss, T.V., and Collingridge, G.L. (1993). A synaptic model of memory: long-term potentiation in the hippocampus. *Nature, 361,* 31-39.

Boal, J.G., Dunham, A.W., Williams, K.T. and Hanlon, R.T. (2000). Experimental evidence for spatial learning in Octopuses (Octopus bimaculoides). *Journal of Comparative Psychology, 114,* 246-252.

Bode, W., Fernandez-Catalan, C., Tschesche, H., Grams, F., Nagase, H., and Masko, S, K. (1999). Structural properties of matrix metalloproteinases. *Cellular and Molecular Life Sciences, 55,* 639-652.

Bohlen und Halback, O.V. (2003). Angiotensin IV in the central nervous system. *Cellular and Tissue Research 311,* 1-9.

Bottari, S.P., Raylor, V., King, I.N., Bogdal, S., Whitebread, S., and DeGasparo, M. (1991). Angiotensin II AT_2 receptors do not interact with guanine nucleotide binding proteins. *European Journal of Pharmacology, 207,* 157-163.

Braszko, J.J. (2002). AT(2) but not AT(1) receptor antagonism abolishes angiotensin II increase of the acquisition of conditioned avoidance responses in rats. *Behavioural Brain Research, 131,* 79-86.

Braszko, J.J., Kulakowska, A., and Karwowska-Polecka, W. (1998). CGP 42112A antagonism of the angiotensin II and angiotensin II(3-7) facilitation of recall in rats. *Pharmacological Research, 38,* 461-468.

Braszko, J.J., Kulakowska, A., and Winnicka, M.M. (2003). Effects of angiotensin II and its receptor antagonists on motor activity and anxiety in rats. *Journal of Physiological Pharmacology, 54,* 271-281.

Braszko, J.J., Kupryszewski, G., Witczuk, B., and Wisniewski, K. (1988). Angiotensin II (3-8)-hexapeptide affects motor activity, performance of passive avoidance, and a conditioned avoidance response in rats. *Neuroscience, 27,* 777-783.

Braszko, J.J., and Wisniewski, K. (1988). Effective angiotensin II and saralasin on motor activity in the passive avoidance behavior of rats. *Peptides, 9,* 475-479.

Braszko, J.J., Wisniewski, K., Kupryszewski, G., and Witczuk, B. (1987). Psychotropic effects of angiotensin II and III in rats: Locomotor and exploratory vs. cognitive behavior. *Behavioural Brain Research, 25,* 195-203.

Braszko, J.J., Wlasienko, J., Koziolkiewicz, W., Janecka, A., and Wisniewski, K. (1991). The 3-7 fragment of angiotensin II is probably responsible for its psychoactive properties. *Brain Research, 542,* 49-54.

Brembs, B., Baxter, D.A. and Byrne, J.H. (2004). Extending in vitro conditioning in *Aplysia* to analyze operant and classical processes in the same preparation. *Learning and Memory, 11,* 412-420.

Broshinan, K.B., Li P., and Ferrario, C.M. (1996). Angiotensin (1-7) dilates canine coronary arteries through kinins and nitric oxide. *Hypertension 27,* 523-528.

Cajal, S.R. (1928). *Degeneration and Regeneration of the Nervous System.* London: Oxford University Press.

Calabresi, P., Napolitano, M., Centonze, D., Marfia, G.A., Gubellini, P., Teule, M.A., Berretta, N., and Bernardi, G. (2000). Tissue plasminogen activator controls multiple forms of synaptic plasticity and memory. *European Journal of Neuroscience, 12,* 1002-1012.

Campagnole-Santos, M.J., Heeringer, S.B., Batista, E.N., Khosla, M.C., and Santos, R.A. (1992). Differential baroreceptor reflex modulation by centrally infused angiotensin peptides. *American Journal of Physiology 263,* R89-R94.

Centonze, D., Napolitano, M., Saulle, E., Gubellini, P., Picconi, B., Martorana, A., Pisani, A., Gulino, A., Bernardi, G., and Calabresi, P. (2002a). Tissue plasminogen activator is required for corticostriatal long-term potentiation. *European Journal of Neuroscience, 16,* 713-721.

Chai, S.Y., Fernando, R., Peck, G., Ye, S.Y., Mendelsohn, F.A.O., Jenkins, T.A., and Albiston, A.L. (2004). The angiotesin IV/AT$_4$ receptor. *Cellular and Molecular Life Sciences, 61,* 2728-2737.

Chauvel, E.N., Llorens-Cortes, C., Coric, P., Wilk, S., Roques, B.P., and Fournie-Zaluski, M.C. (1994). Differential inhibition of aminopeptidase A and aminopeptidase N by new-amino thiols. *Journal of Medicinal Chemistry, 37,* 2950-2957.

Coleman, J.K., Krebs, L.T., Hamilton, T.A., Ong, B., Lawrence, K.A., Sardinia, M.F., Harding, J.W., and Wright, J.W. (1998). Autoradiographic identification of kidney angiotensin IV binding sites and angiotensin IV-induced renal blood flow changes in rats. *Peptides, 19,* 269-277.

Croog, S.H., Levine, S., Testa, M.A., Brown, B., Bulpitt, C.J., Jenkins, C.D., Klerman, G.L., and Williams, G.H. (1986). The effects of antihypertensive therapy on the quality of life. *English Journal of Medicine, 314,* 1657-1664.

Day, L.B., Crews, D. and Wilczynski, W. (2001). Effects of medial and dorsal cortex lesions on spatial memory in lizards. Behavioural Brain Research 118, 27-42.

Decker, M.W., and McGaugh, J.L. (1991). The role of interactions between the cholinergic system and other neuromodulatory sytsems in learning and memory. *Synapse, 7,*151-168.

de Gasparo, M., Catt, K.J., Inagami, T., Wright, J.W., and Unger, T. (2000). International Union of Pharmacology. XXII. The angiotensin II receptors. *Pharmacological Reviews, 52,* 415-472.

de Gasparo, M., and Siragy, H.M. (1999). The AT$_2$ receptor: fact, fancy and fantasy. *Regulatory Peptides, 81,* 11-24.

Deiken, R.F. (1986). Captopril treatment in depression. *Biological Psychiatry, 21*, 1428-1452.

Delorenzi, A., Locatelli, F., Romano, A., Nahmod, V., and Maldonado, H. (1997). Angiotensin II (3-8) induces long-term memory improvement in the crab *Chasmagnathus. Neuroscience Letters, 226*, 143-146.

Delorenzi, A., and Maldonado, H. (1999). Memory enhancement by the angiotensinergic system in the crab *Chasmagnathus* is mediated by endogenous angiotensin II. *Neuroscience Letters, 266*, 1-4.

Denny, J.B., Polan-Curtain, J., Wayner M.J., and Armstrong, D.L. (1991). Angiotensin II blocks hippocampal long-term potentiation. *Brain Research, 567*, 321-324.

DeNoble, V.J., DeNoble, K.F., Spencer, K.R., Chiu, A.T., Wong, P.C., and Timmermans, B.M. (1991). Non-peptide angiotensin II receptor antagonist and angiotensin-converting enzyme inhibitor: effect on a renin-induced deficit of a passive avoidance response in rats. *Brain Research, 561*, 230-235.

Dityatev, A., and Schachner, M. (2003). Extracellular matrix molecules and synaptic plasticity. *Nature Reviews Neuroscience, 4*, 456-468.

Dudai, Y. (2004). The neurobiology of consolidations, or, how stable is the engram? *Annual Reviews in Psychology, 55*, 51-86.

Dulin, N., Madhun, Z.T., Chang, C.H., Berti-Mattera, L., Dickens, D., and Douglas, J.G. (1995). Angiotensin IV receptors and signaling in opossum kidney cells. *American Journal of Physiology, 269*, F644-F652.

Eikmans, M., Baelde, J.J., de Heer, E., and Bruijn, J.A. (2003). ECM homeostasis in renal diseases: a genomic approach. *Journal of Pathology, 200*, 526-536.

Engbring, J.A., and Kleinman, H.D. (2003). The basement membrane matrix in malignancy. *Journal of Pathology, 200*, 465-470.

Ennis, B.W., and Matrisian, L.M. (1994). Matrix degrading metalloproteinases. *Journal of Neuro-Oncology, 18*, 105-109.

Fager, N., and Jaworski, D.M. (2000). Differential spatial distribution and temporal regulation of tissue inhibitor of metalloproteinase mRNA expression during rat central nervous system development. *Mechanisms of Development, 98*, 105-109.

Ferrario, C.M. (2003). Contribution of angiotensin-(1-7) to cardiovascular physiology and pathology. *Current Hypertension Reports, 5*, 129-134.

Ferrario, C.M., Chappell, M.C., Tallant, E.A., Brosnihan, K.B., and Diz, D.I. (1997). Counterregulatory actions of angiotensin-(1-7). *Hypertension, 30*, 535-541.

Frankland, P. W., and Bontempi, B. (2005). The organization of recent and remote memories. *Nature Reviews Neuroscience*, 6, 119-130.

Frey, U., and Morris, R.G. (1998). Synaptic tagging: implications for late maintenance of hippocampal long-term potentiation. *Trends in Neuroscience, 21*, 181-188.

Frey, U., Muller, M., and Kuhl, D. (1996). A different form of long-lasting potentiation revealed in tissue plasminogen activator mutant mice. *Journal of Neuroscience, 16*, 2057-2063.

Gard, P.R. (2002). The role of angiotensin II in cognition and behaviour. *European Journal of Pharmacology, 438*, 1-14.

Georgiev, V.P., Yonkov, D.I., and Kambourova, T.S. (1988). Interactions between angiotensin II and baclofen in shuttle-box and passive avoidance performance. *Neuropeptides, 12*, 155-158.

Gesualdo, L., Ranieri, E., Monno, R., Rossiello, M.R., Colucci, M., Semeraro, N., Grandaliano, G., Schena, F.P., Ursi, M., and Cerullo, G. (1999). Angiotensin IV stimulates plasminogen activator inhibitor-1 expression in proximal tubular epithelial cells. *Kidney International, 56*, 461-470.

Glossmann H, Baukal A, and Catt KJ. (1974). Angiotensin II reeptors in bovine adrenal cortex. Modification of angioensin II binding by guanyl nucleotides. *Journal of Biological Chemistry, 249*, 664-666.

Gold, P.E. (2003). Acetylcholine modulation of neural systems involved in learning and memory. *Neurobiology of Learning and Memory, 80*, 194-210.

Goldbrunner, R.H., Bernstein, J.J., and Tonn, J.C. (1998). ECM-mediated glioma cell invasion. *Microscopy and Research Technology, 13*, 250-257.

Gottschall, P.E., and Deb, S. (1996). Regulation of matrix metalloproteinase expression in astrocytes, microglia and neurons. *Neuroimmunomodulation, 3*, 69-75.

Graeff, F.G., Gentil, C.G., Peres, V.L., and Covian, M.R. (1973). Lever-pressing behavior caused by intraseptal angiotensin II in water satiated rats. *Pharmacology, Biochemistry and Behavior, 1*, 357-359.

Gulpinar, M.A., and Yegen, B.C. (2004). The physiology of learning and memory: Role of peptides and stress. *Current Protein Peptides and Science, 5*, 457-473.

Guo DF, and Inagami T. (1994). The genomic organization of the rat angiotensin II receptor AT_{1B}. *Biochimistry Biophysiology Acta, 1218*, 91-94.

Haas, H.L., Felix, D. and Davis, M.D. (1982). Angiotensin excites hippocampal pyramidal cells by two mechanisms. *Cellular and Molecular Neurobiology, 2*, 21-32.

Hajdu, I., Obal, F., Gardi, J., Laczi, F., and Krueger, J.M. (2000). Octreotide-induced drinking, vasopressin, and pressure responses: Role of central angiotensin and Ach. *American Journal of Physiology. Regulatory and Integrative Comparative Physiology, 279*, R271-R277.

Hall, K.L., Hanesworth, J.M., Ball, A.E., Felgenhaner, G.P., Hosick, H.L., and Harding, J.W. (1993). Identification and characterization of a novel angiotensin binding site in cultured vascular smooth muscle cells that is specific for the hexapeptide (3-8) fragment of angiotensin II, angiotensin IV. *Regulatory Peptides, 44*, 225-232.

Hamilton, T.A., Handa, R.K., Harding, J.W., Wright, J.W. (2001). A role for the AT_4/angiotensin IV system in mediating natriuresis in the rat. *Peptides, 22*, 935-944.

Handa, R.K., Krebs, L.T., Harding, J.W., and Handa, S.E. (1998). Angiotensin IV AT_4-receptor system in the rat kidney. *American Journal of Physiology, 274*, F290-299.

Handsley, M.M., and Edwards, D.R. (2005). Metalloproteinases and their inhibitors in tumor angiogenesis. *International Journal of Cancer, 115*, 849-860.

Hanesworth, J.M., Sardinia, J.F., Krebs, L.T., Hall, K.L., and Harding, J.W. (1993). Elucidation of a specific binding site for angiotensin II(3-8), angiotensin IV, in mammalian heart membranes. *Journal of Pharmacological and Experimental Therapeutics, 266*, 1036-1042.

Harding, J.W., Cook, V.I., Miller-Wing, A.V., Hanesworth, J.M., Sardinia, M.F., Hall, K.L., Stobb, J.W., Swanson, G.N., Coleman, J.K., Wright, J.W., and Harding, E.C. (1992). Identification of an AII (3-8) AIV binding site in guinea pig hippocampus. *Brain Research, 583*, 340-343.

Hayashita-Kinoh, H., Kinoh, H., Okada, A., Komori, K., Itoh, Y., Chiba T., Kajita, M., Yana, I., and Seiki, M. (2001). Membrane-type 5 matrix metalloproteinase is expressed in differentiated neurons and regulates axonal growth. *Cellular Growth and Differentiation, 12*, 573-580.

Hebb, D.O. (1949). *Organization of Behavior: A Neurophsychological Theory*. New York: Wiley.

Heeneman, S., Cleutjens, J.P., Faber, B.C., Creemers, E.E., van Suylen, R.J., Lutgens, E., Cleutjens, K.B., and Daemen, M.J. (2003). The dynamic extracellular matrix: intervention strategies during heart failure and atherosclerosis. *Journal of Pathology, 200*, 516-525.

Hirawa, N., Uehara, Y., Kawabata, Y., Numabe, A., Gomi, T., Ikeda, T., Suzuki, T., Goto, A., Toyo-oka, T., and Omata, M. (1999). Long-term inhibition of renin-angiotensin system sustains memory function in aged Dahl rats. *Hypertension, 34*, 496-502.

Hjorth-Simonsen, A., and Jeune, B. (1972). Origin and termination of the hippocampal perforant path in the rat studied by silver impregnation. *Journal of Comparative Neurology, 144*, 215-231.

Huang, Y.Y., Bach, M.E., Lipp, H.P., Zhuo, M., Wolfer, D.P., Hawkins, R.D., Schoonjans, L., Kandel, E.R., Godfraind, J.M., Mulligan, R., Collen, D., and Carmeliet, P. (1996a). Mice lacking the gene encoding tissue-type plasminogen activator show a selective interference with late-phase long-term potentiation in both Schaffer collateral and mossy fiber pathways. *Proceedings of the National Academy of Sciences, USA, 93*, 8699-8704.

Ikeda, S., Wayner, M.J., Armstrong, D.L., Wright, J.W., Harding, J.W., and Smith, B.G. (1998). The role of angiotensin IV in hippocampal dentate granule cell LTP. *Society of Neuroscience Abstracts, 24*, 330.

Isbil-Buyukcoskun, N., Gulec, G., and Ozluk, K. (2001). A central link between angiotensinergic and cholinergic systems: Role of vasopressin. *Peptides, 22*, 1414-1420.

Iwai, N., and Inagami, T. (1992). Identification of two subtypes in the rat type 1 angiotensin II receptor. *FEBS Letters, 298*, 257-260.

Jaiswal, N., Diz, D.I., Chappell, M.C., Khasla, M.C., and Ferrario, C.M. (1992). Stimulation of endothelial cell prostaglandin production by angiotensin peptides. Characterization of receptors. *Hypertension 21*, 900-905.

Jarvis, M.F., Gessner, G.W., and Ly, C.G. (1992). The angiotensin hexapeptide 3-8 fragment potently inhibits $[^{125}I]$ angiotensin II binding to non-AT_1 or -AT_2 recognition sites in bovine adrenal cortex. *European Journal of Pharmacology, 219*, 319-322.

Jaworski, D.M. (2000a). Developmental regulation of membrane type-5 matrix metalloproteinase (MT5-MMP) expression in the rat nervous system. *Brain Research, 860*, 174-177.

Jaworski, D.M. (2000b). Differential regulation of TIMP mRNA expression in response to intracranial injury. *Glia, 30*, 199-208.

Jaworski, J., Biedermann, I.W., Lapinska, J., Szklarczyk, A., Figiel, I., Konopka, D., Nowicka, D., Filipkowski, R.K., Hetman, M., Kowalczyk, A., and Kaczmarek, L. (1999). Neuronal excitation-driven and AP-1-dependent activation of timp-1 gene expression in rodent hippocams. *Journal of Biological Chemistry, 274*, 28106-28112.

Jeng, A., Gonnell, N., and Skiles, J. (2001). The design, structure, and therapeutic application of matrix metalloproteinase inhibitors. *Current Medicinal Chemistry, 8*, 425-474.

Job, C., and Eberwine, J. (2001). Localization and translation of mRNA in dendrites and axons. *Nature Reviews Neuroscience, 2*, 889-898.

Johnston, C.I. (1990). Biochemistry and pharmacology of the renin-angiotensin system. *Drugs, 39*, 21-31.

Kaczmarek, L., Lapinska-Dzwonek, J., and Szymczak, S. (2002). Matrix metalloproteinases in the adult brain physiology: a link between c-Fos, AP-1 and remodeling of neuronal connections? *EMBO Journal, 21*, 6643-6648.

Kahari, V.M., and Saarialho-Kere, U. (1997). Matrix metalloproteinases in skin. *Experimental Dermatology, 6*, 199-213.

Kakar, S.S., Sellers, J.C., Devor, D.C., Musgrove, L.C., and Neill, J.D. (1992). Angiotensin II type-1 receptor subtype cDNAs: Differential tissue expression and hormonal regulation. *Biochemical and Biophysiological Research Communications, 31*, 1090-1096.

Kambayashi, Y., Bardhan, S., Takahashi, K., Tsuzuki, S., Inui, T., Hamakubo, T., and Inagami, Y. (1993). Molecular cloning of a novel angiotensin II receptor isoform involved in phospotyrosine phosphatase inhibition. *Journal of Biological Chemistry, 268*, 24543-34546.

Kelleher, III, R.J., Govindarajan, A., and Tenegawa, S. (2004). Translational regulatory mechanisms in persistent forms of synaptic plasticity. *Neuron, 44*, 59-73.

Kerins, D.M., Hao, Q., and Vaughan, D.E. (1995). Angiotensin induction of PAI-1 expression in endothelial cells is mediated by the hexapeptide angiotensin IV. *Journal of Clinical Investigation, 96*, 2515-2520.

Kerr, D.S., Bevilaqua, L.R., Bonini, J.S., Rossatao, J.I., Kohler, C.A., Medina, J.H., Izquirdo, I., and Cammarota, M. (2004). Angiotensin II blocks memory consolidation through an AT(2) receptor-dependent mechanism. *Psychopharmacology (Berl), 179*, 529-535.

Kleiner, D.E., and Stetler-Stevenson, W.G. (1993). Structural biochemistry and activation of matrix metalloproteases. *Current Opinions in Cell Biology, 5*, 891-897.

Klug, A., Hailer, N.P., Horvath, T.L., Bechmann, I., and Nitsch, R. (1998). Tracing of the entorhinal-hippocampal pathway in vitro. Hippocampus 8, 57-68.

Köller, M., Krause, H.P., Hoffmeister, F., and Ganten, D., (1979). Endogenous brain angiotensin II disrupts passive avoidance behavior in rats. *Neuroscience Letters 14*, 71-75.

Konoshi, H., Kuroda, S., Inada, Y., and Fujisawa, Y. (1994). Novel subtype of human angiotensin II type 1 receptor: cDNA cloning and expression. *Biochemical and. Biophysiological Research Communications, 199*, 467-474.

Kramár, E.A., Armstrong, D.L., Ikeda, S., Wayner, M.J., Harding, J.W., and Wright, J.W. (2001). The effects of angiotensin IV on long-term potentiation within the CA1 region of the hippocampus in vitro. *Brain Research, 897*, 114-121.

Kramár, E.A., Harding, J.W., and Wright, J.W. (1997). Angiotensin II- and IV-induced changes in cerebral blood flow: Roles of AT_1, AT_2, and AT_4 receptor subtypes. *Regulatory Peptides, 68*, 131-138.

Kramár, E.A., Krishnan, R., Harding, J.W., and Wright, J.W. (1998). Role of nitric oxide in angiotensin IV-induced increases in cerebral blood flow. *Regulatory Peptides, 74*, 185-192.

Kramár, E.A., Armstrong, D.L., Ikeda, S., Waynder, M.J., Harding, J.W. and Wright, J.W. (1999). Angiotensin IV analog facilitates long-term potentiation in the dentate hyrus in vitro. *International Behavioral Neuroscience Society Abstracts, 8*, 39.

Kulakowska, A., Karwowska, W., Wisniewski, K., and Braszko, J.J. (1996). Losartan influences behavioural effects of angiotensin II in rats. *Pharmacological Research, 34,* 109-115.

Kunz, J. (2002). Can atherosclerosis regress? The role of the vascular extracellular matrix and the age-related changes of arteries. *Gerontology, 48,* 267-278.

Kusayama, T. and Watanabe, S. (2000). Reinforcing effects of methamphetamine in planarians. *NeuroReport, 11,* 2511-2513.

Lambert, E., Dasse, E., Haye, B., and Petitfrere, E. (2004). TIMPs as multifacial proteins. *Critical Reviews of Oncological Hematology, 49,* 187-198.

Lashley, K.D. (1950). In search of the engram. In K.D. Lashley (Ed.) *Society for Experimental Biology. Physiological Mechanisms in Animal Behavior.* Cambridge: Cambridge University Press, pp 454-480.

Lee, E.H., Ma, Y.L., Wayner, M.J., and Armstrong, D.L. (1995). Impaired retention by angiotensin II mediated by the AT_1 receptor. *Peptides, 16,* 1069-1071.

Lee, J., Albiston, A.L., Allen, A.M., Mendelsohn, F.A., Ping, S.E., Barrett, G.L., Murphy, M., Morris M.J., McDowall, S.G., and Chai, S.Y. (2004). Effect of I.C.V. injection of AT_4 receptor ligands, NLE^1-angiotensin IV and LVV-hemorphin 7, on spatial learning in rats. *Neuroscience, 124,* 341-349.

Lee, J., Chai, S.Y., Mendelsohn, F.A.O., Morris, M.J., and Allen, A.M. (2001). Potentiation of cholinergic transmission in the rat hippocampus by angiotensin IV and LVV-hemorphin-7. *Neuropharmacology, 40,* 618-623.

Lee, J., Chai, S.Y., Morris, M.J., Mendelsohn, F.A.O., and Allen, A.M. (2003a). Effect of fimbria-fornix lesion on ^{125}I-angiotensin IV (Ang IV) binding in the guinea pig hippocampus. *Brain Research, 979,* 7-14.

Lee, J., Mustafa, T., McDowall, S.G., Mendelsohn, F.A., Brennan, M., Lew, R.A., Albiston, A.L., and Chai, S.Y. (2003b). Structure-activity study of LVV-hemorphin-7: angiotensin AT4 receptor ligand and inhibitor of insulin-regulated aminopeptidase. *Journal of Pharmacological and Experimental Therapeutics, 305,* 205-211.

Lee, J.L.C., Everitt, B.J., and Thomas, K.L. (2004). Independent cellular processes for hippocampal memory consolidation and reconsolidation. *Science, 304,* 839-843.

Lee, S.J., and Benveniste, E.N. (1999). Adhesion molecule expression and regulation on cells of the central nervous system. *Journal of Neuroimmunology, 98,* 77-88.

Lewis, D.J. (1979). Psychobiology of active and inactive memory. *Psychological Bulletin, 86,* 1054-1083.

Li, P., Chappell, M.C., Ferrarion, C.M., and Broshinan, K.B. (1997). Angiotensin (1-7) augments bradykinin-induced vasodilation by competing with ACE and releasing nitric oxide. *Hypertension 29,* 394-400.

Lisman, J. (1989). A mechanism for the Hebb and the anti-Hebb processes underlying learning and memory. *Proceedings of the National Academy of Sciences, USA, 86,* 9574-9578.

Llorens-Cortes, C., and Mendelsohn, F.A.O. (2002). Organsatin and functional role of the brain angiotensin system. *Journal of Renin-Angiotensin-Aldosterone System, 3,* S39-S48.

Loot, A.E., Roks, A.J., Henning, R.H., Tio, R.A., Suurmeijer, A.M., Boomsma, F., and van Gilst, W.H. (2002). Angiotensin-(1-7) attenuates the development of heart failure after myocardial infarction in rats. *Circulation 105,* 1548-1550.

Lukes, A., Mun-Bryce, S., Lukes, M., and Rosenberg, G.A. (1999). Extracellular matrix degradation by metalloproteinases and central nervous system diseases. *Molecular Neurobiology, 19,* 267-284.

Lukowiak K., Sangha, S. McComb, C., Varshney, N., Rosenegger, D., Sadamoto, H. and Scheibenstock, A. (2003). Associative learning and memory in *Lymnaea stagnalis*: How well do they remember? *Journal of Experimental Biology, 206,* 2097-2103.

Mann, D.L., and Spinale, F.G. (1998). Activation of matrix metalloproteinases in the failing human heart, breaking the tie that binds. *Circulation, 98,* 1699-1702.

Manns, J.R., Hopkins, R.O., and Squire, L.R. (2003). Semantic memory and the human hippocampus. *Neuron, 38,* 127-133.

Martin, K.C., Barad, M., and Kandel, E.R. (2000). Local protein synthesis and its role in synapse-specific plasticity. *Current Opinions in Neurobiolology, 10,* 587-592.

Maskos, K., and Bode, W. (2003). Structural basis of matrix metalloproteinase and tissue inhibitors of metalloproteinases. *Molecular Biotechnology, 25,* 241-266.

McEwen, B.S. (2001). Plasticity of the hippocampus: adaptation to chronic stress and allostatic load. *Annals of the New York Academy of Sciences, 933,* 265-277.

McGaugh, J.L. (1966). Time-dependent processes in memory storage. Science, 153, 1351-1358.

McKinley, M.J., Albiston, A.L., Allen, A.M., Mathai, M.L., May, C.N., McAllen, R.M., Oldfield, B.J., Mendelsohn, F.A.O., and Chai, S.Y. (2003). The brain renin-angiotensin system: location and physiological roles. *International Journal of Biochemistry and Cell Biology, 35,* 901-918.

Mehta, J.L., Li, D.Y., Yang, H., and Raizada, M.K. (2002). Angiotensin II and IV stimulate expression and release of plasminogen activator inhibitor-1 in cultured human coronary artery endothelial cells. *Journal of Cardiovascular Pharmacology, 39,* 789-794.

Melo, J.C., and Graeff, F.G. (1975). Effect of intracerebroventricular bradykinia and related peptides on rabbit operant behavior. *Journal of Pharmacological and Experimental Therapeutics, 193,* 1-10.

Mentlein, R., and Roos, T. (1996). Proteases involved in the metabolism of angiotensin II, bradykinin, calcitonin gene-related peptide (CGRP), and neuropeptide Y by vascular smooth muscle cells. *Peptides, 17,* 709-720.

Mesulam, M.M., Mufson, E.J., Wainer, B.H., and Levey, A.L. (1983). Central cholinergic pathways in the rat: An overview based on an alternative nomenclature. *Neuroscience, 10,* 1185-1201.

Miller-Wing, A.V., Hanesworth, J.M., Sardinia, M.F., Wright, J.W., Speth, R.C., Grove, K.L., and Harding, J.W. (1993). Central angiotensin IV receptors: distribution and specificity in guinea pig brain. *Journal of Pharmacological and Experimental Therapeutics, 266,* 1718-1726.

Misanin, J.R., Miller, R.R., and Lewis, D.J. (1968). Retrograde amnesia produced by electro-convulsive shock after reactivation of a consolidated memory trace. Science, 160, 203-204.

Miyashita, Y. (2004). Cognitive memory: cellular and network machineries and their top-down contral. Science, 306, 435-440.

Møeller, I., Allen, A.M., Chai, S.Y., Zhuo, J., and Mendelsohn, F.A.O. (1998). Bioactive angiotensin peptides. *Journal of Human Hypertension, 12,* 289-293.

Møeller, I., Clune, E.F., Fennessy, P.A., Bingley, J.A., Albiston, A.L., Mendelsohn, F.A., and Chai, S.Y. (1999). Up regulation of AT_4 receptor levels in carotid arteries following balloon injury. *Regulatory Peptides, 83,* 25-30.

Morgan, T.M., and Routtenberg, A. (1977). Angiotensin injected into the neostriatum after learning disrupts retention performance. *Science, 196,* 87-89.

Morris, R.G.M., Schenk, F., Tweedie, F., and Jarrard, L.E. (1990). Ibotenate lesions of hippocampus and/or subiculum: dissociating components of allocentric spatial learning. *European Journal of Neuroscience, 2,* 1016-1028.

Mufson, E.J., Ma, S.Y., Dills, J., Chochran, E.J., Leurgans, S., Wuu, J., Bennett, D.A., Jaffar, S., Gilmor, M.L., Levey, A.I. and Kordower, J.H. (2002). Loss of basal forebrain P75(NTR) immunoreactivity in subjects with mild cognitive impairment and Alzheimer's disease. *Journal of Comparative Neurology, 443,* 136-153.

Muir, J.L. (1997). Acetylcholine, aging, and Alzheimer's disease. Pharmacology, Biochemistry and Behavior, 56, 687-696.

Mukoyama, M., Kakajima, M., Horiuchi, M., Sasamura, H., Pratt, R.E., and Dzau, V.J. (1993). Expression cloning of type 2 angiotensin II receptor reveals a unique class of seven transmembrane receptors. *Journal of Biological Chemistry, 268,* 24539-24542.

Murphy, G., Knauper, V., Cowell, S., Hembry, R., Stanton, H., Butler, G., Freije, J., Pendas, A.M. and Lopez-Otin, C. (1999). Evaluation of some newer matrix metalloproteinases. *Annuls of the New York Academic of Sciences 878,* 25-39.

Müller, G.E., and Pilzecker, A. (1900). Experimentelle beitrage zur lehre vom gedachtnis. *Zeitschrift fur Psychologie,* Supplement. 1.

Murphy T.J., Alexander, R.W., Griendling, K.K., Runge M.S., and Bernstein, K.E. (1991). Isolation of a cDNA encoding the vascular type-1 angiotesnin II receptor. *Nature (London), 16,* 233-236.

Muthalif, M.M., Benter, I.F., Uddin, M.R., Harper, J.L., and Malik, K.U. (1998). Signal transduction mechanisms involved in angiotensin (1-7)-stimulated arachidonic acid release and prostanoid synthesis in rabbit aortic smooth muscle cells. *Journal of Pharmacological and Experimental Therapeutics 284,* 388-398.

Nadel, L., and Land, C. (2000). Memory traces revisited. *Nature Reviews, 1,* 209-212.

Nader, K. (2003). Memory traces unbound. *Trends in Neurscience, 26,* 65-72.

Nedivi, E., Hevroni, D., Naot, D., Israeli, D., and Citri, Y. (1993). Numerous candidate plasticity-related genes revealed by differential cDNA cloning. *Nature, 363,* 718-722.

Neves, L.A., Averill, D.B., Ferrario, C.M., Chappell, M.C., Aschner, J.L., Walkup, M.P., and Brosnihan, K.B. (2003). Characterization of angiotensin-(1-7) receptor subtype in mesenteric arteries. *Peptides, 24,* 455-462.

Nicoll, R.A. (1985). The septo-hippocampal projection: A model cholinergic pathway. *Trends in Neuroscience 8,* 533-536.

Olson, M.L., Olson, E.A., Qualls, J.H., Stratton, J.J., Harding, J.W., and Wright, J.W. (2004). Norleucine[1]-angioensin IV alleviates mecamylamine-induced spatial memory deficits. *Peptides 25,* 233-241.

Olton, D.S., Walker, J.A., and Gage, F.H. (1978). Hippocampal connections and spatial discrimination. *Brain Research, 139,* 295-308.

Opdenakker, G., Nelissen, I., and Van Damme, J. (2003). Functional roles and therapeutic targeting of gelatinase B and chemokines in multiple sclerosis. *Lancet Neurology, 2,* 747-756.

Otani, S. (2002). Memory trace in prefrontal cortex: theory for the cognitive switch. *Biological Reviews of Cambridge Philosophical Society, 77*, 563-577.

Pagenstecher, A., Stalder, A.K., and Campbell, I.L. (1997). RNAse protection assays for the simultaneous and semiquantitative analysis of multiple murine matrix metalloproteinase (MMP) and MMP inhibitor mRNAs. *Journal of Immunological Methods, 206*, 1-9.

Paula, R.D., Lima, C.V., and Khosla, M.C. (1995). Angiotensin (1-7) potenitates hypotensive effect of bradykinin in conscious rats. *Hypertension 26,*1154-1159.

Pederson, E.S., Harding, J.W., and Wright, J.W. (1998). Attenuation of scopolamine-induced spatial learning impairments by an angiotensin IV analog. *Regulatory Peptides, 74*, 97-103.

Pederson, E.D., Krishnan, R., Harding, J.W., and Wright, J.W. (2001). A role for the angiotensin AT_4 receptor subtype in overcoming scopolamine-induced spatial memory deficits. *Regulatory Peptides, 102*, 147-156.

Perry, E.K., Perry, R.H., Smith, C.J., Dick, D.J.,Candy, J.M., Edwardson, J.A., Fairbarin, A., and Blessed, G. (1987). Nicotinic receptor abnormalities in Alzheimer's and Parkinson's diseases. *Journal of Neurology Neurosurgery and Psychiatry 50*, 806-809.

Powell, H.W., and Duncan, J.S. (2005). Functional magnetic resonance imaging for assessment of language and memory in clinical practice. *Current Opinions in Neurology, 18*, 161-166.

Power, A.E., Vazdarjanova, A., and McGaugh, J.L. (2003). Muscarinic cholinergic influences in memory consolidation. *Neurobiological of Learning and Memory, 80*, 178-193.

Qian, Z., Gilbert, M.E., Colicos, M.A., Kandel, E.R., and Kuhl, D. (1993). Tissue-plasminogen activator is induced as an immediate-early gene during seizure, kindling and long-term potentiation. *Nature, 361*, 453-457.

Raghavendra, V., Chopra, K., and Kulkarni, S.K. (1999). Brain renin angiotensin system (RAS) in stress-induced analgesia and impaired retention. *Peptides, 20*, 335-342.

Raghavendra, V., Chopra, K., and Kulkarni, S.K. (1998). Involvement of cholinergic system in losartan-induced faciliatation of spatial and short-term working memory. *Neuropeptides, 32*, 417-421.

Raghavendra, V., Chopra, K., and Kulkarni, S.K. (2001). Comparative studies on the memory-enhancing actions of captopril and Losartan in mice using inhibitory shock avoidance paradigm. *Neuropeptides, 35*, 65-69.

Rich, D.H., Moon, B.J., and Harbeson, S. (1984). Inhibition of aminopeptidases by amastatin and bestatin derivatives, effect of inhibitor structure on slow-binding processes. *Journal of Medicinal Chemistry, 27*, 417-422.

Rivera, S., and Khrestchatisky, M. (2000). Matrix metalloproteinases and tissue inhibitors of metalloproteinases in neuronal plasticity and pathology. In M. Baudry, J.L. Davis, and R.F. Thompson (Eds.), *Advances in synaptic plasticity*. Cambridge, MA: The MIT Press, pp. 53-86.

Rivera, S., Tremblay, E., Timsit, S., Canals, O., Ben-Ari, Y., and Krestchatisky, M. (1997). Tissue inhibitor of metalloproteinases-1 (TIMP-1) is differentially induced in neurons and astrocytes after seizures: evidence for developmental, immediate early gene, and lesion response. *Journal of Neuroscience, 17*, 4223-4235.

Roberts, K.A., Krebs, L.T., Kramár, E.A., Shaffer, M.J., Harding, J.W., and Wright, J.W. (1995). Autoradiographic identification of brain angiotensin IV binding sites and differential c-Fos expression following intracerebroventricular injection of angiotensin II and IV in rats. *Brain Research, 682,* 13-21.

Rolls, B.J., Jones, B.P., and Fallows, D.J., (1972). A comparison of the motivational properties of thirst. *Physiology and Behavior, 9,* 777-782.

Rose, J.K., Kaun, K.R., Chen, S.H. and Rankin, C.H. (2003). GLR-1 a non-NMDA glutamate receptor homolog, is critical for long-term memory in *Caenorhabditis elegans. Journal of Neuroscience, 23,* 9595-9599.

Rosenberg, G.A. (2002a). Matrix metalloproteinases in neuroinflamation. *Glia, 39,* 279-291.

Rosenberg, G.A. (2002b). Matrix metalloproteinases and neuroinflammation in multiple sclerosis. *Neuroscientist, 8,* 586-595.

Rubin, R.D. (1976). Clinical use of retrograde amnesia produced by electroconvulsive shock. A conditioning hypothesis. Canadian Psychiatric Association Journal, 21, 87-90.

Rubin, R.D., and Franks, C. (1969). New application of ECT. In R.D. Rubin and C. Franks (Eds), *Advances in Behavior Therapy.* San Diego, CA: Academic Press, pp. 37-44.

Saavedra, J.M. (1992). Brain and pituitary angiotensin. *Endocrine Reviews, 13,* 329-380.

Sadamura, H., Hein, L., Krieger, J.E., Pratt, R.E., Kobilka, B.K., and Dzau VJ. (1992). Cloning, characterization, and expression of two angiotensin receptor (AT-1) isoforms from the mouse genome. *Biochemistry and Biophysics Research Communications, 185,* 253-259.

Salzet, M., Deloffre, L., Breton, C., Vieau, D., and Schoofs, L. (2001). The angiotensin system elements in invertebrates. *Brain Research Reviews, 36,* 35-45.

Sandberg, K., Ji, H., and Catt, K.J., (1994). Regulation of angiotensin II receptors in rat brain during dietary sodium changes. *Hypertension, 23,* I-137-I-141.

Santos, R.A., Campagnole-Santos, M.J., and Andrade, S.P. (2000). Angiotensin-(1-7): an update. *Regulatory Peptides, 91,* 45-62.

Santos, R.A. Campagnole-Santos, M.J., Baracho, N.C., Fontes, M.A., Silva, L.C., Neves, L.A., Oliveira, D.R., Caligiorne SM, Rodrigues, A.R., Gropen, C., Carvalho, W.S., Simoes, E., Silva, A.C., and Khosla, M., 1994. Characterization of a new angiotensin antagonist selective for angiotensin-(1-7): evidence that the actions of angiotensin-(1-7) are mediated by specific angiotensin receptors. *Brain Research Bulletin, 35,* 293-298.

Sarter, M., and Parikh, V. (2005). Choline transporters, cholinergic transmission and cognition. *Nature Reviews Neuroscience, 6,* 48-56.

Sasaki, K., Yamano, Y., Bardhan, S., Iwai, N., Murray, J.J., Hasegawa, M., Matsuda, Y., and Inagami, T. (1991. Cloning and expression of a complementary DNA encoding a bovine adrenal angiotensin II type-1 receptor. Nature (London), 351, 230-233.

Sayeski, P.P., Ali, M.S., Semeniuk, D.J., Doan, T.N., and Bernstein, K.E., 1998. Angiotensin II signal transduction pathways. *Regulatory Peptides, 78,* 19-29.

Seeds, N.W., Williams, B.L., and Bickford, P.C. (1995). Tissue plasminogen activator induction in Purkinje neurons after cerebellar motor learning. *Science, 270,* 1992-1994.

Sekine-Aizawa, Y., Hama, E., Watanabe, K., Tsubuki, S., Kanai-Azuma, M., Kanai, Y., Arai, H., Aizawa, H., Iwata, N., and Saido, T.C. (2001). Matrix metalloproteinase (MMP) system in brain: identification and characterization of brain-specific MMP highly expressed in cerebellum. *European Journal of Neuroscience, 13,* 935-948.

Sellebjerg, F., and Sorensen, T.L. (2003). Chemokines and matrix metalloproteinase-9 in leukocyte recruitment to the central nervous system. *Brain Research Bulletin, 61,* 347-355.

Shepherd, J., Bill, D.J., Dourish, C.T., Grewal, S.S., McLenachan, A., and Stanhope, K.J. (1996). Effects of the selective angiotensin II receptor antagonists losartan and PD123177 in animal models of anxiety and memory. *Psychopharmacology, 126,* 206-218.

Silva-Barcellos, N.M., Frezard, F., Caligiorne, S., and Santos, R.A. (2001). Long-lasting cardiovascular effects of liposome-entrapped angiotesnin (1-7) at the rostral ventrolateral medulla. *Hypertension 38,* 1266-1271.

Simons, J.S., and Spiers, H.J. (2003). Prefrontal and medial temporal lobe interactions in long-term memory. *Nature Reviews Neuroscience, 4,* 637-648.

Skelton, R.W., and McNamara, R.K. (1992). Bilateral knife cuts to the perforant path disrupt spatial learning in the Morris water maze. *Hippocampus, 2,* 73-80.

Skiles, J.W., Gonnella, N.C., and Jeng, A.Y. (2004). The design, structure, and clinical update of small molecular weight matrix metalloproteinase inhibitors. *Current Medicinal Chemistry, 11, 2911-22977.*

Slinker, B.K., Wu, Y., Brennan, A.J., Campbell, K.B., and Harding, J.W. (1999). Angiotensin IV has mixed effects on left ventricle systolic function and speeds relaxation. *Cardiovascular Research, 42,* 660-669.

Sobel, R.A. (1998). The extracellular matrix in multiple sclerosis lesions. *Journal of Neuropathology and Experimental Neurology, 57, 205-217.*

Sounni, N.E., and Noel, A. (2005). Membrane type-matrix metalloproteinases and tumor progression. Biochimie, 87, 329-342.

Speth, R.C., Brown, T.E., Barnes, R.D., and Wright, J.W. (2003). Brain angiotensinergic activity: The state of our current knowledge. *Proceedings of the Western Pharmacological Society, 46,* 11-15.

Speth, R.C., Thompson, S.M., and Johns, S.J. (1995). Angiotensin II receptors: Structural and functional considerations. In A.K. Mukhopadhyay and M.K. Raizada (Eds*.) Current concepts: tissue rennin angiotensin systems as local regulators in reproductive and endocrine organs.* New York: Plenum Press, pp. 169-192.

Squire, L.R., and Kandel, E.R. (1999). *Memory: From Mind to Molecules.* , New York, N.Y: Freedman and Company.

Squire, L.R., Stark, C.E., and Clark, R.E. (2004). The medial temporal lobe. *Annual Reviews of Neuroscience, 27,* 279-306.

Stamenkovic, I. (2003*). Extracellular matrix remodeling: the role of matrix metalloproteinases. Journal of Pathology, 200,* 448-464.

Stanhope, K.J., Choules, M., Yudko, E., and Dourish, C.T. (1994). Re-evaluation of the effects of putative cognitive disrupters in the reinforced-alternation T-maze task in the rat. *British Journal of Pharmacology, 112,* 15P.

Stanhope, K.J., McLenachan, A.P., and Dourish, C.T. (1995). Dissociation between cognitive and motor/motivational deficits in the delayed matching to position test: effects of scopolamine, 8-OH-DPAT and EAA antagonists. *Psychopharmacology ,122,* 268-280.

Steward, O., and Schuman, E.M. (2001). Protein synthesis at synaptic sites on dendrites. *Annual Reviews of Neuroscience, 24,* 299-325.

Stubley-Weatherly, L.A., Harding, J.W., and Wright, J.W. (1996). Effects of discrete kainic acid-induced hippocampal lesions on spatial and contextual learning and memory. *Brain Research, 716,* 29-38.

Sutherland, R.J., and McDonald, R.J. (1990). Hippocampus, amygdala and memory deficits in rats. *Behavioural Brain Research, 37,* 57-79.

Swanson, G.N., Hanesworth, J.M., Sardinia, M.F., Coleman, J.K., Wright, J.W., Hall, K.L., Miller-Wing, A.V., Stobb, J.W., Cook, V.I., Harding, E.C., and Harding, J.W. (1992). Discovery of a distinct binding site for angiotensin II (3-8), a putative angiotensin IV receptor. *Regulatory Peptides, 40*, 409-419.

Szklarczyk, A., Lapinska, J., Rylski, M., MCKay R.D., and Kaczmarek, L. (2002). Matrix metalloproteinase-9 undergoes expression and activation during dendritic remodeling in adult hippocampus. *Journal of Neuroscience, 22*, 920-930.

Tanzi, E. (1893). I fatti c lc induzioni nell'odicrnaistilogia del sistema nervosa. *Riv. Sper. Freniat. Med. Alienazioni. Meni. 19*, 419-472.

Taubenfeld, S.M., Wiig, K.A., Monti, B., Dolan, B., Pollonini, G. and Alberini, C.M. (2001). Fornix-dependent induction of hippocampal CCAAT enhancer-binding protein [beta] and [delta] Co-localizes with phosphorylated cAMP response element-binding protein and accompanies long-term memory consolidation. *Journal of Neuroscience, 21*, 84-91.

Teyler TJ. (1999). Use of brain slices to study long-term potentiation and depression as examples of synaptic plasticity. *Methods, 18*, 109-16.

Teyler, T.J., and DiScenna P. (1987). Long-term potentiation. *Annual Reviews of Neuroscience, 10*, 131-61.

Teyler, T.J., Morgan, S.L., Russell, R.N., and Woodside, B.L. (2001). Synaptic plasticity and secondary epileptogenesis. *International Reviews of Neurobiology, 45*, 253-67.

Thomas, W.G., and Mendelsohn, F.A.O. (2003). Molecules in focus: Angiotensin receptors: form and function and distribution. *International Journal of Biochemistry and Cell Biology, 35*, 774-779.

Tsilibary, E.C. (2003). Microvascular basement membranes in diabetes mellitus. *Journal of Pathology. 200*, 537-546.

Ueda, S., Masumori-Maemoto, S., Ashino, K., Nagohara, T., Gotoh, E., Umemura, S., and Ishii, M. (2000). Angiotensin (1-7) attenuates vasoconstriction evoked by angiotensin II but not by noradrenaline in man. *Hypertension 35*, 998-1001.

Unger, T., Badoer, E., Ganten, D., Lang, R.E., and Rettig, R. (1988). Brain angiotensin: pathways and pharmacology. *Circulation, 77*, 140-154.

Vaillant, C., Didier-Bazes, M., Hutter, A., Belin, M.F., and Thomasset, N. (1999). Spatiotemporal expression patterns of metalloproteinases and their inhibitors in the postnatal developing rat cerebellum. *Journal of Neuroscience, 19*, 4994-5004.

Vaughn, D.E. (2002). Angiotensin and vascular fibrinolytic balance. *American Journal of Hypertension 15*, 3S-8S.

Vauquelin, G., Michotte, Yvette, Smolders, I., Sarre, S., Ebinger, G., Dupont, A., and Vanderheyden, P. (2002). Cellular targets for angiotensin II fragments: pharmacological and molecular evidence. *Journal of Renin-Angiotensin-Aldosterone System, 3*, 195-204.

Vecil, G.G., Larsen, P.H., Corley, S.M., Herx, L.M., Besson, A., Goodyer, C.G., and Yong, V.W. (2000). Interleukin-1 is a key regulator of matrix metalloproteinases-9 expression in human neurons in culture and following mouse brain trauma in vivo. *Journal of Neuroscience Research 61*, 212-224.

Von Bohlen und Halbach, O. (2003). Angiotensin IV in the central nervous system. *Cell and Tissue Research, 311*, 1-9.

Von Bohlen und Halbach O, Albrecht D. (1998). Opposite effects of angiotensin II and IV in the lateral nucleus of the amygdala. Brain Research Bulletin, 47, 311-315.

Vos, C.M., van Haastert, E.S., de Groot, C.J., van der Valk, P., and de Vries, H.E. (2003). Matrix metalloproteinases-12 is expressed in phagocytotic macrophages in active multiple sclerosis lesions. *Journal of Neuroimmunology, 138*, 106-114.

Wang, Y.X., Martin-McNulty, B., Freay, A.D., Sukovich, D.A., Halks-Miller, M., Li, W.W., Vergona, R., Sullivan, M.E., Morser, J., Dole, W.P., and Deng, G.G. (2001). Angiotensin II increases urokinase-type plasminogen activator expression and induces aneurysm in the abdominal aorta of apolipoprotein E-deficient mice. *American Journal of Pathology, 159*, 1455-1464.

Wayner, M.J., Armstrong, D.L., and Phelix, C.F. (1996). Nicotine blocks angiotensin II inhibition of LTP in the dentate gyrus. *Peptides, 17*, 1127-1133.

Wayner, M.J., Armstrong, D.L., Polan-Curtain, J.L., and Denny, J.B. (1993a). Ethanol and diazepam inhibition of hippocampal LTP is mediated by angiotensin II and AT_1 receptors. *Peptides, 14*, 441-4.

Wayner, M.J., Armstrong, D.L., Polan-Curtain, J.L., and Denny, J.B. (1993b). Role of angiotensin II and AT_1 receptors in hippocampal LTP. *Pharmacology, Biochemistry and Behavior, 45*, 455-64.

Wayner MJ, Ono T, and Nolley D. (1973). Effects of angiotensin II on central neurons. *Pharmacology, Biochemistry and Behavior, 1*, 679-691.

Wayner, M.J., Polan-Curtain, J.L., and Armstrong, D.L. (1995). Dose and time dependency of angiotensin II inhibition of hippocampal long-term potentiation. *Peptides, 16*, 1079-82.

Wayner, M.J., Polan-Curtain, J.L., Chiu, S.C., and Armstrong, D.L. (1994). Losartan reduces ethanol intoxication in the rat. *Alcohol, 11*, 343-346.

Wilk, S., and Healy, D.P. (1993). Glutamyl aminopeptidase (aminopeptidase A), the BP-1/6C3 antigen. *Advances in Neuroimmunology, 3*, 195-207.

Wittenberg, G.M., Sullivan, M.R., and Tsien, J.Z. (2002). Synaptic reentry reinforcement based network model for long-term memory consolidation. *Hippocampus, 12*, 637-647.

Woessner, J.F., and Nagase, H. (2000). *Matrix Metalloproteinases and TIMPs*. Oxford, UK: Oxford University Press.

Woolf, N.J. Eckenstein, F., and Butcher, L.L. (1984). Choinergic systems in the rat brain. I. Projections to the limbic telencephalon. *Brain Research Bulletin, 13*, 751-784.

Wright, J.W., and Harding, J.W. (1994). Brain angiotensin receptor subtypes in the control of physiological and behavioral responses. *Neuroscience and Biobehavioral Reviews, 18*, 21-53.

Wright, J.W., and Harding, J.W. (1995). Brain angiotensin receptor subtypes AT_1, AT_2, and AT_4 and their functions. *Regulatory Peptides, 59*, 269-295.

Wright, J.W., and Harding, J.W. (1997). Important roles for angiotensin III and IV in the brain renin-angiotensin system. *Brain Research Reviews, 25*, 96-124.

Wright, J.W., and Harding, J.W. (2004). The brain angiotensin system and extracellular matrix molecules in neural plasticity, learning, and memory. *Progress in Neurobiology 72*, 263-293.

Wright, J.W., Jensen, L.L., Roberts, K.A., Sardinia, M.F., and Harding, J.W. (1989). Structure-function analyses of brain angiotensin control of pressor action in rats. *American Journal of Physiology, 257*, R1551-1557.

Wright, J.W., Kramar, E.A., Meighan, S.E., and Harding, J.W. (2002a). Extracellular matrix molecules, long-term potentiation, memory consolidation and the brain angiotensin system. *Peptides, 23*, 221-246.

Wright, J.W., Krebs, L.T., Stobb, J.W., and Harding, J.W. (1995). The angiotensin IV system: Functional implications. *Frontiers in Neuroendocrinology,16*, 23-52.

Wright, J.W., Miller-Wing, A.V., Shaffer, M.J., Higginson, C., Wright, D.E., Hanesworth, J.M., and Harding, J.W. (1993). Angiotensin II(3-8) [ANG IV] hippocampal binding: potential role in the facilitation of memory. *Brain Research Bulletin, 32*, 497-502.

Wright, J.W., Reichert, J.R., Davis, C.J., and Harding, J.W. (2002b). Neural plasticity and the brain renin-angiotensin system. *Neuroscience and Biobehavioral Reviews 26*, 529-552.

Wright, J.W., Stubley, L, Pederson, E.S., Kramar, E.A., Hanesworth, J.M., and Harding, J.W. (1999). Contributions of the brain angiotensin IV-AT$_4$ receptor subtype system to spatial learning. *Journal of Neuroscience, 19*, 3952-3961.

Yong, V.W., Krekoski, C.A., Forsyth, P.A., Bell, R., and Edwards, D.R. (1998). Matrix metalloproteinases and diseases of the CNS. *Trends in Neuroscience, 21*, 75-80.

Yonkov, D.I., and Georgiev, V.P. (1990). Cholinergic influence on memory facilitation induced by angiotensin II in rats. *Neuropeptides, 16*, 157-162.

Yoshiyama, Y., Asahina, Y.M., and Hattori, T. (2000). Selective distribution of matrix metalloproteinase-3 (MMP-3) in Alzheimer's disease brain. *Acta Neuropathology, 99*, 91-95.

Zaccardi, M.L., Traina, G., Cataldo, E. *and Brunelli, M. (2001). Nonassociative learning in the leech Hirudo medicinalis. Behavioural Brain Research, 126*, 81-92.

Zhu, B., and Herbert, J. (1996). Central antagonism of atrial natriuretic peptides on behavioral and hormonal responses to angiotensin II: mapping with c-Fos. *Brain Research, 734*, 55-60.

Zubenko, G.S., and Nixon, R.A. (1984). Mood elevating effect of captopril in depressed patients. *American Journal of Psychiatry, 141*, 110-111.

In: Trends in Learning Reserch
Editor: Samuel N. Hogan, pp. 41-66

ISBN 1-59454-965-6
© 2006 Nova Science Publishers, Inc.

Chapter 2

LITERACY LEARNING IN COMMUNITIES OF DISCOURSE: READING TO LEARN AND WRITING TO COMMUNICATE

Miriam Alfassi[1]
School of Education
Bar-Ilan University
Ramat-Gan 52900
ISRAEL

ABSTRACT

Reading and writing are complex cognitive activities that are indispensable for adequate functioning in society. To enter the literate society of today students must know how to learn from reading and how to communicate while writing. Recent data indicates that a third of the student population manifest low levels of learning to comprehend and write. Such evidence emphasizes the need to develop effective learning environments that will promote student literacy

According to contemporary theory language plays a major role in education, not only as a subject in the curriculum but mainly as the medium through which meaning is shared and learning and teaching are carried out. Knowledge emerges from the interaction of voices therefore learning involves both individual interpretation and negotiation with others. Hence, discourse plays a crucial mediational role in learning as it allows for new understandings to be negotiated among participants. This implies that literacy is best acquired while learning in depth content that engages students in thoughtful reading, writing and discussion

The reported studies in this chapter translate the above assertions into practice by applying a progressive instructional model designed to include opportunities for learning through negotiation. The instructional model integrates socio-cognitive learning principles and activities in a problem-based environment geared to teach literacy. The

---

[1] Tel. No.: +972-3-5317963,Fax No.: +972-3-5353319,Email: alfasm@mail.biu.ac.il

reported studies examine the efficacy of the instructional model in fostering reading comprehension and writing competence.

The studies situated in junior high school language art classes compare between students engaged in guided inquiry within communities of discourse to students who were exposed to traditional methods of literacy instruction. Quantitative and qualitative methods of analysis are applied to trace the contextual features within the learning environment that promote literacy learning. Findings suggest that designing a learning environment in which students and teachers mediate and negotiate meaning while co-constructing their knowledge provides the context in which students develop cognitive tools for comprehension and generation of text.

INTRODUCTION

One of the major goals of education is to impart high literacy skills that allow students to identify problems in, and reason effectively with printed information. According to contemporary theory the acquisition of high literacy entails teaching students to adapt the use of language, content and reasoning to particular situations and disciplines (Langer, 2001). This calls for students to be provided with significant learning opportunities that demand engagement in thoughtful reading, writing and discussion about content. However, recent research indicates that scholastic instruction includes few assigned writing tasks and very few discussion episodes. Moreover, many of the learning tasks students encounter require the recall and display of assigned information thereby exposing them to learning experiences that rarely promote reasoned and analytic use of language (Applebee, Langer, Nystrand and Gamoran, 2003; Nystrand, 1997).

This poor state of affairs is commensurate with findings on student achievement. These findings indicate that only one third of high-school students write complete responses that contain sufficient information to support their claims, and that only 2% write effective responses containing supporting details and discussion (National Center for Education Statistics, 1999). In addition, reading achievement reports show that fewer than 7% of students in Grades 4, 8 and 12 perform at the advanced level in reading (NAEP, 1998). To ameliorate this state of affairs schools are under pressure to reform their curricula and instructional practices and to integrate reading and writing with activities such as listening, speaking and thinking. The research reported in this paper examines the efficacy of applying integrated literacy instruction within a community of learners engaged in guided inquiry. The literacy instruction is embedded within a disciplinary content, the students read to learn, they negotiate their understandings within small learning groups and then generate materials to teach other fellow students under teacher guidance. These learning applications depart significantly from traditional practices of learning and instruction.

MOVING FROM THE OLD TO THE NEW

Traditionally learning and teaching has been viewed as the *transmission* of skills and knowledge. According to this view knowledge is stored in individual minds, texts, or other artifacts and can be transferred to learners through the use of language which is considered a precise neutral tool for instruction (Wells, 2000). This implies that an oral presentation and/or a written text has a meaning of it's own that is independent of the reader and/or listener (Bruner, 1986). Indeed, literacy is envisioned as a set of discrete skills that once mastered enables learners to read and listen attentively to the knowledge conveyed through authoritative texts and lectures, and then to absorb and remember it for subsequent reproduction. In congruence, reading comprehension and writing are taught sequentially as decontextualized discrete skills mastered through repeated practice and drill performed solitarily by the students (Greeno, 1998).

The contemporary social constructive theory of education views learning and teaching as a process that entails the *transformation* of knowledge and skills. Knowledge emerges from the interaction of voices, therefore learning involves both individual interpretation and negotiation with others (Windschitl, 2002). In this view language is perceived not only as a social means of communication but as a major tool in mediating learning and thinking. Discourse, social speech, plays a crucial mediational role in the learning process as it allows for new understandings to be negotiated among participants. Reading and writing, according to this perspective, cannot be separated from speaking, listening and interacting on the one hand or using language to think about and act on the world on the other hand (Gee, 2001). Reading and writing components, according to this perspective, are best learned and practiced simultaneously within the context of a disciplinary learning task. Thus, the traditional approach to literacy that views meaning as residing within the mind and/or text is at variance with the socio-cognitive theory which views meaning to be socially constructed by teachers and students as they interact with texts, media and each other (Bean, 2000; Au, 1998).

The reconceptualization of literacy learning implies that the instruction of reading and writing needs to move beyond the understanding of relations internal to the text to include an interactive process in which interpersonal behaviors are the basis for the meaning making and generating of text. Indeed, emanating from the path-breaking work of Vygotsky (1962, 1978) and related research (Brown and Campione, 1996; Gallimore and Tharp, 1990; Neeedles and Knapp, 1994) recent developments in instructional psychology suggest that literacy is best taught within interactive learning environments that stimulate problem solving and analysis in conjunction with reading, writing and computer skills (Wilkinson and Stilliman, 2000). Such environments are designed to include small groups of students engaged in guided learning while collaborating and negotiating with each other, thereby evoking students to become thoughtful literate users of language while acquiring skills and knowledge (Schultz and Fecho, 2000).

In this chapter we suggest an instructional program designed to create a learning environment that imparts in dialogic interaction with others higher cognitive processes such as reading, writing, and argumentation while learning deep disciplinary content. The program situated within communities of discourse is based on the instructional model Fostering Communities of Learners derived from the work of Brown and Campione (1990, 1994, 1996).

FOSTERING COMMUNITIES OF LEARNERS (FCL)

FCL is designed to promote the critical thinking and reflection skills underlying multiple forms of higher literacy. The learning principles underlying FCL are embedded in Vygotsky's (1962, 1978) language-centered sociocultural and sociohistorical theories of learning that have profoundly influenced educational research. Vygotsky (1962, 1978) asserted that higher mental processes are developed through social speech, discourse, being gradually internalized. The developmental learning process occurs through participation in collaborative activity with an adult or more able peer. In embracing Vygotsky's approach FCL has departed from the focus on individual learners engaged in separate and independent learning activities by emphasizing the interrelated shared activities within which individuals participate while learning (Hicks, 1996; Greeno, 1998).

FCL is embedded in a disciplinary content and includes a system of interacting activities that result in a metacognitive environment (Karpov and Haywood, 1998). The three activities that are central to FCL are research, sharing information, and the performance of a consequential task. All students engage in independent and group *research* on a joint or shared topic, teachers provide guidance and direction to students and members of each research group *share* their expertise with their classmates by preparing computer-based teaching materials. To motivate shared learning students are required to *perform* a consequential task that requires them to learn all aspects of the joint topic. While participating in the research-share-perform cycles students collaboratively construct and negotiate meaning and action thereby transforming the classroom into a community of discourse.

FCL is based on a set of learning principles. The learning principles guide the various implementations of the research-share-perform cycle that is the backbone of the instructional model. The key principles as presented above include (a) creating a metacognitive environment in which students apply active and strategic learning (b) aligning instruction and assessment to allow for guided learning and (c) designing curriculum situated within deep disciplinary knowledge that includes elements of student choice. To apply the FCL instructional model these learning principles need to be translated into classroom activities through flexible use and creative adaptation (Brown and Campione, 1996).

Most studies conducted on FCL are situated within the biological sciences. In these studies students discover and derive under teacher guidance general scientific rules or concepts while applying high literacy. Research to date demonstrates that students exposed to FCL acquire knowledge better, use it more flexibly and show higher gains on measures of reading comprehension than students exposed to traditional instruction (Brown and Campione 1994, 1998; Engle and Conant, 2002). However, research also indicates that guided discovery of scientific knowledge is time consuming, difficult for teachers to orchestrate and may result in students deriving erroneous concepts (Brown and Campione, 1994; Heller and Gordon, 1992; Tudge, 1992; Karpov and Haywood, 1998). The instructional program reported in this chapter attempts to integrate the learning principles and activities of FCL in a problem-based environment geared to teach literacy. The curriculum includes the learning of a problem based theme situated in deep disciplinary content in addition to direct instruction of reading and writing strategies that is delivered opportunistically. Learning of the problem based theme is deductive rather than inductive. The learner is presented with a higher order generalization from which more specific conclusions are derived and answers are discovered.

The higher order generalization is usually introduced as a dilemma. The dilemma has more than one possible correct answer, thus allowing for a plethora of solutions that may be acceptable if appropriately supported, thereby enriching students' argumentation and critical thinking skills. During collaborative discovery of possible answers, students are exposed to methods of analysis aimed at identifying, modeling and applying essential characteristics of strategic reading, writing and argumentation. Once internalized these methods become cognitive tools that mediate students' independent problem solving while learning. Hence, the main goal of the instructional program is to equip students with literacy as a critical tool while learning.

READING TO LEARN AND WRITING TO COMMUNICATE (RLWC)

The *RLWC* instructional program embedded in communities of discourse rests on the assertion that the process of becoming literate is inherently social in nature. Indeed, reading and writing are carried out by individuals. However these activities do not take place in isolation but rather occur in relation to a discourse community of other readers and writers. This implies that fostering students' literacy requires not only the presence of readers, writers and texts but also the interaction between and among them (Lensmire, 1994; Smagorinsky, 2001). To provide opportunities for students to engage with each other while reading, writing and discussing, literacy acquisition is situated within a community of discourse that share mutual goals and interest.

The instructional program is anchored in a problem-based curriculum that involves collaborative student decision-making. The curriculum is based on an ill-structured problem that is messy and complex in nature; requires inquiry information gathering and reflection; and has no simple, fixed solution. The ill-structured problem is presented at the beginning of the program and serves as the organizing center and context for learning. Inquiry occurs through participation in the FCL activities of research, sharing information and the performance of a consequential task. While participating in the research-share-perform cycles, students use speech reading and writing in exploratory ways as they tentatively propose and reflect on ideas in the pursuit of answers to authentic questions embedded in a disciplinary context.

Teachers guide and orchestrate students' collaborative inquiry processes while providing guided assistance tailored to the needs of individual students. The students' manifestation is used by the teacher as a form of informal assessment to create instructional scaffolding (e.g., cuing, prompting, questioning, and remodeling) that provides students with the required information to reassess their performance. Once students move to self-directed stages of understanding the scaffolding is gradually diminished.

Literacy is acquired and practiced while learning deep disciplinary content. Students read to learn and engage in understanding texts collaboratively thereby promoting comprehension monitoring. They write to clarify their ideas and communicate their knowledge to their fellow students. The written materials go through several revisions guided by the classroom teacher. The teacher responds to students' writing through written prompts aimed at fostering students' self editing and self reflecting procedures. On the basis of student manifestation, the teacher determines writing conventions that are not applied by most students and addresses those conventions through direct instruction. In addition personal computers are used to facilitate the co-construction of knowledge among learners (Roth, 1995; Windschitl, 2002). These activities foster students' literacy, argumentation and communication skills and create an intentional learning environment (Scardemelia and Breiter, 1991) in which students are encouraged to monitor their own and others' comprehension and to reflect on their progress to date (Brown and Campione, 1996).

To implement the program three specific features were devised: a problem based curriculum situated in a disciplinary content, a model for qualitative assessment of writing to be used as a scaffold and self-management sheets to support thoughtful writing.

Course Curriculum

As mentioned above the instructional program is anchored in a problem-based curriculum that is ill structured. The ill -structured problem is presented first and serves as the organizing center and context for learning. For example, one of the selected topics for a course curriculum was Creation of a Nation. This theme was designed to arouse and sustain interest while developing hypothetical reasoning. The major goal of the curriculum was to discover the elements that unite a crowd of people from different cultures into a nation. To achieve this goal the students were presented with the ethnic diversity of their social environment and were asked to think if and how different ethnic backgrounds can be shaped into a unified society. To explore this question the students were exposed to eight different historical figures of their society that lived in the same period of time. Each figure had made a significant contribution and had become a man or woman of distinguished valor in his or her realm. The work of these people of valor represents the many elements that unify a society into a nation, contribute to its welfare and give people a common base of communication and understanding. At the end of the course the students were required to compare between the different historical figures and their contributions according to specific criteria delineated by the students through guided instruction. These comparisons enabled the students to reflect on the plight of human spirit to achieve progress within their society while contributing to its' unity.

A Model for Qualitative Assessment of Writing

This model was developed for teachers to provide a scaffold to developing writers. The scaffold is tailored to the specific writing competence of each student and includes a qualitative assessment. The model is based on the Vygotskian concept of Zone of Proximal Development (ZPD) that is defined as the difference between what a person can do alone and what he or she can do with assistance from a more knowledgeable other (Vygotsky, 1978). In congruence, the model is designed to meet the challenge of engaging developing writers in writing tasks that match their abilities while helping them develop the necessary proximal strategies for progress.

The model is comprised of three components (a) progress feedback through which the teacher mirrors to the student writing strategies successfully applied in the generated text (actual level of functioning) (b) opportunistic prompts through leading questions posed by the teacher as a response to incoherence or poor wording (e.g., Do you think you could connect these two sentences? Remember there are many conjunctions and connecting words, which do you think would be the most appropriate?) (c) a declaration of expected student manifestation in the revised writing task (expected level of functioning) (e.g., in your next submission please divide your essay into introductory, body and summary paragraphs). The model provides guidance and ongoing feedback to individual students, it breaks down the writing task into manageable parts and sets attainable proximal goals allowing each student to experience success.

Self-Management Sheets

The sheets were devised in order to prompt students to use reflective thinking during all phases of the writing process. According to Hayes and Flower's model the cognitive monitoring processes applied while writing are planning, text generation and revision (Hayes and Flower, 1980; Hayes, 1996). Planning includes idea generation, organization and goal setting and revision includes reading and editing. The self management sheets require the student to activate the monitoring subprocesses mentioned above. On the first sheet students are asked to relate to three features of their writing assignment: The topic, the intended audience and the goals. On the second sheet they are required to brainstorm on the topic, to delineate the different main ideas, to organize them consecutively and to specify their supporting details. These sheets were provided prior to every writing assignment to fulfill the role of a suggested outline and preliminary draft. The third self-management sheet relates to the reading, reviewing and editing process of a writing draft. Students are required to mark four features within their writing assignment: organization (introduction, body and conclusion), topic sentences, connecting words and questionable writing conventions (repetitive ideas or sentences, poor wording or sentence structure). In addition students are asked to reflect on the writing process by referring to their choice of title, stating the positive features and/or strong points of their composition and listing encountered difficulties.

The three above features: the problem based curriculum situated in deep disciplinary content, the qualitative assessment of writing and the self management sheets create opportunities to externalize interactive, responsive, flexible and reflective processes that underlie high literacy, i.e., thoughtful reading, writing and discussion.

EVALUATING THE SUCCESS OF THE PROGRAM

To evaluate the success of the *RLWC* program several studies have been conducted. These studies include different measures of reading and writing in addition to quantitative and qualitative research methods. All studies compare between students who were exposed to literacy instruction within communities of discourse in a problem based instructional environment to a group of students who were exposed to more traditional methods of literacy instruction. Students were randomly assigned to one of the two conditions that were similar in reading load and number of writing assignments. The composition of the experimental and control groups with respect to gender, ethnic origin and age was similar. In addition the Standard Progressive Matrices (SPM) was administered in all studies to verify that students of the experimental and control groups were of comparable intelligence. Literacy instruction was delivered to all students once a week for ninety minutes for the duration of 16 weeks.

The Intervention

The experimental group in the reported studies participated in the instructional program *Reading to Learn and Writing to Communicate (RLWC)* embedded in communities of discourse. The first lessons of the intervention were conducted as benchmark lessons in which the teacher read a passage that introduced the problem-based theme. While reading the teacher explicitly expalined the reasoning and mental processes involved in comprehension of the text. This included a detailed explanation of the reading strategies applied in addition to mental modeling of their use. In addition the teacher modeled thinking and self-reflection while arousing relevant topics to be researched and discussed. Although the teacher provided the tasks and themes of the curriculum students were responsible for doing their own research. This allowed students to partially select and design their own curriculum. All classroom activities were orchestrated by the teacher who participated in group discussions and provided guidance tailored to the needs of the learners.

Students formed research groups. Each group was assigned responsibility for one of the sub-themes of the curriculum. The group applied the reciprocal teaching method (Palincsar and Brown, 1984) while reading collaboratively an introductory text on the assigned sub-theme. Each student was assigned a segment of the text and read it out loud at his or her turn. After reading the text, the student asked questions that a teacher might ask on the segment, summarized the content for other students, discussed and clarified any remaining difficulties, and finally made a prediction about future content. While performing these activities the students in each group gave feedback to one another and the teacher provided guidance to the student expert.

Once a group completed reading the introductory text each student was required to submit a written summary including a reasoned choice of two related topics of interest for further research. Each summary was qualitatively assessed by the teacher and returned to the student for revision. The teacher's qualitative assessment initiated a whole class discussion on the need to plan, organize and sequence paragraphs logically, after which the self-management sheets were introduced to the students. Once the revisions were complete, each group decided upon the topics of interest to be explored. The students engaged in independent and group research, yielding their own curriculum units. This included a search for relevant materials in the class, school library and computer lab. The allocation and collection of relevant materials lead to discussions within which students presented their findings and devised collaboratively learning materials to share and teach their peers.

The students separated into learning groups, each student was responsible for teaching the sub-theme researched by his or her research group to members of his/her learning-group. After peer teaching, the learning groups were required to synthesize the knowledge by completing an integrative task. This evoked group discussions that enabled students to negotiate for understanding. To conclude all activities the students were required to individually complete a consequential writing task and a short quiz that related to the problem based theme and its' subtopics.

During the intervention, cycles of research-share-perform were carried out a few times in addition to whole class instruction that was applied opportunistically. Reading and writing activities were carried out individually and as a joint activity. Joint reading activities included reciprocal teaching that was applied at the beginning of the intervention. Initially, the adult teacher gave direct instruction of the reading strategies and modeled the reciprocal teaching activities but gradually the students became capable of assuming their role as the "expert". Thereafter, students initiated the reciprocal teaching method opportunistically when faced with a comprehension failure. Students' writing samples were composed after group discussions with the intention to be used as learning materials by fellow students. The writing samples, accompanied with self-management sheets, went through several revisions guided by the classroom teacher who applied as a scaffold the *Model for Qualitative Assessment of Writing (MQAW)*. The *MQAW* opened the floor to a written dialogue between reader and writer that culminated in the co-construction of the text. In addition, the *MQAW* allowed the teacher to determine writing conventions that were not applied by most students and then address them through direct instruction. The direct instruction related to authentic writing difficulties encountered by the students and informed them about the required competencies to be applied in their next writing sample.

All members of the control group were exposed to direct instruction of discrete reading and writing skills such as: finding topic sentences, differentiating between facts and opinions, generating paragraphs according to topic sentences, using conjunctions to build compound and complex sentences (but, and, or etc.). The literacy skills were taught using different content realms through direct teacher instruction and completion of individual worksheets. Teaching phases included clear and explicit directions, followed by guided practice in which teachers directed students through the use of the skill that was then practiced, solitarily by the students. In addition students were exposed to different writing formats (description, persuasion etc.) and were given explicit explanations on how to write a research paper. This included generating ideas on a given topic, analyzing the key elements of a research question, collecting information from reference books, making outlines, organizing and sequencing paragraphs logically and listing bibliography references. Towards the end of the course the control students worked on individual research projects. Students were expected to apply the taught literacy skills while researching and writing up their projects. All assignments were graded and returned to the student.

The principal hypothesis of the reported studies is that students exposed to the instructional program *RLWC* designed to promote the critical thinking and reflection skills underlying multiple forms of higher literacy will show greater improvements in reading and academic writing competence than students exposed to traditional methods of literacy instruction. The results include qualitative and quantitative data and analyses of representative samples that summarize the general findings in each realm.

QUANTITATIVE DATA AND ANALYSES

Reading

Reading Comprehension

To examine whether students improved their reading comprehension two different reading measures were applied, a multiple–choice standardized reading measure and reading assessments with open-ended questions.

The standardized measure of reading achievement, the Ortar Reading Test (1987), was administered to examine whether students transfer the learned strategic reading to a variety of texts on a measure that is similar to high stakes testing. The test includes short reading passages of 35 to 190 words followed by several multiple-choice questions. The questions tap understanding of details as well as whether students can integrate information.

In addition to the standardized measure reading assessments were carried out to examine whether students transfer the learned strategic reading to other authentic texts that are different in content but similar in structure and length to some of the authentic readings they were exposed to during intervention. The reading assessment is characteristic of the type of tests and quizzes that are administered to students as measures of achievement in content related courses.

The reading assessments include expository reading passages of approximately 400-600 words each. Students are presented with the reading passage only. Once they complete reading the passage they return the text and answer ten comprehension questions that require short answers. The ten comprehension questions per passage are constructed using the Pearson and Johnson (1978) classification of question type:

1. Four text explicit questions - answer is explicitly mentioned in text.
2. Four text implicit questions - answer is inferred by integrating information presented in text.
3. Two script implicit questions - answer is inferred by relating text to prior knowledge concerning the topic.

To verify that the passages and the accompanied questions conformed to a similar reading comprehension ability the passages and questions were administered to several other students. An analysis of the results confirmed that the reading passages and questions were similar and could be considered as equivalent forms. In all cases, two independent raters (qualified reading specialists) agreed on the classification and the appropriateness of the questions.

As can be seen in Figure 1 and Figure 2 the experimental group manifested higher gains in reading comprehension than the control group. Further analyses indicated that the difference between the groups is statistically significant on the reading assessment only. As can be seen in Figure 2 the reading assessment passages administered at the beginning of the investigation yielded a mean score of 59.9% for the experimental group and 56.3% for the control group. After intervention, the mean score of the experimental group showed a significant improvement rising to 70 %. In contrast, despite the intervention of traditional literacy instruction the control group's score remained unchanged, at 56.3%. The significant difference between the groups on the reading assessment demonstrates that embedding reading strategy instruction in discourse communities in which teachers and students mediate and negotiate meaning while co-constructing their knowledge provides significantly better results than traditional methods of literacy instruction.

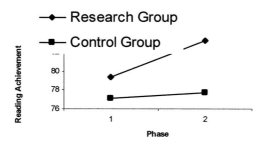

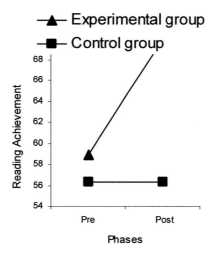

Figure 1. Means of reading achievement on the standardized measure for experimental and control groups

Figure 2. Means of reading achievement on reading assessments for experimental and control groups

The finding of significant differences between groups on the reading assessment only and insignificant higher gains on the standardized comprehension test for the experimental group when compared to the control group was revealed across many different studies. This discrepancy in findings may be explained by the different demands that these measures place on a student's ability to comprehend. A comparison between both measures demonstrates that the measures differ in: whether the text is available during the test, quantity of information (often indicated by passage length), density of information, format of the comprehension check and the text's structure and genre (Alfassi, 1998; Johnston and Pearson, 1983).

An analysis comparing both reading comprehension measures shows that on the standardized multiple-choice test *recognition* of the correct answer is the major strategy applied. For successful performance on such a test, reading the question first and then reading the given text for the answer is a desirable procedure. On the other hand, the major comprehension strategy involved in answering the open-ended questions on the reading assessment is *recall*, as the text is not available to the students once they answer questions. Hence, the reading assessment requires students to learn through reading, i.e., to study the text in order to retrieve from memory the information needed to answer test-like questions. Such learning requires students' to apply proactive reading methods (Zimmerman, 2000). Indeed, successful performance on the reading assessments is determined by the extent that students activate relevant prior knowledge, allocate attention to important information and monitor ongoing activities to assess comprehension. Hence, these assessments are geared toward gauging students' ability to read for meaning (i.e., study large segments of expository text) a skill crucial for academic success. The unsatisfactory score on the reading assessment obtained by all students prior to intervention may suggest that the students are using ineffective methods for reading to learn.

Furthermore, a close examination of the different reading measures shows that the open-ended reading assessment relates directly to the strategies and genre practiced within the *RLWC* program. Indeed, students exposed to the *RLWC* intervention read expository text and engaged in discussion based activities. While performing these activities students were invited to make predictions, summarize, generate text related questions, clarify understanding and muster relevant evidence to support an interpretation thereby promoting comprehension monitoring necessary for independent learning (Applebee et al, 2003; Glaser, 1990). These comprehension strategies were collaboratively practiced while learning deep disciplinary content. This is in contrast to the traditional method of literacy instruction in which reading comprehension was practiced through neutral sequential activities carried out as discrete exercises that were mastered individually and then used whenever the students saw fit. Hence, this analysis suggests that the even though the standardized reading measure taps reading comprehension it does not sample the type of reading strategies fostered in the intervention. The siginificant improvement of the control group from prior to after the literacy intervention on the standardized test only is commensurate with other findings mentioned within the literature. These findings suggest that teaching routines through the acquisition of discrete skills tends to produce high scores on multiple choice tests that employ recognition and reactive methods for learning (Darling-Hammond, 1996).

Reading Rate and Reading Accuracy

Many experimenters and theorists have suggested that reading rate is dependent on the effectiveness of decoding and level of comprehension of text (Carver, 1990). Typically, more efficient decoding is presumed to lead to improved comprehension, and the successful integration of these two skills is thought to lead to more rapid word identification. As a consequence, reading rate has become a diagnostic measure of reading ability (Perfetti, 1991; Stanovich, 1981).

To examine whether students improved their reading abilty over the phases of intervention two different reading measures were applied, reading accuracy and reading rate.

The reading rate was measured by timing the student's oral reading. Oral reading rate was represented in words per minute (WPM) for each test passage. Reading accuracy was measured by using the number of words identified incorrectly for each passage. Each substitution, addition, mispronunciation or deletion was scored as a reading error (see Ekwall, 1979). The total number of errors was subtracted from the total number of words in the passage to yield the percentage of words read incorrectly.

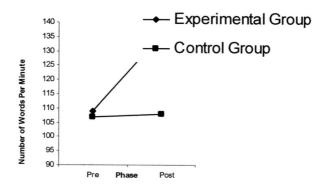

Figure 3. means of reading rate for experimental and control groups

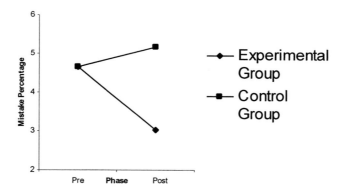

Figure 4. Means of decoding ability according to mistake percentage for experimental and control groups

Reading rate and reading accuracy measures revealed significant intervention effects between phases of the study. On both measures the students of the experimental group improved their performance significantly from prior to after intervention whilst the control group portrayed no improvement at all. The significant improvement in reading accuracy and reading rate over the phases of intervetion is additional support to the effectiveness of the *RLWC* interventional program in fostering reading.

The findings on the different reading measures support the contemporary view of learning that posits that social processes create the context within which students develop the cognitive and linguistic tools for comprehension and understanding associated with literacy (Applebee et. al, 2003). In addition, the results lend further support to findings that demonstrate that teaching students proactive reading strategies leads to independent and successful strategy use (Alfassi, 2004; Sinatra, Brown and Reynolds, 2002) thereby fostering learning from expository text. Indeed, the reported findings demonstrate the efficacy of embedding literacy instruction in a problem based environment that includes collaborative learning of in depth content in addition to direct instruction of reading strategies.

Writing

Expository Writing Competence

To examine students' writing competence samples of their expository writing were collected. Consistent with procedures used by writing researchers (Hout, 1990; Shell, Murphy, and Bruning, 1989; Needles and Knapp, 1994) direct evaluations were conducted on students' writing samples. A writing prompt was selected to represent expository writing assigned in school. The writing prompt drew on an experience common to all children, it was based on little prior knowledge and focused on a topic that would be of interest to most children. For example: "Think about your school. Do you find it to be a safe environment for you and most students? Elaborate on the different aspects of the presented issue while expressing your own view". Students were allowed as much time as needed to complete the essay. The same writing prompt was given at the different phases of the study.

The writing essays were independently scored by two different raters, using a semi-holistic scoring method. The scorers were unaware of each other's ratings or the students' identities. Sub-scores were assigned for systematic and focused response, relevance and amount of supporting details, development and coherency, and organization and structure. Scores on each category ranged from inadequate response (1) to excellent response (6). When scorers' judgments differed a student's final score was the mean score. The four sub-scores were then summed, resulting in a total score ranging from 6 to 24. Interrater reliability was found to be $r = .82$ which is within the range of interrater reliability estimates obtained for holistic scoring (.68 to .89) when adequate methods are used (White, 1985).

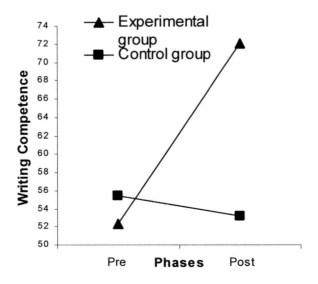

Figure 5. Means of writing competence for experimental and control groups

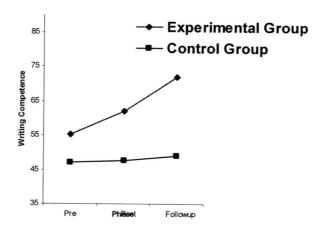

Figure 6. Means of writing competence for experimental and control groups on the three phases of intervention

The writing assessments administered at the beginning of the investigation revealed no significant difference between the mean score of the experimental group and the control group. All groups, as can be seen in Figures 5 and 6 scored a failing grade portraying unsatisfactory academic writing competence. This finding is commensurate with other findings that demonstrate that students who are considered proficient learners lack in their writing competence, accentuating the importance of devising innovative intervention programs such as the one suggested in this chapter.

As can be seen in Figure 5 the achieved mean score of the experimental group improved significantly after instruction to a satisfactory grade equivalent to average performance (70%). In contrast the mean score of the control group remained an unchanged failing grade. These results demonstrate that integrating reading, writing and discussion into communities of discourse in a problem based environment yields significant improvements in academic writing competence when compared to more traditional methods of literacy instruction.

In an additional study samples of students writing were collected at three different phases: prior to intervention, immediately after training and after 12 weeks of maintenance in which the students were not exposed to literacy instruction. As can be seen in Figure 6 findings indicated that the experimental group improved its performance significantly from the first phase to the second and also from the second phase to the third. These findings indicate that the significant differences found between the groups on the writing assessments as a result of instruction not only were maintained after 12 weeks but also continued to expand over time. These results demonstrate the benefits of embedding instruction in communities of discourse engaged in inquiry where students construct their knowledge while completing authentic writing tasks for a genuine audience. Such an intervention provides significantly better results than more traditional methods of instruction.

Moreover, the results suggest that the growth in writing competence demonstrated by the students is structural i.e., durable and pervasive as students' writing competence continued to grow well after the intervention has ceased. This fits well with Feuerstein's theoretical entity of structural cognitive modifiability (Feuerstein et al., 1980), that is defined as change that is self-perpetuating and is differentiated from temporary change by its manifested permanent and pervasive growth over time. These findings provide further support to the main findings of this research, namely that the *RLWC* intervention is an effective method to foster and modify complex cognitive skills such as writing.

To further explain the differences in writing performance demonstrated by the experimental and control groups an analysis was conducted of the instructional context in which the act of writing was fostered. The comparison is based upon the assertion stated in the literature that different instructional contexts may effect differentially the learning, acquisition and manifestation of student writing (Hayes, 1996; Schultz and Fecho, 2000). Table 1 presents a comparison of the two instructional methods.

As can be seen in Table 1, one of the main features of the *RLWC* program is that students write to teach their fellow students thereby providing students with authentic writing tasks that have purpose and meaning (Langer, 1987). This is in contrast to more traditional methods of instruction in which school writing is often characterized as an artificial non-authentic activity. Writing tasks such as abstracting chapters, and completing essay exams and research papers are carried out by students solely for the purpose of being evaluated and are not geared to add or transform the teacher's knowledge. As such, these writing activities do not provide the writer with the opportunity to use writing for authentic and real-world purposes such as persuasion, description and expression of the writer's voice (Boice, 1994; Bruning and Horn, 2000; Sitko, 1998).

Table 1. Features of Writing Instruction in the Traditional and *RLWC* Classroom

Feature	Traditional	RLWC
Writing purpose	To teach students to communicate coherently through text	To teach students to communicate coherently through text
		A tool to explore ideas - a "thinking device"
Curriculum	Discrete sequential writing skills Fragmented	Authentic simultaneous use of reading, writing and discussion
Content		Deep disciplinary content
Writing Prompt	Different themes	Recurrent themes
Writing Instruction	Pre-set program	Opportunistic – according to students' needs
Practice	Solitary	Collaborative
Audience	Teacher	Peers
Number of Reviews	One	Many
Assessment	Common set criteria Standardized	Individualized Aimed at a vary of ZPD's
Evaluation	Grade End product	Scaffold Writing process

In addition, in the *RLWC* program idea generation and information gathering are shared activities. Students share with each other the information they gather, discuss the topics at hand and then on that basis go on to create learning materials for their fellow students. This is in contrast to the more traditional methods of writing in which students carry out individually in solitary all aspects of an undertaken writing assignment. Furthermore, writing in the *RLWC* program is used as a tool for exploring ideas and serves a dialogic function. Student writing is critically reviewed by teacher and/or peers and then revised by the student who then deliberately improves and develops the text. Thus, students and teachers are involved in the joint construction of written texts.

An additional feature of the suggested program is the *Model for Qualitative Assessment of Writing (MQAW)* developed to foster writing competence. The model provides the students with a supportive environment that includes positive reinforcement and affirmation that the employed strategies are useful. The literature suggests that the more students perceive writing strategies to be useful the more likely they are to apply them and that in turn will promote skill acquisition (Bandura, 1997). The reported findings further support this contention. In addition the model furnishes the teacher with a tool for goal setting and progress monitoring of the student, two facilitative variables of writing competence (Graham, 1997; Bruning and Horn, 2000). By applying the *MQAW* model on students' writing samples, the teacher directs each student to specific writing strategies to be applied in his or her next writing assignment. As such, the teacher evaluation is individualized and geared towards development of the writing process itself. This is in contrast to more traditional methods of evaluation in which teachers assess student writing as an end product according to a common set criterion that all students are expected to meet.

In sum, the significant improvement of students exposed to the *RLWC* program in academic writing competence demonstrates the effectiveness of embedding literacy instruction in communities of discourse engaged in guided inquiry where students construct their knowledge through social interaction while completing authentic writing tasks for a genuine audience. Furthermore, these findings support the view that scaffolding plays an important role in fostering students' budding knowledge and writing expertise (Shultz and Fecho, 2000; Stefanou, Perencevich, Dicinto and Turner, 2004). Indeed, the reported findings support the social constructive view that context and capacity are intricately intertwined (Lee and Smagorinsky, 2000) and demonstrate that fostering writing requires designing a learning environment that includes the above features.

QUALITATIVE DATA AND ANALYSES

In an attempt to capture processes that occur during exposure to literacy instruction in communities of discourse lessons were vidoetaped and analyzed. Through direct observation student behaviour and class discourse were recorded and are reported in the following section. The qualitative analyses enable to extract and portray elements of the *RLWC* intervention that appear to contribute to the fostering of high literacy.

Episode 1: David is a student with average intelligence who is diagnosed with ADHD. For the first few lessons David did not participate in class activities. He rocked his chair from side to side, walked around the classroom, and usually ended up back in his chair with his head on the table. During these episodes the teacher called on him attempting to focus his attention but to no avail. During small group activities, David joined only upon teacher request. He did not participate in class activities and disconnected himself by listening to his MP3 player which was usually confiscated.

At the beginning of the fifth lesson David appeared to be listening to the group discussion that ended with a decision to prepare a Power Point presentation. David approached his peers and said "I can help prepare the presentation. I know to download real neat stuff from the net. I'm great at this!". For the next few lessons David took an active role in designing the group's presentation and presenting it to the class. During a class discussion on peer teaching he said :

"In order to teach others I have to study the material the best I can and to dwell deeply into it, so that I'll be ready to answer any question I might be asked. I think peer teaching is an excellent way to get you down to work....it certainly worked for me....".

The change in David's behavior was apparent in the following lessons. He participated in class activities and collaborated with his peers. In one of the last lessons he is observed reading an expository text together with two other peers. They encountered difficulty in word clarification and one of his peers called the teacher for assistance. David intervened and commented "Jason, come on we can do this by ourselves! Look this word is in a sentence, I'll read the sentence again, then you will tell me the sentence in your own words. If it makes sense to us then that means we understood the gist and it really doesn't matter if we don't understand the exact meaning of the word itself......".

An analysis of this excerpt suggests that the turning point in David's behaviour occurs once he becomes a valued member who contributes to the group. This fits well with the contention that school membership is a preliminary condition to school engagement (Wehlage, Rutter, Smith, Lesko and Fernandez, 1989). David's school engagement is demonstrated in his involvement in classwork that entailed intention, concentration, and commitment. The fact that he and his peers were proactive in selecting the learning experiences for a genuine audience gave him a sense of responsibility and ownership. *"In order to teach others I have to study the material the best I can... so I'll be ready to answer any question."* Indeed, the newly-gained sense of ownership appeared to foster motivation and student engagement as suggested within the literature (Ryan and Deci, 2000; Vatterott, 1995). Furthermore, this excerpt portrays how the cooperative learning component embedded within the intervention allows for student diversity and ensures that expertise is deliberately distributed across the members of the classroom. It is clearly demonstated how the distribution of expertise allows the members of the community to benefit from and to contribute to the pool of knowledge. In addition, it shows how reading for meaning is collaboratively learned and practiced. The students tackle the comprehension breakdown independently by verbalizing their understanding and applying self monitorinfg skills *"..you will tell me the sentence in your own words. If it makes sense to us then that means we understood... ."* It is impotrant to note that at the beginning of the intervention students applied the reciprocal teaching method using all four strategies while reading text. In this episode which is towards the end of the intervention, David and Jason appropriately apply only one of the strategies to overcome their misunderstanding thereby demonstrating the internalization of active comprehension processing that resulted in self regu35altion

Episode 2. Amanda, Danielle and Julie are students with average grades. They were observed while attempting to compose a biography that would shed light on the special features of a famous literary figure. Danielle is dictating to Amanda, Julie is scribbling on a piece of paper and does not appear to be involved in the activity.

Danielle (stops dictating to Amanda) : " Hey! We have a problem. I don't know how to continue.... I don't understand something in the historical background of the character."

Julie (stops scribbling): "Why don't you read out loud what's written in the encyclopedia on the historical backround of the figure-maybe we'll understand."

Danielle (reads out loud from the encyclopedia): "During World War I Rachel Blustein lived in Odessa where she taught in a high school. In addition to teaching Rachel translated many poems of well known Russain poets. In 1919 Rachel returned to the land of Israel and joined a group of settlers in Dagania. To her dismay, she had to terminate her work on the farm as she had contracted tuberculosis. Due to her sickness she moved to Jerusalem and became a teacher....."

Amanda: "I don't understand why Rachel left the land of Israel in the first place.... More than that it says that her sickness prevented her from working on the farm, wasn't she a teacher? And if she was sick with tuberculosis why did she want to work on a farm at all?"

Julie: (takes a different encyclopedia and looks into it) "Here it says that Rachel came to the land of Israel during the second wave of immigration (1904-1914) which most of its members were young people inspired by socialist ideals. I think we will be able to understand more about Rachel's whereabouts and her decision to work on the farm if we figure out the ideology of the members of the second wave of immigration."

Danielle: "Good idea! Let's ask Jordan if his group is learning about someone who came to the land of Israel during the same period of time. (Danielle calls Jordan) Hey Jordan! Tell me do you know anything about the second wave of immigration?"

Jordan: "Sure enough, why are you asking?"

Danielle: "Can you explain to me their ideology? We can't figure out why our character decided to go live on a farm and work the land."

Jordan: "The members of the second wave of immigration had experienced pogroms in Russia. These pioneers were determined to establish in the land of Israel independent rural communities where they would not only defend themselves but they would also provide their economical needs by working the land."

Danielle: "but our character was a teacher......how does she get to work the land on a farm?????"

Amanda: Wait! here it says that in 1913 she went to France to study agriculture. So she did have interest in this field. If she was a member of the second wave of immigration she must have held the same ideas and believed in working the land and maybe that is why she left the country to learn agriculture. Remember the country then was desolate and they really didn't have the know how .... what to plant where and so on... ."

Julie: "That makes sense. I think Amanda is right. I suggest we first present the ideology of the memebers of the second wave of immigration and only then we will present our character. This will enable the reader to understand Rachel's decisions and whereabouts."

Amanda: "Great! Now that we know how we are going to go about it lets' get down to work. Danielle can you continue... ."

In this excerpt collaboration between peers is portrayed. It is important to note that throughout this episode the teacher was available to answer questions. The students independently approached their peers demonstrating their perception that the teacher is not the sole source of information in the classroom. The students also referred to different texts in search for relevant information.

This episode portrays students actively attempting to extract meaning from text while externalizing through verbalization covert self monitoring skills. They are simultaneously concentrating on the material (*"but our character was a teacher... ... how does she get to work the land on a farm?????, Wait! here it says that in 1913 she went to France to study agriculture..."*) and on themselves checking if their reading is resulting in understanding (*"That makes sense..."*). Collaboratively, the group, with its' variety of expertise and engagement learns the text while reading for meaning. One student raises a problem, another provides required information and a third suggests a solution to the problem while providing supporting facts. Indeed, their understanding is gained by provision of social support that simplifies the task at hand and ensures the construction of meaning (Brown and Palinscar, 1989). In addition, the students discussion provides the floor for verbalization and externalization of covert metacognitive writing strategies such as planning their writing while relating to an intended audience.

Episode 3. One of the groups in the class was presented with a biography on Eliezer Ben-Yehuda. Eliezer Ben-Yehuda is regarded by many to be the father of the modern Hebrew language, he is credited for making Hebrew a language of living and vibrant use after two thousand years of not being spoken. The students read the following paragraph that instigated the discussion to be reported.

"Most of the Jewish inhabitants of Jerusalem were pious Jews, who wished to live their lives in the holy center of Judaism. Most knew Hebrew though the prayers and study books, but the spoken language was normally in the native language of origin in addition to Yiddish and Ladino. They were opposed to Ben Yehuda's will to revive ancient Hebrew into an everyday spoken language. They maintained that Hebrew was a sacred language to be used only for religious purposes. The orthodox Community subsequently hounded and persecuted Ben-Yehuda, eventually excommunicating him"

Teacher: Who would like to ask a question?

Matt: Was Hebrew a spoken language at the time of Ben-Yehuda?

Dan: No, it states in the text that Hebrew was spoken only when praying or learning sacred scriptures.

Stephanie: It says they spoke Yiddish.

Teacher: What is Yiddish? Who spoke that language?

Debbie: Yiddish is similar to German but not exactly. Most Jews from European origin spoke that language.

Matt: Weren't there at that time Jews who lived in Israel that immigrated from other continents like Africa? They didn't speak Yiddish did they?

Debbie: No, they spoke Ladino. By the way what language is that?

Teacher: Well, can someone answer Debbie's question? (Quiet) Ladino is the spoken and written Hispanic language of Jews of Spanish origin.

Michael: So that creates a problem. If the people in the land of Israel at the time were from different places they spoke different languages. So how could they communicate with each other?

Judy: Ah-ha! I am beginning to understand Ben-Yehuda's theory. He wanted people to immigrate to the land of Israel from all over the diaspora. He understood that to unite these people there is a need for something basic like maybe a common language....

Josh: O.K. But why did he have to choose to revive an ancient language used for sacred purposes only? He knew that by doing this he was arousing the anger of the religious people.

Dan: Maybe he thought it would be easier to revive a language everybody knew from their religious practices instead of suggesting a new one.

Teacher: Dan do you think he chose Hebrew because it was the easiest way to go about it?

Judy: It's a pity he didn't choose English!

Michael: Dan, you are thinking of the difficulties Ben-Yehuda was facing. I don't think you understand why he was so decisive about reviving Hebrew. It is true that by choosing a different language he would have avoided the opposition from the orthodox people and life would have been easier for him. But I think this was a matter of principle as this specific language was meaningful to all.

Stephanie: Judy, do you really think he should have chosen English? We don't live in England do we????

Judy: What has one got to do with the other? It's a fact that today we all use English. It's an international language that is important to know. The British governed over the country and it would have come in handy then and it certainly would be helpful today if we all spoke English instead of Hebrew.

Michael: But Hebrew is the language of the Jews for generations........

Teacher: Hmmm....maybe there is a point in what Judy is suggesting. English is certainly an international language that we use while surfing the net and when we go overseaes.

Gil: That does not make sense at all every nation has it's own language. Why would he choose the language of a different nation? He wanted to bond the people through the use of a unique language. How else could he unite them into a nation?

Debbie: Then why not choose Yiddish or Ladino?

Gil: Because Hebrew was a language known to all and that already was a common denominator. A common language meaningful to all unites and bonds people into a nation.

This excerpt portrays the role of discourse in developing understanding of processes that underlie a course of events as presented within written text. The understanding is gained through external verbalization of hypothetical thinking voiced and responded to by memebers of a collaborative learning group. The assumptions voiced are challenged (*"but why did he have to choose to revive an ancient language used for sacred purposes only...."; "..do you really think he should have chosen English? We don't live in England do we????*) logically supported (*"Maybe he thought... a language everybody knew from their religious practices...would be easier to revive than suggesting a new one;" "It's a fact that today we all use English"*) and evaluated (*"That does not make sense at all..."*) thereby conrtibuting to the verbalization of a higher order generalization (*"...a common language...unites and bonds people into a nation*). Indeed, the higher order generalization, crucial to solving the problem-based theme presented to the students, is formed through group negotiation facilitated by the teacher.

The literature suggests that comprehension strategy instruction can be characterized as a process in which teachers attempt to make learning sensible and students make sense of learning (Dole, Duffy, Roehler and Pearson, 1991). The teacher in this episode contributes to the group negotiations by providing required information (*"Ladino is the spoken and written Hispanic language of Jews of Spanish origin"*), planning the understanding to be developed (*"What is Yiddish? Who spoke that language?"; "Dan do you think he chose Hebrew because it was the easiest way to go about it?"*) and kindling the discussion among peers (" *Well, can someone answer Debbie's question?; Hmmm...maybe there is a point in what Judy is suggesting.."*). Most of the teachers comments are pointers for further thinking. She is problematizing the issues at hand forcing the students to support their views and refine them i.e., make sense of what they are saying. This negates the typical instructional discourse in which teachers seek to elicit specific "official" answers originating in text and transmitted oneway, mainly from teachers to students.

The above analysis portrays the group as a discourse community in which meaning is constantly negotiated and refined. Most of the discourse handled by the students includes ideas planted by and expanded on, by both teacher and students. In addition, the discourse is characterized by modes of speculation, evidence and proof. Such discourse, coined within the literature as dialogical has been found to correlate positively with achievement (Bahktin, 1984; Nystrand, Wu and Gamoran, 2003). This analysis adds to those findings and suggests that the *RLWC* program situated in communities of discourse is characterized by dialogic learning and instruction that fosters students thoughtful reading and writing.

The qualitative analyses presented above support the current view of reading comprehension as a process of emerging expertise where readers create meaning through the integration of existing and new knowledge, and the flexible use of strategies to foster, monitor, regulate and maintain comprehension (Alexander and Jetton, 2000; Dole et al., 1991; Wittrock, 1998; Glaser, 1990). The studies also support the contention that enhancing students' ability to construct meaning from text requires teachers to provide students with clear explanations about strategies while allowing them to engage in meaningful dialogue around substantive ideas (Alexander and Jetton, 2000; Pressley, 2000). As mentioned above, the socio cognitive approach asserts that learning involves the construction of *meaning (sense making)* that emerges through exploration (Wells, 2000). The qualitative data supports this assertion and portrays how such meaning is achieved through the process of articulating ideas that involves both individual interpretation and negotiation with others.

CONCLUSION

The quantitative and qualitative findings presented in this chapter support the contention that literacy instruction is an active social constructive process in which discussion and guided exploration of ideas are central to the developing understandings of readers and writers. In addition the findings support the claim that literacy is best acquired while learning in depth content that engages students in thoughtful reading writing and discussion for a purposeful goal (Gee, 2000; Langer, 2001). Indeed, the reported studies translate these theoretical assertions into practice by applying the FCL principles embedded in a problem based curriculum through which students *read to learn and write to communicate* thereby transforming their experience into knowledge.

Overall, the findings of this chapter demonstrate the educational benefits of the contemporary view of literacy learning. The results illustrate that *RLWC* is a viable interventional program that can be implemented successfully in language arts classes. Furthermore, the results indicate that *RLWC* promotes dialogic learning and engages students in thoughtful reading, writing and discussion about content that in turn foster high literacy. These results add to recent research in cognitive instruction and support the need to modify prevailing methods of literacy learning to include a learning environment in which teachers and students mediate and negotiate meaning while co-constructing their knowledge and applying complex tasks of reading, writing and discussions.

REFERENCES

Alfassi, M. (1998). Reading for meaning: The efficacy of reciprocal teaching in fostering reading comprehension in high school students in remedial reading classes. *American Educational Research Journal, 35,* 309-332.

Alfassi, M. (2004). Reading to learn: Effects of combined strategy instruction on high school students. *Journal of Educational Research, 97,* 171-184.

Applebee, A. N., Langer, J., Nystrand, M., and Gamoran, A. (2003). Discussion based approaches to developing classroom instruction and student performance in middle and high school English. *American Educational Research Journal, 40,_685-730.*

Au, K. H. (1998). Social constructivism and the school literacy learning of students of diverse backgrounds. *Journal of Literacy Research, 30,* 297-319.

Bakhtin, M. (1984). *Problems of Dostoevsky's poetics* (translated and edited by Caryl Emerson). Minneapolis; University of Minnesota Press.

Bandura, A. (1997). *Self -efficacy: The exercise of control.* New York: W. H. Freeman and Company.

Bean, T. W. (2000). Reading in the content areas: Social constructivist dimensions. In M. L. Kamil, P. B. Mosenthal, P. D. Pearson, and R. Barr (Eds.), *Handbook of reading research Vol. 3* (pp. 629-644). New Jersey: Lawrence Erlbaum Associates.

Boice, R. (1994). *How writers journey to comfort and fluency.* Westport, CT: Praeger.

Brown, A. L., and Campione, J. C. (1990). Communities of learning and thinking: Or a context by any other name. *Contributions to Human Development, 21,* 108-126

Brown, A. L., and Campione, J. C. (1994). Guided discovery in a community of learners. In K. McGilly (Ed.), *Classroom lessons: Integrating cognitive theory and classroom practice* (pp. 229-270). Cambridge, MA: MIT Press.

Brown, A. L., and Campione, J. C. (1996). Psychological theory and the design of innovative learning environments: On procedures, principles, and systems. In L. Shauble and R. Glaser (Eds.), *Innovations in learning: New environments for education* (pp. 289-325). Mahwah. NJ: Erlbaum.

Brown, A. L., and Campione, J. C. (1998). Designing a community of young learners: theoretical and practical lessons. In N. M. Lambert and B. L. McCombs (Eds.), *How students learn: Reforming schools through learner-centered education* (pp. 153-186). American Psychological Association. Washington, DC.

Bruner, J. (1986). *Actual minds, possible worlds.* Cambridge, MA: Harvard University Press.

Bruning, R., and Horn, C. (2000). Developing motivation to write. *Educational Psychologist, 35,* 25-37.

Carver, R. P. (1990). *Reading rate: A review of research and theory.* Academic Press, San Diego, CA.

Darling-Hammond, L. (1996). The right to learn and the advancement of teaching: Research, policy, and practice for democratic education. *Educational Researcher, 25(6),* 5-17.

Engle, R. A., and Conant, F. R. (2002). Guiding principles for fostering productive disciplinary engagement: Explaining an emergent argument in a community of learners classroom. *Cognition and Instruction, 20,* 399-483.

Ekwall, E. E. (1979). *The Ekwall reading inventory.* Allyn and Bacon, Boston

Feuerstein, R., Rand, Y., Hoffman, M. B., and Miller, R. (1980). *Instrumental enrichment: An intervention program for cognitive modifiability.* Baltimore: University Park Press.

Gallimore, R., and Tharp, R. (1990). Teaching mind in society: Teaching, schooling and literate discourse. In L. C. Moll (Ed.), *Vygotsky and Education.* (pp.175-205) Cambridge: Cambridge University Press.

Gee, J. P. (2000). Discourse and socoicultural studies in reading. In M. L. Kamil, P. B. Mosenthal, P. D. Pearson, and R. Barr (Eds.), *Handbook of reading research Vol. 3* (pp. 195-207). New Jersey: Lawrence Erlbaum Associates.

Gee, J. P. (2001). Reading as situated language: A sociocognitive perspective. *Journal of Adolescent and Child Literacy, 44,* 714-725.

Glaser, R. (1990). The reemergence of learning theory within instructional research. *American Psychologist, 45,* 29-39.

Graham, S. (1997). Executive control in the revising of students with learning and writing difficulties. *Journal of Educational Psychology, 89,* 223-234.

Greeno, J. G. (1998). The situativity of knowing, learning and research. *American Psychologist, 53,* 5-26.

Hayes, J. R., and Flower, L. (1980). Identifying the organization of writing processes. In L. W. Gregg and E. R. Sternberg (Eds.), *Cognitive processes in writing.* Hillsdale, NJ: Lawrence Erlbaum Associates.

Hayes, J. R. (1996). *The science of writing.* Mahwah, NJ: Lawrence Erlbaum Associates.

Heller, J. I, and Gordon, A. (1992). Lifelong learning. *Educator, 6,* 4-19.

Hicks, D. (1996). *Discourse, learning, and schooling.* Cambridge: Cambridge University Press.

Hout, B. (1990). The literature of direct writing assessment: Major concerns and prevailing trends. *Review of Educational Research, 60,* 237-263.

Johnston, P., and Pearson, D. (1983). Assessment: Responses to exposition. In A. Berger and H. A. Robinson (Eds.), *Secondary school reading: What research reveals for classroom practice* (pp. 127-141). Urbana: University of Illinois.

Karpov, Y. V., and Haywood, H. C. (1998). Two ways to elaborate Vygotsky's concept of mediation: Implications for instruction. *American Psychologist, 53(1),* 27-36.

Langer, J. (Ed.) (1987). *Language, literacy, and culture: Issues of society and schooling.* Norwood, NJ: Ablex.

Langer, J. A. (2001). Beating the odds: Teaching middle and high school students to read and write well. *American Educational Research Journal, 38,* 837-880.

Lee, C. D., and Smagorinsky, P. (2000). Introduction: Constructing meaning through collaborative inquiry. In C. D Lee and P. Smagorinsky (Eds.), *Vygotskian perspectives on literacy research: Constructing meaning through collaborative meaning* (pp. 1-18). Cambridge, MA: Cambridge University Press

Lensmire, T. J. (1994). *When children write; Critical revisions of the writing workshop.* New York Teachers College Press.

National Assessment of Educational progress (1998). *National writing summary data tables for grade 8 teacher data.* Retrieved, from http// www.nces. ed. gov / nationreportcard / TABLES/index.shtml.

National Center for Education Statistics (1999). *Report in brief: NAEP 1998 trends in academic progress.* Washington, DC: US Department of Education

Needles, M. C., and Knapp, M. S. (1994). Teaching writing to children who are underdeserved. *Journal of Educational Psychology, 86(3),* 339-349.

Nystrand. M. (1997). *Opening dialogue: Understanding the dynamics of language and learning in the English classroom.* New York: Teachers College Press.

Nystrand M. and Wu, L, Gamoran, A., Zeiser, S., and Long, D. A. (2003). Questions in time: Investing the structure and dynamics of unfolding classroom discourse. *Discourse Processes, 35,* 135-198.

Ortar, G. (1987). *"Lets read": A reading comprehension test for schools.* Jerusalem: Achiever.

Palincsar, A., and Brown, A. (1984). Reciprocal teaching of comprehension fostering and comprehension-monitoring activities. *Cognition and Instruction, 1,* 117-175.

Pearson, D., and Johnson, D. (1978). *Teaching reading comprehension.* New York: Holt, Rinehart and Winston.

Perfetti, C. (1991). Representation and awarenwss in in the acquisition of reading competence. In L. Riben and C. Perfetti (Eds.), *Learning to Read* (pp. 33-37). New Jersey: Lawrence Erlbaum Associates.

Pressley, M. (2000). What should comprehension instruction be the instruction of? In M. L. Kamil, P. B. Mosenthal, P. D. Pearson, and R. Barr (Eds.), *Handbook of reading research Vol. 3* (pp. 545-563). New Jersey: Lawrence Erlbaum Associates.

Roth, W. M. (1995). *Authentic school science: Knowing and learning in open-inquiry science laboratories.* Boston: Kluwer.

Ryan, R. M., and Deci, E. L. (2000). Self- determination theory and the facilitation of intrinsic motivation, social development, and well-being. *American Psychologist, 55,* 68-78.

Scardamalia, M. and Breiter, C. (1991). Higher levels of agency for children in knowledge building: A challenge for the design of new knowledge media. *The Journal of the Learning Sciences, 1,* 37-68

Shell, D. F., Murphy, C. C., and Bruning, R. H. (1989). Self efficacy and outcome expectancy mechanisms in reading and writing achievement. *Journal of Educational Psychology, 81,* 91-100.

Shultz, K., and Fecho, B. (2000). Society's child: Social context and writing development. *Educational Psychologist, 35,* 51-62.

Sinatra, G. M., Brown, K. J., and Reynolds, R. E. (2002). Implications of cognitive resource allocation for comprehension strategies instruction. In C. C. Block and M. Pressley (Eds.), *Comprehension instruction: Research-based best practices* (pp. 62-76). New York: Guilford Press.

Sitko, B. (1998). Knowing how to write: Metacognition and writing instruction. In D. J. Hacker, J. Dunlosky and A. C. Graesser (Eds.), *Metacognition in educational theory and practice* (pp. 93-113). Mahwah, New Jersey: Lawrence Erlbaum Associates.

Smagorinsky, P. (2001). If meaning is constructed. What's it made from? Toward a cultural theory of reading. *Review of Educational Research, 71,* 133-169.

Stanovich, K. E.(1981). Relationships between word decoding, speed, general, retreival ability and radiing progress in first-grade children. *Journal of Educational Psychology, 75,* 809-815.

Stefanou, C. R., Perenevich, K. C., DiCintio, M., and Turner, J. (2004). Supporting autonomy in the classroom: Ways teachers encourage student decision making and ownership. *Educational Psychologist, 39*, 97-110.

Tudge, J. (1992). Vygotsky: The zone of proximal development and peer collaboration: Implications for classroom practice. In L. C. Moll (Ed.), *Vygotsky and ecuation: Instructional implications and applications of sociocultural psychology* (pp. 155-172). New York: Cambridge University Press.

Vatterott, C. (1995). Student-focused instruction: Balancing limits with freedom. *Middle School Journal, 27*(11), 28-38.

Vygotsky, L. S. (1962). *Language and thought.* Cambridge, MA: Harvard University Press.

Vygotsky, L. (1978). *Mind in society; The development of higher psychological processes* (M. Cole, V. John-Steiner, S. Scribner and E. Souberman, (Eds. and Trans.). Cambridge, MA: Harvard University Press.

Wehlage, G. G., Rutter, R. A., Smith, G. A., Lesko, N., and Fernandez, R. R. (1989). *Reducing the risk: Schools as communities of support.* New-York: The Falmer Press.

Wells, G. (2000). Dialogic inquiry in education: Building on the legacy of Vygotsky. In C. D. Lee and P. Smagorinsky (Eds.), *Vygotskian perspectives on literacy research: Constructing meaning through collaborative meaning* (pp. 51-85) Cambridge, MA: Cambridge University Press.

White, E. M. (1985). *Teaching and assessing writing.* San-Francisco: Jossey-Bass.

Wilkinson, L. C., and Silliman. E. R., (2000). Classroom language and literacy learning. In M. L. Kamil, P. B. Mosenthal, P. D. Pearson, and R. Barr (Eds.), *Handbook of reading research, Vol. 3* (pp. 337-360). New Jersey: Lawrence Erlbaum Associates.

Windschitl. M. (2002). Framing constructivism in practice as the negotiation and dilemmas: An Analysis of the conceptual, pedagogical, cultural and political challenges facing teachers. *Review of Educational Research, 72,* 131-176.

Zimmerman, B. J. (2000). Attaining self regulation: A social cognitive perspective. In M. Boekaerts, P. R. Pintrich, and M. Zeidner (Eds.), *Handbook of self regulation* (pp. 13-35). New York; Academic Press.

In: Trends in Learning Reserch
Editor: Samuel N. Hogan, pp. 67-80

ISBN 1-59454-965-6
© 2006 Nova Science Publishers, Inc.

Chapter 3

WRITING ERRORS INDUCED IN NORMAL SUBJECTS: A COMPARISON WITH WRITING ALTERATIONS IN ALZHEIMER'S PATIENTS

Rita Moretti [1], Paola Torre and Rodolfo M. Antonello
Dipartimento di Medicina Clinica e Neurologia, U.C.O. di Clinica Neurologica,
Università degli Studi di Trieste

ABSTRACT

Writing is a complex process requiring visual memory, attention, phonological and semantic operations and motor performance. For that reason, it can easily be disturbed by interfering with attention, memory, by interfering subvocalization, and so on. Using 23 female third-year students (23.4 ± 0.78 years old) from the University of Trieste, we investigated the production of errors in three experimental conditions (control, articulatory suppression and tapping). In the articulatory suppression condition, the participants produced significantly more linguistic impairments (such as agrammatism, unrelated substitutions, sentence omissions, and semantically deviant sentences), which are similar to linguistic impairments found in aphasia. On the tapping condition there were more perseverations, deletions, and substitutions, both of letters and of words. We then have considered 50 patients suffering from Alzheimer's Disease (CDR average' score=1.76±0.56): we evaluated their writing production, in the spontaneous, under dictation and on copy tasks. We collected the samples and analysed their production, with the same schema of mistake' classification score. We compared the results, and try to find a correlation with specific items of the AD population.

These data suggest that writing is not an automatic skill. Only after many years of experience and practice of processing information (through cortical subcortical channels) can writing be considered an automatic skill. Limited experimental conditions can disrupt the writing system in normal subjects, probably interfering with the cortical subcortical loops, and link normality to pathology. In neurodegeneration, such as in Alzheimer'

---

[1] Corresponding Autor: Rita Moretti M.D., Dipartimento di Medicina Clinica e Neurologia, U.C.O. di Clinica Neurologica, Università degli Studi di Trieste, Ospedale di Cattinara 34149 Trieste, Italy or e-mail (moretti@univ.trieste.it).

Disease, writing is precociously impaired and the disruption is early macroscopically evident.

Writing is an expression of language. However, even the most prolific authors speak more than they write, and for the bulk of the population, writing is far and away the least used of their language skills. Traditional neuropsychologists seem to have thought about writing as a skill, and appear to assume it to be closely dependent upon speech skills. Within cognitive neuropsychology, the study of writing processes has tended to concentrate on the writing in aphasic writers.

Writing is a cognitive system with a complex architecture consisting of many functionally independent procedural and memory components. It involves central and peripheral processes, where the central process integrates the output modalities involved in the spelling of familiar and unfamiliar words (Beauvois, and Derousne, 1981; Shallice, 1981; Alexander, Fischer, and Friedman, 1982; Bub, and Kertesz, 1982; Alexander, Friedman, Loverso, and Fischer, 1992). The peripheral processes realize the motor output of spelled words, with their allographic variants (Papagno, 1992). A popular view in the classical literature on dysgraphia states that writing requires the mediation of "inner speech" (Luria, 1970). More specifically, writing takes place through the acoustic analysis of the input, the recoding of each phoneme of the stimulus into a grapheme, and the recoding of graphemes in motor schemes (Luria, 1970). Children who were asked to open their mouths and keep them open while writing something produced more letter omissions, mis-spellings, and repetitions than the control group. In recent years, this phonological mediation hypothesis has been modified. For example, the dissociation between poor writing of familiar words and good writing of novel words in specific clinical cases (Beauvois, and Derousne, 1981; Ellis and Young, 1988) had been interpreted as evidence for the existence of two functionally independent routines: a lexical mechanism, which does not require phonological mediation and is used for spelling known words, and a phonological mechanism, which requires phonological mediation and is used for spelling words not previously encountered.

Many years have underwent since it was noted that the ability to write depende critically on both linguistic and motoric functions and that agraphia might be related to apraxia and visuospatial impairment. However, till that moment, some Authors have demonstrated that apractic agraphia were not intimately bound to apraxia of the limbs (Roeltgen, and Heilman, 1983). We report a clinical case of a 71-year-old man, with an eighth-grade education, in his usual state of health until two days before admission, when he noted difficulty in writing and a slight clumsiness of his right hand. At examination, he was right-handed (+22 at Briggs and Nebes Test) (Briggs, and Nebes, 1975); the medical history was remarkable for mild congestive heart failure and atrial fibrillation; he was alert and oriented. Calculations, right/left discrimination, stereognosis, graphestesia and memory appeared normal. He had no neglect, nor extinction. He exhibited a moderate right central facial weakness but no clear weakness or sensory loss in his extremities. Reflexes were symmetric. A CT of the head shoed a small area of presumed infarction involving the left-superior temporo-parietal cortex. Neuropsychological exams noted a slight dysprosodia, without a slow rate of speech. No aphasia was noted with the Aachner Aphasia Test (Luzzati, Wilmes, and DeBleser, 1992). Reading aloud and for comprehension was normal, as well preserved were his denomination, oral spelling, and his praxis (Christensen, 1975). The patient's writing was assessed under different conditions: he was asked to copy, write to dictation and spontaneously letters, words and sentences. He exhibited a profound impairment in grapheme production under all conditions and when writing single letters as well as entire sentences. Morphological, lexical and semantic aspects were not influenced by his writing impairment, which seems to interest only the motor sub-system, and in particular, its spatial realization. When he was asked to write with anagram letters, he did well, both with his right and left hand, and moreover, writing was not influenced by closing his eyes. He did not ameliorate when asked to write larger letters, and moreover, he noted that writing into a specific spatial pattern was very difficult. For example, he could not complete crossword puzzle anymore. His coordination pattern was equally disrupted when he intended to write following the horizontal line of a paper. He was tested three times during hospitalization, and he gradually began to improve, after the first week: firstly, we assisted to a better motor execution of the graphemic pattern, and lastly, to an improvement of spatial realization of his writing production.

Attention is also involved in writing. Writing was found to be impaired in a large number of acutely confused patients (Chedru, and Geschwind, 1972) without focal brain lesions. These impairments involved the motor and spatial aspects of writing as well as spelling and syntax, with a high error rate in terms of omissions and substitutions of consonants and of grammatical morphemes. Any visual scene contains multiple objects, where each object is composed of multiple features such as colour, shape, motion and location. Writing process needs the selection of the objects of interest (letters) based on any feature or combination of features. Such sort of spatial cueing enhances visual performance in a large variety of visual tasks, including threshold and supra-threshold detection of luminance increments and discriminations involving shape and colour (Eriksen, and Hoffman, 1972). Two locations are also selected in the context of a large class of vasomotor behaviours including orienting to peripheral stimuli; overt orienting refers to a set of processes by which stimuli of interest in a visual scene are detected in the periphery of the visual field and rapidly brought into the fovea by means of rapid saccadic eye movements. On the contrary, covert orienting is relevant for the fact that the behaviourally relevant stimuli can be attended to in the absence of exploratory saccadic eye movements. It is a well-known fact that we can move our attention around in visual space without moving our eyes; yet when the eyes do move, there appears to be an obligatory shift of attention. Therefore, cover orienting and overt orienting implicate oculomotor programming in the generation of attentional shifts. Both the systems are involved in writing, where higher vision is fundamental for its realization (Corbetta, 2001). Ullman (1984) proposed that the computation of various spatial relations between objects requires the application of visual routines to selected stimulus locations. However, because of computational limitations visual routines can be applied only to one or two locations. The analysis of the visual scene therefore requires a mechanism for selecting and switching the focus of processing from one location to another. Writing, as a cognitive system under lied by many functionally independent procedural and memory components, tightly relies on visuo-spatial attention. A recent work (Olive, and Kellogg, 2002) used interference reaction time for detecting auditory probes to measure attentional demands of copying, and composing a text in children and adults. With motor execution being relatively automatic, adults were able to attend fully to the high-level processes required in mature, effective composition. One reason that children fail to engage in such high-level processes is that motor processes deplete available attention.

Importantly, writing errors are not exclusive to aphasic patients as normal individuals also make errors in writing (Ellis, 1979). The errors referred here to are not spelling errors, but unintentional "slips of the pen", which can be perceived to be incorrect as soon as one becomes aware of them. One of the insights gleaned from studies of normal errors has to do with the planning of writing. If an error involves the intrusion of an element (e.g. a letter or a word) due later in a sequence, then the intruding element mostly likely must already have been selected from memory (Lashley, 1951; Miceli, Silveri and Caramazza, 1988). The orthographic representation is stored in the graphemic output buffer (Wing, and Baddeley, 1980; Miceli, et al. 1988), which seems to be part of the working memory. Information apparently decays in this buffer very rapidly (Wing, and Baddeley, 1980), and has to be refreshed for normal writing. The stored graphemic representations specify the identity and order of the component letters and their status as consonants or vowels. Different methods were proposed for classifying errors by collecting samples of spontaneous writing from Broca's, Wernicke's, and conduction aphasics (Sgaramella, Ellis, and Semenza, 1991), or by collecting a corpus of mistakes produced by normal persons (Ellis, 1979). We used a modified classification of mistakes, which gave good results in the study of the writing production in different neurological population (Moretti, Torre, Antonello, Carraro, Zambito-Marsala, Ukmar, Capus, Gioulis, Cazzato, and Bava, 2002). Spelling mistakes were not considered for this study. The remaining errors were classified into word-level (movement and selection) and letter-level (movement and selection) types of mistakes.

This study was conducted, at the beginning, precisely to evaluate various experimental manipulations of writing, in three conditions (spontaneous, copying, and dictation) in normal subjects: normal standard state, articulatory suppression and tapping. The articulatory suppression may interfere with phonological control, or reduce the number of the so-called parasitic thoughts, by activating the articulatory loop from the working memory. The tapping condition might interfere with motor development of intended act. Four questions have arisen in our minds, when we began the study:

1. do normal subjects produce movement or selection mistakes?
2. do normal subjects produce more mistakes in different experimental conditions?
3. could we distinguish specific types of mistakes in different experimental conditions, specific to the condition?
4. which type of writing modality (spontaneous, dictation or summary) is more sensitive to external stimuli?

The null hypothesis form is that there will be no significant differences in the number of errors between the conditions. What we found suggest that there are different and specific errors in the two experimental conditions (articulatory suppression and tapping), when compared to normal standard situation. The number of mistakes are significantly different, allowing us to reject the null hypothesis and claim support to the possibility to get in the way of writing procedure with two given stimuli, by altering the articulatory loop of the working memory, or by interfering with motor execution of the act.

But then, we decided to test 30 patients, suffering from Alzheimer's Disease (AD), at the very beginning of their clinical history, and to evaluate their writing production, in three conditions (spontaneous, copying, and dictation). We have detected their mistakes, evaluate them with the same criteria proposed for the normal subject group, and then compared them with the corpus collected from the samples of normal subjects.

We discuss the results, trying to examine the possible brain correlates with graphemic output realisation.

METHOD

Subjects

30 female third-year students (22.15 ± 0.54 years old) from the Faculty of Medicine at the University of Trieste. We chose a group of female students due to the probable minor hemispheric lateralization of linguistic areas (see data and literature in: Fabbro, and Bava, 1990). The participants have been enrolled randomly from an original group of 67 volunteers. We decided to limit the number of participants due to the duration of the tests (trials before test, instructions, explanations, and effective time for the test amount for more than four hours for each subjects), but have expanded their number, starting from a previous experience (Moretti, Torre, Antonello, Fabbro, Cazzato, and Bava, 2003). All the students were right handed according to the Briggs and Nebes test (Briggs, and Nebes, 1975). None of the subjects had ever suffered from language impairment, of learning disability or other neurological or auditory impairments.

30 patients, diagnosed as suffering from probable AD, in accordance with NINCDS-ADRDA (McKahnn, Drachman, Folstein, Katzmann, Price, and Stadlan, 1984), (73,84 ± 7,14 years old), right handed according to the Briggs and Nebes test (Briggs, and Nebes, 1975), at the very beginning of their clinical history, according to the Clinical Dementia Rating (CDR) (mean score= 1.765 ± 0,14) (Hughes, Berg, Danizger, Coben, and Martin, 1982), have been examined.

Materials and Procedures

The normal subjects' tasks were to write on set topics, to take dictation, to copy, and to summarize. The students were asked to write 3 compositions, given the following instructions: "Describe a trip near Trieste"; "Describe Your favourite topic at University"; "Describe your best friend". Then the subjects were asked to write a dictation of 90 words and non-words (see Appendix 1A) and 30 sentences, chosen from the Bilingual Aphasia Test (Paradis, 1987; Paradis, and Canzanella, 1990) (see Appendix 1B). Subjects were told that it might be possible that some phonemes, put together, could be presented to them, and in that case, it was part of the experiment, so they should write the same sounds they have heard. No specific mention has been made to the presence of non – words in the test. All the words, non-words and sentences were recorded and were allowed 5 seconds between words and 10 seconds between sentences. The students were then asked to summarize three tales recorded on audio tape (see Appendix 1C), given a maximum time of ten minutes each, and to copy three written passages, each of which contained 87 words (see Appendix 1D), given a maximum time of five minutes each.

The subjects had to carry out the trials under the following conditions: normal control; articulatory suppression (the subject must pronounce indefinite sounds such as "bla-bla" aloud; this causes an articulatory suppression of the subvocalizing enhancement of the memory process); tapping (the subject must tap with the forefinger of the left hand while writing with the right hand).

The order of the various conditions was counterbalanced across the subjects.

They were requested to execute their task on different pieces of paper (white sheets, without lines). No preference was indicated by the examiner whether to write in cursive or in print.

The AD patients were asked to write five sentences, spontaneously; then they were asked to write a dictation of 30 words and 30 non words, and 5 sentences. They were asked to summarize a short story they have heard extracted from the Bilingual Aphasia Test (Paradis, 1987; Paradis, and Canzanella, 1990) and to copy five sentences from the same test. They were requested to execute their task on different pieces of paper (white sheets, without lines). No preference was indicated by the examiner whether to write in cursive or in print.

All the material was classified and corrected independently by two trained neurologists (with a good inter-rater reliability, kappa=0.79) and then the results were compared: spelling mistakes were not taken into account, nor were doubtful strokes, or inaccurate or imprecisely written letters. For disagreements between-raters, after comparison, there was a discussion and a final decision derived from a mutual consensus.

Spelling mistakes were not considered: "aqua" for "acqua", or "a" instead of "ha", or "artilio" for "artiglio", "perche" for "perché". The remaining significant errors were classified into word-level (movement and selection) and letter-level (movement and selection) types of mistakes. Letter Movement mistakes comprised adjacent and nonadjacent letter reversals (such as "catrolina" for "cartolina" or "fanira" "farina") and perseverations of single letters (such as "lamponee" for "lampone") (Kirk, Blonder, Wertman, and Heilman, 1991). Letter Selection mistakes comprised insertions (such as "penotola" for "pentola"), substitutions (such as "penta" for "penna") and deletions (such as "penola" for "pentola") (Kirk et al., 1991). Word Movement errors comprised perseverations (such as "andammo al al mare" for "andammo al mare") and regularizations of non-words (such as "catrame" for "catrumo") (Sgaramella, et al., 1991). Word Selection errors comprised omissions (such as "andammo mare" for "andammo al mare"), additions (such as "partirono per di Torino" for "partirono per Torino"), verbal substitutions (such as "cantina" for "catino"), and unrelated substitutions (such as "catrumpo" for "catrame") (Sgaramella, et al., 1991) of single words (data and Literature have been reported in: Moretti, Torre, Antonello, Fabbro, Cazzato, and Bava, 2003).

Statistical analysis was performed using the Statistical Package for the Social Sciences (SPSS-PC, version 10.0). In the comparison between groups, paired samples t-test, and analysis of variance (ANOVA) were used, as appropriate.

RESULTS

All the 30 students completed all the trials. We try to proceed accordingly to the four preliminary questions, presented in the introduction:

1. Do normal subjects produce movement or selection mistakes?The total number of errors was 943. The subjects produced 169 mistakes (19% of the total errors) under the control condition; in particular, they produced 19 letter-movement, 121 letter selection, 20 word-movement and 9 word-selection mistakes.
2. Do normal subjects produce more mistakes in different experimental conditions?

The total number of errors was 932. The subjects produced 169 mistakes (19% of the total errors) under the control condition, 330 (35%) under the tapping condition, and 433 (46%) under the articulatory suppression condition. In particular, they produced 20 letter-movement, 109 letter selection, 21 word-movement and 19 word-selection mistakes in normal condition; they produced 43 letter-movement, 235 letter selection, 17 word-movement and 35 word-selection mistakes in tapping condition; finally, they produced 44 letter-movement, 302 letter selection, 42 word-movement and 45 word-selection mistakes in articulatory suppression condition. (Table 1)

Table 1. Summary of mistakes in the three experimental conditions

	NORMAL	TAPPING	ARTICULATORY SUPPRESSION
Letter movement mistakes	20	43	44
Letter selection mistakes	109	235	302
Word movement mistakes	21	17	42
Word selection mistakes	19	35	45
TOTAL	169	330	433

3. Could we distinguish specific types of mistakes in different experimental conditions, specific to the condition?

All the individual results were analyzed with an analysis of variance (condition: control, articulatory suppression and tapping; type of error: letter-level, word-level). The factor condition was significant ($F(2, 30) = 21.45$; $p<.001$). Type of error was also found to be significant ($F (1,15) = 59.91$; $p<.001$). The interaction condition/error type was significant ($F (2,30) = 8.67$; $p<.001$). Therefore, according to the Bonferroni test, the subjects produced significantly fewer errors under the control condition than under the tapping and articulatory suppression conditions. Moreover, the subjects produced significantly more errors in the articulatory suppression condition (Table 2).

4. Which type of writing modality (spontaneous, dictation or summary) is more sensitive to external stimuli?

Considering the single task proposed, subjects'errors could be divided as follows: 110 were found among dictated words; 183 were found among dictated non-words; 104 were found among dictated sentences; 166 were made in the summary task; 220 were made in the copy task; 149 were found in the composition task (Table 3). Paired samples t-tests (2-tailed) were done within tasks, considering letter-level and movement-level. In the word dictation task, the number of errors in the control condition was significantly different from articulatory suppression condition ($p<0.01$). No difference could be detected at the word level. In the non word dictation task, no significant difference emerged among the three different conditions, as far as letter level is concerned; the number of mistakes is significantly different in the articulatory suppression condition ($p<0.01$) in the word-level.

Table 2. Synopsis of qualitative analysis of total number of mistakes on different writing tasks

	Types of mistakes	Control	Tapping	Articulatory suppression
Letter movement errors	Adjacent letter reversals	10	6	15
	Perseverations	10	31	15
	Non adjacent letters Reversals	0	6	14
Letter selection errors	Insertions	7	20	34
	Substitutions	76	124	143
	Deletions	26	91	125
Word movement errors	Perseverations	0	2	13
	Regularizations	21	15	29
Word selection	Omissions	11	12	22
	Additions	0	8	0
	Verbal substitutions	4	6	11
	Unrelated substitutions	4	9	12

Table 3. Synopsis of mistakes in three experimental conditions

	CONTROL				TAPPING				ART. SUPPRESSION				TOTAL
	Letter		Word		Letter		Word		Letter		Word		
	Sel	Mov	Sel	Mov	Sel	Mov	Sel	Mov	Sel	Mov	Sel	Mov	
Word-dictation	4	6	2	8	28	2	0	0	42	12	6	0	110
Non Word-dictation	27	0	8	8	38	0	4	14	32	4	18	30	183
Sentences dictation	16	0	0	0	14	8	0	0	54	2	10	0	104
Summary	16	10	2	0	45	8	8	0	50	8	9	10	166
Copy	27	0	4	5	69	16	11	3	74	8	1	2	220
Composition	19	4	3	0	41	9	12	0	50	10	1	0	149
Total	109	20	19	21	235	43	35	17	302	44	45	42	932

In the sentence task, paired sample t-tests suggested a significant difference among the number of mistakes in control versus articulatory suppression condition ($p<0.01$) at letter level. No difference was demonstrated at the word-level. In the copy task, paired sample t-tests suggested a significant difference in the number of letter-level mistakes in control versus tapping ($p<0.001$) and versus articulatory suppression ($p<0.001$). When compared to word level mistakes, only the control versus tapping conditions were significantly different ($p<0.001$).

In the summary task, paired sample t-tests suggested a significant difference in the number of letter level mistakes in the control versus the tapping ($p<0.05$) and versus the articulatory suppression conditions ($p<0.001$). When compared to word level mistakes, the control versus tapping conditions were significantly different ($p<0.01$), as were the control versus articulatory suppression ($p<0.001$). Lastly, in the composition task, paired sample t-tests put in evidence a significant difference in the number of letter-level mistakes in control versus tapping ($p<0.01$) and versus articulatory suppression ($p<0.001$). When compared word-level mistakes, control versus tapping condition is significantly different ($p<0.01$), as well as control versus articulatory suppression ($p<0.001$).

The AD patients were asked to write five sentences, spontaneously; then they were asked to write a dictation of 30 words and 30 non words, and 5 sentences. They were asked to summarize a short story they have heard extracted from the Bilingual Aphasia Test and to copy five sentences from the same test. Now, considering the corpus of mistakes made by the AD patients, it must be said that it is more consistent than that of the normal subjects, even in the articulatory suppression condition (Table 4). Considering the obvious reduction of given stimuli to the AD group (inferior to 54%, when comparing to the normal subjects stimuli), there is a larger corpus of mistakes in AD condition. AD patients made 785 mistakes in the only normal condition, which is significantly superior to the number of mistakes made by the normal subjects in all the condition (169; $p<0.001$), but even superior to the whole number of mistakes made by the normal subjects in the three conditions, if hypothesized that the number of stimuli is the same of the AD patients ($p<0.001$). Copy is the most preserved task, considering the ratio mistakes/given items (100/145=0.68). The other are the following: word dictation ratio mistakes/given items is 135/30=4.5; non word dictation ratio mistakes/given items is 167/30=5.66; sentences dictation ratio mistakes/given items is 97/45=2.15; summary ratio mistakes/given items (considering an average number of words produced of 45.3) is 141/45.3=3.11; composition ratio mistakes/given items (considering an average number of words produced of 40.23) is 145/40.23=3.604 (Table 5).

There is a significant number of mistakes in the letter-movement corpus of mistakes, when considering the letter level ($p<0.05$); no difference can be detected in the word-level groups.

Table 4. Summary of mistakes in the AD group

	NORMAL	AD
Letter movement mistakes	20	309
Letter selection mistakes	109	247
Word movement mistakes	21	125
Word selection mistakes	19	104
TOTAL	169	785

Table 5. Synopsis of mistakes in AD patients

	AD				*TOTAL*
	Letter		Word		
	Sel	Mov	Sel	Mov	
Word-dictation	40	49	25	21	135
Non Word-dictation	56	45	31	35	167
Sentences dictation	34	34	24	5	97
Summary	49	56	21	15	141
Copy	27	56	6	11	100
Composition	41	69	18	17	145
Total	**247**	**309**	**125**	**104**	**785**

DISCUSSION

The analysis of a group of subjects studied under standardized conditions represents, first of all, a contribution to the description of writing errors in normal subjects, characteristically described as slips of the pen. New corpora of slips of the pen and of forced errors in normal spellers seem to be of interest, to the extent that they allow further insight into theoretical issues germane to the development of theories of spelling.

Even if the theoretical background of writing is not completely understood, the idea of looking at the disrupting effect of interfering tasks on writing might offer explanations for errors; on the contrary, the results can only be taken to show that normal subjects write more accurately if their attention is unperturbed, which is hardly surprising. To answer the four questions established in the introduction, our results demonstrate that normal subjects produced, in normal conditions, movement and selection mistakes. In normal conditions, letter – level mistakes were more frequent than word-level mistakes. When imposed experimental conditions, they interfere with writing production, heavier the articulatory suppression than the tapping condition, but both of them deeper than control condition. Moreover, during articulatory suppression condition, one can observe the doubling up of "paraphasic" mistakes, such as verbal or unrelated substitutions; the number of types of errors is clearly and significantly reduced, as well as the number of words produced. They were not analyzed parametrically, though there were a higher number of omissions of free grammatical morphemes, associated with a more conspicuous number of semantically deviant sentences, in the articulatory suppression condition. In the tapping condition, on the other hand, high percentage of perseverations of letters and omissions of words was found. Finally, tapping and articulatory suppression interfere with all the writing tasks executed by our volunteers, heavier and differently considering the larger amount of word-level mistakes produced.

Then, it might be hypothesized that articulatory suppression and tapping work somehow to interfere writing process. Once, it might be supposed that articulatory suppression interferes with the phonological mediated linguistic control. The writing process can be divided into different parts (Luria, 1970): words can be divided into phonemes, phonemes are converted into graphemes, and only then writing is possible. The importance of phonetic analysis in writing had been demonstrated in children; when learning to write, they are more likely to anticipate stressed than atonics syllables. In cases reported of sensory alalia (Luria, 1970), patients lose the ability to do phonetic analysis and are only able to copy written language. Stuttering children or children with uranoschisis, develop writing impairments, once interpreted due to the inaccuracy of their phonetic analysis. However, the phonological mediation hypothesis of writing is no longer tenable, especially in the light of recent evidence from adult aphasia (Ellis and Young, 1988). Thus, a "surface dysgraphic" patient may lose the capacity to retrieve once-familiar spellings from some form of lexical store, without losing the capacity to retrieve spoken word-forms; similarly, a "phonological dysgraphic" patient may lose the capacity for phoneme-grapheme conversion required to generate plausible spellings for unfamiliar words or non words without losing the capacity for grapheme-phoneme conversion in reading (Beauvois and Derousne, 1981). As clearly pointed out by Ellis and Young (1988), the cognitive neuropsychology of spelling and writing is not built solely upon patients in whom spelling and writing are impaired. For example, patients who can spell words correctly despite not having access to their correct spoken forms show that spelling of familiar words is not done by phoneme-grapheme conversion (Shallice, 1981). Baddeley (1982; Baddeley, Lewis, and Vallar, 1984; Baddeley, Papagno, and Vallar, 1988) proposed that articulatory suppression may reduce the number of the so-called parasitic thoughts, by activating the articulatory loop from the working memory. He determined that during tests of articulatory suppression, the number of spontaneous thoughts were significantly fewer compared to those registered during the quiet state. More recent experimental designs (Hanley, 1997) confirm that vision, and supplement it. A more precise study design (Calvo, and Eysenck, 1996) demonstrates that articulatory suppression interferes with the articulatory loop, which has been considered by those authors as a sort ancillary mechanism enhanced in the reading operational system when other strategies, such as regressive fixations and control of speed cannot be used. As far as has been demonstrated in a previous work (Moretti, Torre, Antonello, Carraro, Zambito-Marsala, Ukmar, Capus, Gioulis, Cazzato, and Bava, 2002) that reading and writing strongly depend on the integrity of oculomotor regressive fixation and attention, one might suppose that articulatory suppression might interfere with the attention system and above all, disrupting the articulatory loop, eliminates the possible auxiliary control system which guarantees correct execution of writing.

Tapping, considered as a movement itself, interferes both with attention input and with motor development of actions. When tapping is done with the left hand, functional imaging has put in evidence a bilateral activation of motor and supplementary motor areas(Moretti, Torre, Antonello, Ukmar, Longo, and Bava, 2002). Nobody described tapping as interference stimulus in writing process. Bilateral activation of motor and supplementary motor areas might interfere with motor control exerted by the right hand, dedicated at the same moment to a complex distal motor act. When tapping with the left hand, our volunteers persevered and repeat the last letter, or syllables, of the words or delete the last portions of words. There is an interesting analogy between the tapping condition and writing disturbances in acute confusional states (Chedru, and Geschwind, 1972), where an increase in substitution and perseveration of the last letter of words is found. This fact leaves us the possibility that tapping might interfere somehow in attention control of complex motor act, perhaps limiting the bimanual coordination requested in the specific task.

What can be created, as an experimental model, with the results of the tapping and articulatory suppression conditions, might be considered a pseudo-agraphic situation (Sgaramella, et al., 1991). When the type of errors is considered, it must be emphasized that, under the articulatory suppression condition, subjects produced "unrelated word substitution," an increased number of semantically deviant sentences, an increase in the number of omissions of free grammatical morphemes, a reduction of total number of words, and an increase in types of errors specific which stand out as a variety typical only among pathological conditions. On the contrary, when tapping is activated, there is an higher number of perseveration in letters and syllables.

On the contrary, in the AD patients, the corpus of mistakes is higher than normal subjects, in all the three experimental conditions. The study is rather new, as far as we know of another one, systematic study,on writing in AD patients, but the latter did not consider different writing conditions (such as dictation, spontaneous writing, summary and copying) (LaBarge, Smith, Dick, and Storandt, 1992).

The study described graphic errors made in writing a simple sentence in 368 healthy older adults and individuals in different stages of dementia of the Alzheimer type. Errors of agraphia were present in both healthy and demented people and, in general, increased with the severity of dementia. The errors of agraphia were not correlated with measures of aphasia or psychometric measures of language and motor performance. Writing skill may represent procedural memory, and agraphia errors indicate alterations in long-term memory in dementia of the Alzheimer type (LaBarge, Smith, Dick, and Storandt, 1992).

What we have seen in our AD patients corresponds to an increase of mistakes, in all the tasks, with a relative preservation of copy. Thus, it seems that in AD condition, writing, an overlearned skill is disrupted in several parts, in the graphemic motor control, in phonological and in semantic procedure. Graphemic area has been postulated for distinguishing grapheme motor control and other motor skills coordination (Rothi and Heilman, 1981): however, nothing is known about the parietal role (real or putative) in spatial execution of graphemic patterns. We hypothesize that parietal lobe mediate visual input and high-definition control for specific-motor engrams (and among them, graphemes). As far as writing is concerned, parietal lobe may be involved in regularization of visuokinesthesic engrams (Liepmann and Maas, 1907) which realize the selection, timing and spatial relationships of learned motor skills, such as graphemes. Sitting at the junction of the temporal, parietal, and occipital lobes, the inferior region of the parietal area, particulary vulnerable to AD (which includes the angular and supramarginal gyri) has no strict anatomical boundaries, is partly coextensive with the posterior-superior temporal gyrus, and includes part of area 7 as well as area 37. It maintains rich interconnections with the visual, auditory, and somesthetic associations areas including the middle (basal) temporal lobe, the superior colliculus via the pulvinar, the lateral geniculate nucleus of the thalamus, and massive interconnections with the frontal lobes, inferior temporal region, and other higher order assimilation areas throughout the neocortex. Hence, the inferior parietal lobule has auditory and thus (in the left hemisphere) language capabilities. Given its location at the border regions of the somesthetic, auditory, and visual neocortices, and containing neurons and receiving input from these modalities, as the inferior parietal lobule evolved it became increasingly multimodally responsive; a single neuron simultaneously receiving highly processed somesthetic, visual, auditory and movement related input from the various association areas. Hence, many of the neurons in this area are multi-specialized for simultaneously analyzing auditory, somesthetic, and spatial-visual associations, and have visual receptive properties which encompass almost the entire visual field, with some cells responding to visual stimuli of almost any size, shape, or form (Moretti et al., 2005, in press). It has been argued that the sensory motor engrams necessary for the production and perception of written language are stored within the parietal lobule of the left hemisphere. In fact, given that the parietal lobes are concerned with the hands and lower visual fields, they not only guide and observe hand movements, but learn and memorize these actions, including those involved in writing. Hence, when lesioned, patients sometimes have difficulty writing and forming letters due to an inability to access these engrams. Writing samples may be characterized by mispellings, letter ommissions, distortions, temporal-sequential misplacements, and inversions. Sometimes agraphia is accompanied by alexia (Data and literature in: Rhawn, 2000).

Writing could be easily disrupted: it is an overlearned, extra-sophisticated skill, which requires fine and highly precise movements, depending on acquired rules. It is drammatically different from the other motor sequences, almost automatic of acts of real life: that is probably only a part of the truth and much more must be said on this topic.

In conclusion, it can be seen that writing is actually fragile and it is possible to disturb it because it depends on many components. Moreover, writing is not, or is only very rarely, an automatic skill. Limited experimental conditions can produce errors which somehow make normal subjects performance mimic those of subjects with specific pahologies.

REFERENCES

Alexander, M., Fischer, R., and Friedman, R. (1982) Lesion localization in apractic agraphia. *Archives of Neurology* , 49, 246-251.

Alexander, M., Friedman, R., Loverso, F., and Fischer, R. (1992) Lesion localization of phonological agraphia. *Brain and language*, 43, 83-95.

Baddeley, A. D, Lewis, V., And Vallar, G. (1984) Exploring the articulatory loop. *Quarterly Journal of Experimental Psychology*, 36A, 233-252.

Baddeley, A. D, Papagno, C., and Vallar, G. (1988) When long-term learning depends on short-term storage. *Journal of Memory and Language*, 27, 586-595.

Baddeley, A. D. (1982) Amnesia: a minimal model and interpretation. In L. S. Cermak (Ed.), *Human memory and amnesia.* Hillsdale, NJ: Erlbaum. Pp. 305-336.

Beauvois, M. F., and Derousne, J. (1981) Lexical or orthographic agraphia. *Brain*, 104, 21-49.

Briggs, G., and Nebes, R. (1975) Patterns of hand preference in a student population. *Cortex*, 11, 230-23

Bub, D., and Kertesz, A. (1982) Deep agraphia. *Brain and Language*, 17, 146-165.

Calvo, M. G., and Eysenck, M. W. (1996) Phonological working memory and reading in test anxiety. *Memory*, 4(3), 289-305.

Chedru, F., and Geschwind, N. (1972) Writing disturbances in acute confusional states. *Neurpsychologia*, 10, 343-353.

Corbetta, M. (2001) *A neuroimaging exploration of human attention.* American Academy of Neurology (AAN), Phildelphia, 7FC.006, 98-108.

Ellis, A. (1979) Slips of the pen. *Visible language,* XIII (3), 265-282.

Ellis, A., and Young, A. (1988) Spelling and writing. In: A. Ellis, and A. Joung, (Eds.), *Human cognitive neuropsychology.* Hillsdale , NJ: Erlbaum. Pp. 163-191.

Eriksen, C. W., and Hoffman, J. E. (1972) Temporal and spatial characterisitcs of selectinve encoding from visual displays. *Perception and Psychophysics*, 12, 210-204.

Fabbro, F., and Bava, A. (1990) *Asimmetrie dell'encefalo umano: filogenesi ed ontogenesi.* Firenze: Editrice Il Sedicesimo.

Hanley, J. R. (1997) Does articulatory suppression remove the irrelevant speech effect? *Memory*, 5(3), 423-431.

Hughes C., Berg L., Danizger W., Coben L., and Martin R. (1982) A new clinical scale for the staging of dementia. *Brit. J. Psychiatry*, 140: 566-572.

Kirk, A., Blonder, L. X., Wertman, E., and Heilman, K. M. (1991) Phonolexical agraphia: superimposition of acquired lexical agraphia on developmental phonological dysgraphia. *Brain*, 114/4, 1977-1996.

Labarge E., Smith D. S., Dick L., and Storandt M. (1992) Agraphia in dementia of the Alzheimer type, *Archives of Neurology*,49; 11: 121-134.

Lashley, K. (1951) The problem of serial order in behavior. In: L. A. Jeffress (Ed.), *Cerebral mechanism in behavior: the Hixon Symposium*, New York: J. Wiley. Pp. 112-136.

Liepman H., and Maas O. (1907) Einfall von linksseitiger Agraphie und Apraxie bei Rechtseitiger Lahmung. Translated by C. Wirsig and RT Watson *Monatschrift fur Psychologie und Neurologie*, 10, 214-227.

Lurjia, A. R. (1970) *Neuropsicologia del linguaggio grafico*. Padova: Editore Messaggero.

McKahnn G., Drachman D., Folstein M., Katzmann R., Price D., and Stadlan E.M. (1984) Clinical diagnosis of AD: report of the NINCDS-ADRDA work group under auspices of the Department of health and human services task forces on AD. *Neurology*, 34: 939-944.

Miceli, G., Silveri, M., and Caramazza, A. (1988) The role of the phoneme to grapheme conversion system and of the graphemic output buffer in writing. In: R. Coltheart, G. Sartori (Eds.), *The cognitive Neuropsychology of the language*. Hillsdale, NJ: Erlbaum. Pp. 235-251.

Moretti R., Torre P., Antonello R.M., Fabbro F., Cazzato G., Bava A. (2003). Writing errors by normal subjects. *Perceptual and Motor Skills*; 97: 215-229.

Moretti, R., Torre, P., Antonello, R. M., Carraro, N., Zambito-Marsala, S., Ukmar, M., Capus, L., Gioulis, M., Cazzato, G., and Bava, A. (2002) Peculiar aspects of reading and writing performances in patients with olivopontocerebellar atrophy. *Perceptual and Motor Skills*, 94, 677-694.

Moretti, R., Torre, P., Antonello, R. M., Ukmar, M., Longo, R., and Bava, A. (2002) Learned movements in a left-handed pianist: an f-MRI evaluation. *Journal of Clinical Neuroscience*, 9 (6), 680-684.

Olive, T., and Kellogg, R. T. (2002) Concurrent activation of high- and low-level production processes in written composition. *Mem. Cognit.*, 30 (4), 594-600.

Papagno, C. (1992) A case of peripheral dysgraphia. *Cognitive Neuropsychology*, 9(3), 259-270.

Paradis, M. (1987) *The assessment of bilingual aphasia*. Hillsdale, NJ: Erlbaum.

Paradis, M., And Canzanella, M. (1990) *Test per l'afasia in un bilingue: versione italiana*. Hillsdale, NJ: Erlbaum.

Rhawn J. (2000) *The inferior parietal lobe. Neuropsychiatry, Neuropsychology, Clinical Neuroscience*. Academic Press, New York.

Rothi L.J., and Heilman K.M. (1981) Alexia and agraphia with spared spelling and letter recognition abilities. *Brain and Language*, 12, 1-13.

Sgaramella, T., Ellis, A., and Semenza, C. (1991) Analysis of the spontaneous writing errors of normal and aphasic writers. *Cortex*, 27, 29-35.

Shallice, T. (1981) Phonological agraphia and the lexical route in writing. *Brain*, 104, 413-431.

Ullman, S. (1984) Visual routines. *Cognition*, 18, 97-159.

Wing, A., and Baddeley, A.D. (1980) Spelling errors in handwriting: a corpus and a distributional analysis, In U. Frith (Ed.), *Cognitive Processes in Spelling*. New York: Academic Press. Pp. 252-285.

In: Trends in Learning Reserch
Editor: Samuel N. Hogan, pp. 81-98

ISBN 1-59454-965-6

Chapter 4

INDIVIDUAL DIFFERENCES IN SECOND LANGUAGE LEARNING AMONG UNIVERSITY STUDENTS

Georgia Andreou,* Eleni Andreou** and Filippos Vlachos*
*Department of Special Education, University of Thessaly, Greece
**Department of Primary School Education, University of Thessaly, Greece

ABSTRACT

In this chapter, we make an overview of the literature on the learning styles, approaches to studying and the role of gender and handedness on second language (L2) learning and we report our findings from a three-fold research we undertook at the university of Thessaly in a sample of 452 undergraduate students. In the first part of our research we investigated the influence of gender, handedness and Faculty choice on the performance of phonological, syntactical and semantic tasks in L2. In the second part we examined further how Greek students' approaches to studying in combination with gender, academic discipline and professional degree in English affect performance on verbal fluency tasks in English as a second language. In the third part of our research we investigated the relationship between Greek students' learning styles and performance in English phonological, syntactic and semantic tasks, in combination with their gender and discipline.

Our results showed that handedness alone did not influence the students' performance on L2 tasks. Gender was found to play an important role in our results with females performing better than males in both syntax and semantics. Approaches to studying alone or in combination with students' gender and professional degree in L2 influenced students' performance on syntactical L2 tasks, in which they used a deep or strategic approach, but not on phonological or semantic ones. Concerning learning styles, our study revealed that university students have a tendency to prefer a divergent learning style while performing phonological and semantic tasks and an accommodative learning style while performing syntactical tasks in L2.

In conclusion, our research findings suggest that individual differences influence the way people learn and succeed in language study. However, more research is needed in the field in order to make individual differences practical in the classroom and enable the most learners possible to learn a foreign language in their preferred styles using their own approaches to studying.

INTRODUCTION

Competence in more than one language can be approached at both individual and social levels. While many discussions about learning a second language focus on teaching methodologies, little emphasis is given to the contextual factors -individual, social, and societal- that affect students' learning. These contextual factors can be considered from the perspective of the language, the learner, and the learning process. This chapter discusses such perspectives as they relate to learning any second language, with a particular focus on how they affect adult learners of English as a second language.

Over the past several years there have been important changes in our understanding of the nature of effective second language (L2) learning. The study of individual differences in second language learning, such as gender, handedness, Faculty choice, learning styles and approaches to studying, has received considerable attention and has shown that there are a number of dimensions of learner differences which are generally acknowledged to affect the way people learn foreign languages, how they perform in actual language use and the eventual levels of success they achieve (Lujan-Ortega et al., 2000).

In addition, following the expansion in student numbers in higher education there has been a shift in emphasis in the approaches taken to teaching and learning (Sadler-Smith, 1996). Policy has moved towards student-centered methods and demands made on higher education students for greater autonomy and flexibility in their approaches to learning aimed at enabling them to achieve the maximum benefit from their time in higher education. Given the fact that a whole theory, the Linguistic Coding Deficiency Hypothesis (LCDH) (Sparks et al., 1989), was established after the observations of university second language (L2) educators that while some of their students learnt a FL quickly and easily, while others, given the same opportunities to learn, failed repeatedly, individual differences in second language learning among university students should be particularly taken into account.

FACTORS ASSOCIATED WITH L2 LANGUAGE LEARNING IN HIGHER EDUCATION

Language Factors

Several factors related to peoples' first and second languages shape their second language learning. These factors include the linguistic distance between the two languages, peoples' level of proficiency in the native language and their knowledge of the second language, the dialect of the native language spoken by the peoples (i.e., whether it is standard or nonstandard), the relative status of the peoples' language in the community, and societal attitudes toward the peoples' native language.

One of the factors we will discuss in this chapter is how peoples' level of proficiency in the native language (L1) may influence their L2 learning and more specifically how peoples' possible underlying linguistic coding deficits in L1 may interfere with their ability to learn a L2.

It is a common belief that university level L2 learners have acquired a certain competency in all of the linguistic codes, namely phonological, syntactic and semantic, in their L1. However, this is not always the case. The suggestion that L2 learning problems may occur in association with, or perhaps as a result of, L1 learning problems was first made in studies associated with students with learning disabilities (Carrol, 1973) and later confirmed in other studies (Cline, 2000; Downey et al., 2000; Ganschow et al., 2000; Sparks et al., 1999). Informal reports at several universities showed that substantial numbers of students were being referred for suspected learning disabilities after university entry. The referrals were made because of the students' inability to meet the L2 requirement at the university, giving rise to speculation that subtle native language problems became evident primarily because of the demands that the study of a new and unfamiliar symbol system placed on these students (Carrol, 1973). Prior to this, only one reference was made by Dinklage (1971) about Harvard university students, that addressed the possibility of language disabilities among students who had difficulties in L2 classes. Dinklage stated that these bright students who could not seem to learn a L2 exhibit three types of problems: 1) difficulty with the written (reading and writing) aspects of their native language 2) inability to distinguish the sounds of the L2 and, thus, difficulties with an oral communication approach to L2 learning and 3) memory problems for sounds and words. He supported the idea of an underlying language processing disability as the cause of L2 learning.

In other words, prior to 1980 the study of L2 learning for individuals who had found learning to read and write in their native language extremely problematic had been an under-researched area throughout the world (Ganschow et al., 2000). Since the 1980s, Ganschow and Sparks have conducted pioneering research into the nature of difficulties, why they are encountered and how they can be minimized. They suggested, in the form of the Linguistic Coding Dificiency Hypothesis (LCDH), that some individuals have difficulty in learning their native language in oral and/or written form and this difficulty is likely to affect ability to learn L2. The LCDH theory, with its emphasis on the specific components of language, i.e., phonological, syntactic and semantic, provides an explanation for why university students who appear to have learnt their native language adequately, in fact, have problems that have gone unnoticed but have been compensated for over the years. Generally, the problem areas are subtle, e.g., relatively weak spelling or a slow rate of reading. For the most part, the compensatory strategies used by these students mask their linguistic coding deficits in the native language and they often succeed well in academic settings. Most of the university students reported in studies by Lefebvre (1984), Pompian and Thun (1988) and Sparks, Ganschow and Pohlman (1989) were identified as learning disabled after university entry because of foreign language learning difficulties. What happens to these students is that their compensatory strategies become unworkable when they are placed in situations where they must learn a totally unfamiliar and new linguistic coding system. In the context of the LCDH it has been suggested that students who fail to reach a high level of proficiency in L2 might display a broad range of linguistic coding deficits. Studies have consistently shown that students who achieve higher scores on L2 tasks have significantly stronger native and second language aptitude skills than students who achieve lower L2 scores (Ganschow et al., 1998; Ganschow et al., 1994; Ganschow et al., 1991; Sparks et al., 1995). The most successful L2 learners are those who have strong skills in all of the linguistic codes, in particular the phonological code, which seems to have the most immediate impact on a student's performance in L2 tasks (Sparks et al., 1993).

Biological Factors

The neural substrates of L2 acquisition are largely unknown. It has been recently reported that L1 and L2 are represented differentially in cortical areas during discourse production or listening tasks (Dehaene et al., 1997; Kim et al., 1997). However, other imaging studies have reported common neural substrates of L1 and L2 during word generation tasks (Klein et al, 1995; Chee et al., 1999).

On the other hand, over the past 30 years evidence from a variety of sources supports the view that verbal behavior is a lateralized function (Springer et al., 1998). The two hemispheres of the brain seem to have somewhat different functions. The left hemisphere generally controls the majority of language function and the right hemisphere appears to be involved in maintaining focus of attention, and also possibly prosody. Right hemisphere lesions have been known to severely affect ability to analyze metaphors, summarize complex texts, as well as disrupt prosody in otherwise normal language.

In experimental neurolinguistics the role of the right hemisphere in language processing has been discussed extensively over the last decades. Especially such language-related aspects as intonation (emotional prosody), pragmatics, semantics and non-verbal communication (gesticulation and facial expressions) have been proposed to be primarily processed by the right hemisphere (Van Lancker, 1997). Moreover, the right hemisphere has been assumed to play a key role at the beginning of the language acquisition process, when someone is beginning to learn a second language. It has been assumed that the right (non language-dominant) hemisphere "helps" the left hemisphere in so far as it adopts a holistic strategy to make the language learning process easier in its initial stages. The initial stages are the first years of the acquisitional process, when a learner is not yet experienced enough to develop grammatical "automatisms" in the second language (left hemisphere) and thus resorts to imagery and holistic thinking to tackle the acquisitional problems.

According to Obler (1981) and Galloway and Krashen (1980), the initial stages of adult second language acquisition recapitulate children's right-to-left hemispheric shift in relative hemispheric dominance during L1 acquisition. This is in line with the assumption of Paradis (1994), who states that monolingual children have to rely on right hemisphere-based pragmatic processing during their first years of language acquisition, in order to derive an interpretation for utterances in that language for which the required automatic linguistic competence has not yet been fully internalized.

Two biological variables, gender and handedness are the main factors often associated with language lateralization and their influence will be discussed in this chapter. Many previous studies have shown gender differences in performance on a variety of cognitive tasks (Crow et al., 1998; Janowski et al., 1998). One of the differences reported is a female superiority on verbal fluency tasks. In general, females are reported to be more verbally fluent than men (Stumpf, 1995), although mixed results have also been obtained. For instance, a female advantage for quickly producing words from a particular semantic category has been reported (Gordon et al., 1986) but no sex difference for rapidly producing words beginning with a particular letter was found (Gordon et al., 1986). There are also some other studies which found no gender difference for either type of fluency measure (Hampson et al., 1992; Moffat et al., 1996) or a task of rapid articulation (Gouchie et al., 1991). It seems that language has evolved by a process of increasing hemisphere specialization. Therefore, studies on hemisphere specialization for language functions which reveal stronger lateralization in men than women and even gender related differences in interhemispheric transmission time in the human brain (Nowicka et al., 2001) may account for female superiority on verbal tasks.

Since handedness is related to cerebral language representation, it has often been associated with performance on native and foreign language verbal tasks. Left-handers differ from right-handers on cognitive task performance. One of the most striking differences between left- and right-handers' brains is the lateralization of language. It has been claimed that if a certain functional asymmetry (defined as the anatomical hemisphere of the brain in which a certain function, like language, is localized) is observed in right-handers, the corresponding function in left-handers will be less lateralized and possibly lateralized in the other direction (Springer et al., 1998). In other words, language localized to the left hemisphere (LH) for right-handers would be less localized to the LH, or even dominant in the right hemisphere (RH), for left-handers.

Although some studies found no relationship especially between verbal ability and relative hand skill in the two sexes (Bishop, 1990; Crow et al., 1998; Palmer et al., 1996; Resch et al., 1997), degrees of handedness may be important since it has been suggested (Bishop, 1990; Orton, 1937; Zangwill, 1960) that failure to develop unequivocal dominance in one hemisphere predisposes to pathology. Given the fact that left-handers are a more heterogenous population than right-handers in language function organization and patterns of interhemispheric communication, some studies showed inferior achievements of left-handers in foreign language achievement (Lamn *et al.,* 1999; Lamn, 1997). It seems that left-handers are less equipped for the developing of adequate phonological skills needed for reaching high levels of proficiency in L2. In addition, left-handedness seems to be a more affective factor than sex since studies have shown that left-handers of both sexes are overrepresented in the lowest level L2 classes and were underepresented in the higher level L2 classes, compared with right-handers of both sexes (Lamn et al., 1999).

CAREER CHOICE AND LEARNING STYLES

Furthermore, success in L2 higher education learning is related to career choice. Discipline-based research (Willcoxson et al., 1996) has shown that specific learning style preferences are typically found in disciplines which belong to pure sciences such as Foreign Languages and Humanities and are different from those adopted by students in disciplines such as Civil Engineering and Computer Science or Mathematics, which belong to exact sciences. This finding indicates that common learning style preferences may act as a facilitating factor for students of Humanities who learn a foreign language.

Educational leaders nowadays recognize that the process of learning is critically important and the way individuals learn is the key for an educational improvement (Demirbas et al., 2003). An individual's preferred method for receiving information in any learning environment is the learning style of that individual. Learning can be defined as an internal process that is different for every individual and learning style can be described as the way individuals acquire new information. Each learner's preferred ways of perception, organization and retention of new information are distinctive and consistent. Learning styles have been extensively discussed in the educational psychology literature (Claxton et al., 1987; Schmeck, 1988) and specifically in the context of language learning by Oxford and her colleagues (Oxford, 1990; Oxford et al., 1991; Wallace et al., 1992; Oxford et al., 1993) and over 30 learning style assessment instruments have been developed in the past decades (Guild et al., 1985; Jensen, 1987).

Kolb (1984) suggested that an individual learner's style may be identified by assessing her/his position on each of the bipolar dimensions by using a test called Learning Styles Inventory (LSI). There are 12 open-ended questions that have four different alternative responses in LSI. Each question asks respondents to rank-order four sentence endings in a way that best describe their learning preference in any learning setting. After answering all 12 questions, four scores are calculated. These scores are clustered under four modes of the learning cycle which reflect the individual's tendency to learn through Concrete Experience (CE) or through the construction of theoretical frameworks (Abstract Conceptualization-AC) combined with the tendency to learn either through Active Experimentation (AE) or through reflection (Reflective Observation-RO). In the next stage, by subtracting CE from AC and RO from AE scores two combined scores are found out. These combined scores show the position of the individual learner in the two bipolar scales. More specifically, they refer to the major different ways by which students learn: the first (AC-CE) is "how a student perceives" new information or experience and the second (AE-RO) is "how a student processes what s/he perceives". In other words, these combined scores give the learning style preference of that individual. The learning style preferences resulting from the two bipolar scales were described by Kolb (1984) as accommodating (AE/CE), divergent (CE/RO), assimilating (RO/AC) and convergent (AC/AE). These four different learning styles, were labeled according to the individual's preferred information perceiving and processing modes. Each learning style has its own strengths and weaknesses but that does not mean that one is better than the other. More specifically: *Accommodating* learners are best at CE and AE, with their greatest interest lying in doing things (Kolb, 1984). They grasp their environments concretely through their feelings and utilize action to transform information obtained. They are risk-takers and enjoy seeking out new experiences. This kind of learners tends to solve problems in an intuitive, trial-and-error manner and instead of their own analytic ability, they rely on others for information. *Diverging* learners are best at CE and RO. This kind of learners are interested in people and tend to be imaginative and emotional. They have the ability to synthesize and/or assimilate a wide range of totally different observations into a comprehensive explanation that enables them to generate many ideas (Hsu, 1999). They are less concerned with theories and generalizations. Their approach to situations is in a less thoughtful, systematic or scientific way, therefore their abilities to make decisions are inhibited. *Assimilating* learners have the opposite learning strengths of accommodating learners. Their dominant learning abilities are AC and RO. They experience their world symbolically and transform it to information through thought. They are less interested in people and more concerned with abstract concepts, but are less concerned with the practical use of theories (Smith et al., 1996). It is more important for assimilating learners that the theory is logically sound and precise. *Converging* learners have opposite learning strengths of the diverging learners. Their dominant learning abilities are AC and AE. They bring a logical, pragmatic and unemotional perspective to any situation. They are more concerned with the relative truth than absolute truth. The knowledge of converging learners is organized, so that through hypothetical-deductive reasoning, they can focus their knowledge on specific problem. According to Smith and Kolb's description (1996), converging learners are unemotional and prefer to deal with things rather than people.

Results obtained using Kolb's Learning Style Inventory (1985) in discipline based research demonstrate some measure of agreement among researchers regarding the learning style preferences typically found in specified disciplines and more agreement if disciplines are subsumed under descriptions such as arts or sciences. It was found that arts students tend to favour divergent or assimilating learning styles (Kolb, 1985; Kruzich et al., 1986; Willcoxson et al., 1996), social science students tend to have accommodating (Kruzich et al., 1986; Wilson, 1986) and exact science students convergent learning style preferences (Katz, 1988; Reading-Brown et al., 1989; Willcoxson et al., 1996). Regarding L2 learning, there is a great deal of theoretical and empirical support (Jones, 1997; Reid, 1987; Rossi-Le, 1995) that students tend to favour kinesthetic and tactile styles (they prefer active participation/experiences and hands-on work). However, very few studies looked at the links between styles and discipline (e.g. science versus arts). Melton (1999) found that arts students favoured kinesthetic and individual styles, while science students did not. It was also found that science students have stronger preference for group styles, while arts students have a stronger preference for auditory and individual styles (Peacock, 2001).

A careful consideration should be given to learning styles since a mismatch between learning and teaching styles causes learning failure and frustration with implications for both learners and teachers (Drew et al., 2002; Felder et al., 1995). On the contrary, matching teaching styles to learning styles can significantly enhance academic achievement and student attitudes and specifically in foreign language instruction (Oxford et al., 1991; Wallace et al., 1992). Students learn best when they are actively involved in the learning process and when they are in learning situations that meet their learning style needs (Claxton et al., 1987; Earley, 1994; Felder et al., 1995; Hartman, 1995; Kramsch, 1993).

APPROACHES TO STUDYING

Learning styles are closely related to approaches to studying since students with undirected learning styles fail to adopt any consistent strategies when studying. Teachers who use teaching and learning strategies that correspond to their students' learning styles are more likely to reach a larger number of students. Research conducted by Malett et al., (1983) found that university students who became aware of their learning styles consciously adopted approaches to studying which corresponded to their preferred learning styles. This resulted in improvement of work habits, time on task and an increase in grade point averages. The choice of proper approaches to studying affects second language learning outcomes and it is among the most important variables influencing performance in second language. Choosing effective approaches to studying makes learning easier, faster, more enjoyable, more self-directed and more transferable to new situations and contributes to more independent, autonomous and lifelong learning (Allwright, 1990; Little, 1991; Oxford, 1990). Therefore, there is a need to identify and inculcate those approaches which are associated with success and ensure they are congruent with the academic values of higher education. Students' approaches to studying should be widely understood and accepted by teachers in higher education in order to improve the effectiveness of student learning.

Interviews with university students have shown that contrasting approaches to studying are adopted. Marton and Saljo (1976), in a study of how Scandinavian students tackled the task of reading academic articles and texts, identified two contrasting approaches, *deep* and *surface*. Students who adopted a deep approach started with the intention of understanding the meaning of the article, questioned the author's arguments and related them to both previous knowledge and personal experience. This approach contrasted with that of other students who started with the intention of memorizing the important facts and hence were described as adopting a surface approach. During the 1970s and 1980s, using a combination of large-scale surveys and in-depth interviews, Entwistle and his co-workers developed a series of inventories, each consisting of study orientations made up of a number of subscales. The Approaches to Studying Inventory (ASI) assessed, by means of a self-report type format, students' perceptions of their approaches to studying. There have been a number of versions of the ASI including a long form (64 items in 16 subscales), a short form (18 items in three scales) and a more recent version, the Revised Approaches to studying Inventory (RASI) (Entwistle et al., 1994). The RASI is one of the most widely used questionnaires consisting of 44 items and it has been designed to measure student approaches to studying in a higher education context. The items have been conceptualized and designed from six learning orientations, corresponding to six subscales of the subscales of the Inventory: *deep approach, surface approach, strategic approach, lack of direction, academic self-confidence and metacognitive awareness of studying.* However, only the concepts of deep, surface and strategic approaches are widely applied and understood by academics, while the others are not (Tait et al., 1996). For this reason, a shorter version of RASI, a 30-item version, is recommended (Duff, 1997) because it comprises items that relate only to these three approaches to studying.

Deep learning has been one of the most influential constructs to emerge in the literature on effective learning in higher education (Boyle et al., 2003). Students identified as having a *deep approach* report they try to work out the meaning of information for themselves, do not accept ideas without critical examination of them, relate ideas from their studies to a wider context and look for reasoning, justification and logic behind ideas. The deep approach refers to a deeper level of understanding whereby the learner understands the content, the argument and the meaning of the learning materials and is able to apply a critical point of view and can justify and interact with the learning materials. Deep processing involves processes of a high cognitive level, searching for analogies, relating to previous knowledge and theorizing about what is learned. Deep learners are intrinsically motivated by intrinsic interest (Boyle et al., 1003) and it was proved that high levels of intrinsic motivation are positively related to grades in higher education (Lin et al., 2003). In the deep approach, there is a personal commitment to learning, which means that the student relates the content to personally meaningful contexts or to existing prior knowledge. Ehrman (1996) describes deep processing as: an active process of making associations with material that is already familiar, examining interrelationships within the new material, elaborating the stimulus through associations with it and further development of it, connecting the new material with personal experience and considering alternative interpretations. The learner may use the new material to actively reconstruct his or her conceptual frameworks.

Students identified as having a *surface approach* see themselves as relying on rote learning of material, accepting ideas without necessarily understanding them, and emphasizing the acquisition of factual information in isolation to a wider picture and would express anxiety about their studies in terms of organization and volume of material. The surface approach involves a superficial mastery of the learning materials, which brings about a low level of conceptual understanding. Surface motivated students focus on what appears to be the most important items and memorizes them. Because of this focus, they do not see interconnections between the meanings and implications of what is learned. Surface learners in higher education are extrinsically motivated by the desire to obtain qualifications or a job (Boyle et al., 2003). Ehrman (1996) describes surface processing as: completion of the task with minimum conceptual effort, with the result that much less information will stay in memory, because it has been encountered much less and there is no emotional or cognitive investment in it.

Inventories developed to measure the above mentioned approaches have demonstrated a link between the intention to understand and learning processes which relate ideas and use evidence (Entwistle et al., 1983). Deep and surface approaches form almost unrelated factors in analyses of these inventories. In relation to everyday studying, a third dimension has been identified, a *strategic approach,* which describes an intention to achieve the highest possible grades through effort and well-organized studying. Students reporting a strategic approach perceive themselves as having clear goals related to their studies and being hard workers, ensuring that they have the appropriate resources and conditions for successful study, and feel that they are generally well organized (Sadler-Smith, 1996). Investigations using such inventories have indicated that a deep strategic approach to studying at university is likely to lead to high grades, while a surface approach combined with low scores on the strategic dimension is associated with poor academic performance (Au et al., 1999).

Research has shown that there is a clear relationship between a deep approach and a deep level of understanding an academic article (Marton et al., 1976). Another study (Svensson, 1977) has shown that only 23% of the students classified as surface learners passed all their semester examinations while 90% of the students classified as deep learners passed all their semester examinations. Ramsden and Entwistle (1981) examined the relationship between approaches to studying and self-reported ratings of of academic progress. Discriminant function analysis was conducted to discriminate between those who believed they were doing very well and those who believed they were doing badly. Organized study methods and a strategic approach were among the variables which characterized those students who believed they were doing very well. On the other hand, disorganized study methods and surface approach were found to be consistently related to low academic grades awarded (Watkins, 1982). On the whole, it was suggested (Drew et al., 1998; Murray-Harvey, 1993) that approaches to studying are important factors in determining academic performance with organized study methods and a strategic approach being the best predictors of high achievement (Harper et al., 1986). Appropriate approaches to studying make such a difference to learning success that many have attempted to design and execute training programmes on approaches to studying, especially for inexperienced learners (Ehrman et al., 2003). More specifically, in order to increase L2 proficiency some researchers and teachers have provided instruction that helped students learn how to use more relevant and more powerful approaches to studying. Positive effects of instruction emerged for proficiency in speaking (Dadour et al., 1996; O' Malley et al., 1985) and reading (Park-Oh, 1994) and led to increased L2 learning motivation (Nunan, 1997).

OUR RESEARCH FINDINGS

In view of the above findings, we undertook a three-fold research in a sample of 452 undergraduate students (146 males and 306 females) at the university of Thessaly, Greece. Two hundred and thirty-two of them were enrolled in the Faculty of Humanities and 220 in the Faculties of Civil Engineering and Computer Science.

In the first part of our research (Andreou, Vlachos, and Andreou, in press) we investigated the influence of level in L2, sex, handedness and Faculty choice on the performance of phonological, syntactical and semantic tasks in L2. A within-subjects mixed-design ANOVA (handedness X sex X faculty X L2 level) was performed on phonological, syntactical and semantic tasks. The main effect which was statistically significant (p< .05) for all three tasks was obtained for L2 level [phonology: $F(1) = 67.626$, p< .00; syntax: $F(1) = 4.128$, p< .04; semantics: $F(1) = 11.806$, p< .00], indicating that subjects with a professional degree performed generally better than those who did not have, in phonological tasks (13.88 vs 6.80 out of 20), in syntactical tasks (8.02 vs 6.11 out of 10) and semantic tasks (35.30 vs 25.67 out of 40). A statistically significant main effect for syntax and semantics was obtained for sex [syntax: $F(1) = 8.262$, p< .00; semantics: $F(1) = 5.093$, p< .02], indicating that females performed better than males in syntax (7.50 vs 6.57) and semantics (31.47 vs 30.80). No statistically significant main effects were found for faculty and handedness when taken alone but there were two-way statistically significant interactions of handedness X certificate for semantics [$F(2) = 3.992$, p< .01], of sex X faculty for syntax [$F(1) = 6.793$, p< .00] and semantics [$F(1) = 15.704$, p< .00] and of faculty X certificate for syntax [$F(1) = 6.123$, p< .01]. A three-way statistically significant interaction was also obtained for handedness X faculty X certificate for syntax only [$F(2) = 3.075$, p< .04].

In the second part of our research we investigated the relationship between Greek students' learning styles and performance in English phonological, syntactic and semantic tasks, in combination with their sex and discipline. Learning styles were assessed by Kolb's self-report Learning Style Inventory (LSI, 1985). In order to determine the relative contribution of each of the learning styles to performance on L2 verbal fluency tasks three multiple regressions were performed. When phonology served as the dependent variable, R was significantly different from zero [$R^2 = .23$, $F(4, 447) = 2.58$, p<.05]. Inspection of the predictor variables revealed that only divergent learning style (beta = .22, t = 1.96, p<. 05) significantly predicted scores on phonological tasks. For the regression on syntax and semantics R was also significantly different from zero [$R^2 = .39$, $F(4, 447) = 4.54$, p<.001 and $R^2 = .25$, $F(4, 447) = 8.04$, p<.001, respectively]. Scores on syntactical tasks were significantly predicted by accommodative learning style preference (beta = .19, t = 1.87, p<.05) and scores on semantics by divergent learning style preference (beta = .25, t = 2.31, p<.05).

In the third part (Andreou, Andreou, and Vlachos, 2004), we examined further how Greek students' approaches to studying in combination with sex, academic discipline and professional degree in English affect performance on verbal fluency tasks in English as a second language. Approaches to study were assessed by a 30-item version of Entwistle and Tait's RASI (Duff, 1997). The mixed design analysis of variance (MANOVA) (approaches to studying X sex X faculty X L2 certificate) which was computed for each verbal fluency task revealed statistically significant main effects for sex [F(1) = 10.82] and approaches to studying [F(1) = 3.26] on syntax, for faculty [F(1) = 10.86] on phonology and for certificate on phonology [F(1) = 250.16], syntax [F(1) = 25.71] and semantics [F(1) = 102.55]. Two-way statistically significant interaction effects were observed for sex X faculty on semantics [F(1) = 4.02] and for sex X certificate on phonology [F(1) = 8.93]. A three-way statistically significant effect was also obtained for sex X certificate X approaches to studying on syntax [F(1) = 2.46].

Table 1. summarizes in words the factors which contribute to high score achievement in university students' L2 tasks.

Table 1. Factors contributing to high score achievement in university students' L2 tasks

Variables	Verbal Phonology	Fluency Tasks Syntax	Semantics
Level (High/Low)	High*	High*	High*
Sex (Male/Female)	-	Female*	Female*
Learning Styles (Accomodative/Divergent/ Convergent, Assimilative)	Divergent*	Accomodative*	Divergent*
Approaches to studying (Deep/Surface /Strategic)	-	Deep*/Strategic*	-

*statistically significant (p< .05) differences

CONCLUSION

Our findings indicated that the students who reached a high level in L2 showed a superiority in all three linguistic codes, phonology, syntax and semantics. In other words, students who had obtained a professional degree in L2 performed better than those who had not, in all three tasks, phonological, syntactical and semantic. This finding confirms earlier findings, discussed in the context of the Linguistic Coding Deficiency Hypothesis (LCDH), which have shown that subjects who achieve high scores in L2 tasks have strong language aptitude skills (Ganschow et al., 1998; Ganschow et al., 1994; Karapetsas et al., 2001; Sparks et al., 1995).

Handedness alone did not influence our students' performance on L2 tasks, but only in combination with L2 level. This confirms earlier studies which found no relationship between language abilities and relative hand preference (Bishop, 1990; Crow et al., 1998; Palmer et al., 1996; Resch et al., 1997). However, some studies claim that degrees of handedness are important and that left handers are less equipped for the developing of adequate phonological skills needed for reaching high levels of proficiency in L2 (Lamn et al., 1999; Lamn, 1997) and probably that's why the combination of handedness and certificate played an important role in our results.

Gender was found to play an important role in our results, alone and in combination with faculty. Females performed better than males in both syntax and semantics confirming earlier studies which found a female advantage for verbal skills (Gordon et al., 1986; Stumpf, 1995).

The fact that sex combined with faculty influenced our results could be explained by studies on hemispheric specialization for language functions which reveal stronger lateralization in men than women and a female superiority on verbal tasks. Stronger verbal skills on the part of females influences their career choice leading them to choose Faculties such as Humanities which belong to pure sciences rather than exact sciences.

The linguistic code which was mostly influenced by all factors was syntax. This is probably related to the native language spoken by the subjects tested in second language tasks. The native language of our sample was Greek which is a language with free word order while the second language tested was English, a language with strict word order (Goodluck, 1986). Therefore, all our factors had an impact on syntax probably because Greek syntax is completely different from English syntax. In Greek, the same sentence may be expressed in different word orders even with the subject missing while in English, words follow a strict word order in a sentence.

Concerning learning styles, our research findings suggest that university students prefer a divergent learning style while performing phonological and semantic tasks. It is concrete experience and reflective observation that these students apply on L2 phonology and semantics. They like to use their imagination, synthesize and generate ideas and they are less concerned with theories when they are to perform phonological and semantic tasks in L2. On the other hand, they prefer an accommodative learning style while performing syntactical tasks. They have a tendency to learn L2 syntax through a combination of concrete experience and active experimentation. They utilize action to transform information obtained and seek out new experiences when they are to perform syntactical tasks. Therefore, teachers should take into account that while teaching L2 phonology or semantics they should use pedagogic techniques that favour concrete experience and reflective observation such as handouts, videos, class or group discussions. They could also encourage note-taking and reading, write key information on the board, give oral explanations and instruction and generally encourage active participation. On the other hand, while teaching L2 syntax they should use techniques that favour concrete experience and active experimentation such as problem solving activities which involve practical experimentation. Where experimentation does occur, as in the learning of a foreign language, it consists of the oral or written testing of hypotheses. That is, reflection upon personal experience (upon responses to one's use of language) leads to concept development (the formation of new hypotheses about the construction of the language) and the testing of the concepts developed, again through personal experience.

Regarding approaches to studying, our findings are in line with previous research, which reveals that studying orientations are one of the important factors in determining academic performance (Drew et al., 1998; Murray-Harvey, 1993). However, our results suggest that approaches to studying alone or in combination with students' sex and professional degree in L2 seem to influence students' performance only on syntactical L2 tasks and not on phonological or semantic ones. This is probably related to the native language spoken by the subjects tested in L2 tasks. Their native language was Greek which, as it was mentioned above, is a language with strict word order as opposed to the subjects' L2 which was English, a language with strict word order. Therefore, a surface approach, which is based on rote learning and superficial mastery of the learning materials, seems to lead to lower performance on syntactical tasks in English as L2. On the other hand, a deep approach, which involves processes of a high cognitive level and intrinsic motivation, is positively related to higher performance on syntactical tasks in English as L2.

Based on our findings, two main aspects need to be addressed concerning approaches to studying. Firstly, there are students who habitually employ a surface approach to higher education studies in subjects which require a deep level approach. These students need study skills assistance to develop the capability of appropriately utilizing a deep approach. Secondly, there are students who would normally make appropriate use of the deep approach but because of factors such as surface assessment demands, high workloads, overprescriptive courses or an inhospitable learning environment, resort to a surface approach. This second problem can only be ameliorated if the factors influencing students towards a surface approach are addressed by curriculum design, instructional design or institutional policy. In general, research (Ramsden et al., 1981) indicates that the propensity of students who resort to a surface approach can be reduced by ensuring that questions and examinations demand a deep approach, workloads are reasonable and courses have sufficient flexibility to offer relevance and induce intrinsic interest. Any initiatives along these lines would be in keeping with the desire to produce graduates who are true independent learners as well as to reduce the use of a surface approach.

In conclusion, it is obvious both from previous studies and from our research findings that individual differences influence the way people learn and succeed in language study. Therefore, L2 level, sex, handedness, faculty choice, learning styles and approaches to studying may be important factors for teachers in higher education to take into account when designing and delivering their programmes and providing guidance for students. This is especially true in a higher education system where all students are being required to a) take the initiative in learning b) move away from an overreliance on lecturers c) accept that a student-centered approach to learning is active as opposed to passive and d) accept they should learn not just for the purposes of assessment but for their own intellectual growth, pleasure and fulfillment. This places demands on higher education teachers who need to design instruction that meets the needs of their students and enables the most learners possible to learn as much as they can and give them every advantage, including a program that enables them to start out in a relatively comfortable and stress-free way. This means giving them the opportunity to learn in their preferred way, which can happen in the interests of keeping classrooms paced to the majority or to a standard curriculum.

While this digest has focused on second language learning from the perspective of individual differences, it is important to point out that a wider, social and cultural, context of second language development has a tremendous impact on second language learning. Therefore, further research is needed to extend our knowledge on factors which may affect students' L2 learning. For example, further examination of gender differences in adult L2 learning styles will elucidate the influence of second language learners' cultural background and of the educational settings in which they learn the target language on the choice of their approaches to studying by gender. Although this study contributes useful information to the understanding of some of the individual differences among L2 adult learners, yet there is need for further research to cross-validate findings from the present study taking into account more/or different factors that may influence L2 learning.

REFERENCES

Allwright, D. (1990). *Autonomy in language pedagogy. CRILE working paper 6. Centre for Research in Education*. Lancaster: University of Lancaster.

Andreou, E., Andreou, G. and Vlachos F. (2004). Studying orientations and performance on verbal fluency tasks in a second language. *Learning and Individual Differences,* 15, 23-33.

Andreou, G., Vlachos, F. and Andreou, E. (in press). Affecting factors in second language acquisition. *Journal of Psycholinguistic Research,* 34 (4).

Au, C. and Entwistle, N. (1999). Memorizations with understanding in approaches to studying: cultural variant or response to assessment demands? *Paper presented at the European Association for Research on Learning and Instruction Conference.* Gothenburg.

Bishop, D. (1990). *Handedness and Developmental Disorders*. London: Mackeith.

Boyle, E., Duffy, T. and Dunleavy, K. (2003). Learning styles and academic outcome: The validity and utility of Vermunt's Inventory of Learning Styles in a British higher education setting. *British Journal of Educational Psychology,* 73, 267-290.

Carrol, J. (1973). Implications of aptitude test research and psycholinguistic theory for theory for foreign language teaching. *International Journal of Psycholinguistics,* 2, 5-14.

Chee, M., Tan, E. and Thiel, T. (1999.) Mandarin and English single word processing studied with functional magnetic resonance imaging. *Journal of Neuroscience,* 19, 3050–3056

Claxton, C. and Murrell, P.(1987).*Learning Styles: Implications for Improving Educational Practice*. (ASHE-ERIC Higher Education Report No. 4). ASHE: College Station.

Cline, T. (2000). Multilingualism and dyslexia: challenges for research and practice. *Dyslexia*, 6 (1), 3-12.

Crow, J., Crow, R., Done, J. and Leask, S. (1998). Relative hand skills predicts academic ability: global deficits at the point of hemispheric indecision. *Neuropsychologia,* 36(12), 1275-1282.

Dadour, S., Robbins, J. (1996). University- level studies using strategy instruction to improve speaking ability in Egypt and Japan. In Oxford, R. (ed.) *Language Learning Strategies Around the World: Cross-cultural Perspectives* (pp. 1-25). Manoa: University of Hawaii Press.

Dehaene, S., Dupoux, E., Mehler, J., Cohen, L., Paulesu, E., Perani, D., Van de Moortele, P-F., Lehéricy, S. and Le Bihan, D. (1997). Anatomical variability in the cortical representation of first and second language. *Neuroreport,* 8, 3809–3815

Demirbaş, O. and Dermikan, H.(2003). Focus on architectural design process through learning styles. *Design Studies,* 24, 437-456.

Dinklage, K. (1971). Inability to learn a foreign language. In Blaine G.B. and McArthur C. C. (eds.) *Emotional problems of the student* (pp. 185-206). New York: Regents.

Downey, D., Snyder, L. and Hill. B. (2000). College students with dyslexia: persistent linguistic deficits and foreign language learning. *Dyslexia*, 6 (2), 101-111.

Drew, P. and Watkins, D. (1998). Affective variables, learning approaches and academic achievement: A casual modelling investigation with Hong Kong tertiary students. *British Journal of Educational Psychology,* 68, 173-188.

Drew, F. and Ottewill, R. (2002). Learning styles and the potential for learning on institution-wide language programmes: an assessment of the results of the pilot study. *Language Learning Journal,* 26, 11-18.

Duff, A. (1997). A note on the reliability and validity of a 30- item version of Entwistle and Tait' s Revised Approaches to Studying Inventory. *British Journal of Educational Psychology,* 67, 529-539.

Earley, P.(1994).Self or group: cultural effects of training on self-efficacy and performance. *Administrative Science Quarterly,*39,89-117.

Ehrman, M. (1996). *Understanding second language learning difficulties.* Thousand Oaks, CA: Sage

Ehrman, M. and Leaver, B. (2003). Cognitive styles in the service of language learning. *System,* 31(3), 393-415.

Entwistle, N. and Ramsden, P. (1983). *Understanding student learning.* London: Croom Helm.

Entwistle, N. and Tait, H. (1994). *The Revised Approaches to Studying Inventory.* Edinburgh: University of Edinburgh, Centre for Research into Learning and Instruction.

Felder, R. and Henriques, E. (1995). Learning and teaching styles in foreign and second language education. *Foreign Language Annals,* 28, 21-31.

Galloway, L. and Krashen, S. (1980). Cerebral organization in bilingualism and second language. In Scarcella, R. and Krashen, S. (eds.), *Research in Second Language Acquisition* (pp.74-80). Newbury House: Rowley, Mass.

Ganschow, L. and Sparks, R. (2000). Reflections on foreign language study for students with language learning problems: research, issues and challenges. *Dyslexia,* 6 (2), 87-100.

Ganschow, L., Sparks, R., Javorsky, J., Pohlman, J. and Bishop-Marbury, A. (1991). Identifying native language difficulties among foreign language learners in college: A foreign language learning disability?. *Journal of Learning Disabilities,* 24, 530-541.

Ganschow, L., Sparks, R., Anderson, R., Javorsky, J., Skinner, S. and Patton, J. (1994). Differences in anxiety and language performance among high- and low-anxious college foreign language learners. *Modern Language Journal,* 78, 41-55.

Ganschow, L., Sparks, L. and Javorsky, J. (1998). Foreign language learning difficulties: An historical perspective. *Journal of Learning Disabilities,* 31, 248-258.

Goodluck, H. (1986). Language acquisition and linguistic theory. In Fletcher, P. and Garman, M. (eds.), *Language acquisition* (2nd ed., pp. 49-68). New York: Cambridge University Press.

Gordon, H. and Lee, P. (1986). A relationship between gonadotropins and visuospatial function. *Neuropsychologia,* 24, 563-576.

Gouchie, C. and Kimura, D.(1991). The relationship between testosterone levels and cognitive ability patterns. *Psychoendocrinology,* 16, 323-334.

Guild, P.,and Garger, S.(1985*).Marching to Different Drummers.* Alexandria, VA: Association for Supervision and Curriculum Development.

Hampson, E. and Kimura, D.(1992). Sex differences and hormonal influences on cognitive function in humans. In Becker, J., Breedlove, S. and Crews, D. (eds.), *Behavioral Endocrinology* (pp. 357-398). Cambridge, MA: MIT Press.

Harper, G. and Kember, D.(1986). Approaches to studying of distance education students. *British Journal of Educational Technology*, 17, 212-222.

Hartman, V. (1995).Teaching and learning style preferences: transitions through technology. *VCCA Journal, 9,*18-20.

Hsu,C. (1999). Learning styles of hospitality students: Nature or nurture? *HospitalityManagement,* 18(1), 17-30.

Janowsky, S. , Chavez, B., Zamboli, D. and Orwoll, E.(1998). The cognitive Neuropsychology of sex hormones in men and women. *Developmental Neuropsychology,* 14(2/3), 421-440.

Jensen,G. (1987).Learning Styles. In Provost, J. and Anchors, A. (eds.),*Applications of the Myers-Briggs Type Indicator in Higher Education* (pp.181-206). Palo Alto: Consulting Psychologists Press.

Jones, N. (1997). Applying learning styles research to improve writing instruction. *Paper presented at RELC Seminar on Learners and Language Learning.*

Karapetsas, A. and Andreou, G. (2001). Visual field asymmetries for rhyme and semantic tasks in fluent and nonfluent bilinguals. *Brain and Language*, 78, 53-61.

Katz, N. (1988). Individual learning style: Israeli norms and cross- cultural equivalence of Kolb's Learning Style Inventory. *Journal of Cross- cultural Psychology,* 19, 361-379.

Kim, K., Relkin, N., Lee, K. and Hirsch, J. (1997). Distinct cortical areas associated with native and second languages. *Nature,* 388,171–174.

Klein, D., Milner, B., Zatorre, R., Meyer, E. and Evans, A. (1995). The neural substrates underlying word generation: a bilingual functional-imaging study. *Proceedings of the National Academy of Science USA,* 92, 2899–2903.

Kolb, D. (1984). *Experiential Learning: Experience as the Source of Learning and Development.* New York: Prentice- Hall.

Kolb, D. (1985). *Learning Style Inventory.* Boston: McBer and Co.

Kramsch, C. (1993).*Context and Culture in Language Teaching.* Oxford: Oxford University Press.

Kruzich, J., Friesen, B. and Van Soest, D.(1986). Assessment of Students and faculty learning styles: research and application. *Journal of Social Work Education,* 22, 22-30.

Lamn, O. (1997). Sinistrality and developmental reading difficulties. In Shirmon, J. (ed.), *Studies in the Psychology of Language* (pp. 228-247). Jerusalem: Magnes.

Lamn, O. and Epstein, R. (1999). Left handedness and achievements in foreign language studies. *Brain and Language*, 70, 504-517.

Lefebvre, R. (1984). A psychological consultation program for learning disabled students. *College Student Personnel,* 7, 361-362.

Lin, Y. G., McKeachie,W. and Kim,Y. (2003).College student intrinsic and/or extrinsic motivation and learning. *Learning and Individual Differences,* 13, 251-258.

Little, D.(1991). *Learner Autonomy 1: Definitions, Issues and Problems.* Dublin: Authentik.

Lujan-Ortega, V. and Clark-Carter, D. (2000). Individual differences, strategic performance and achievement in second language learners of Spanish. *Studia Linguistica,* 54, 280-287.

Malett, S., Kirschenbaum, D. and Humphrey, L. (1983).Description and subjective evaluation of an objective successful study improvement program. *Personnel and Guidance Journal,* 61, 341-345.

Marton, F. and Saljo, R.(1976). On qualitative differences in learning : I. Outcome and process. *British Journal of Educational Psychology*, 46, 4-11.

Melton, C. (1990). Bridging the cultural gap: a study of Chinese students' learning style preferences. *RELC Journal,* 21, 29-54.

Moffat, S. and Hampson, E.(1996). A curvilinear relationship between testosterone and spatial cognition in humans: Possible influence of hand preference. *Psychoendocrinology*, 21, 323-337.

Murray-Harvey, R.(1993). Identifying characterisitics of successful tertiary students using path analysis. *Australian Educational Researcher*, 20, 63-81.

Nowicka, A. and Fersten, E.(2001). Sex- related differences in interhemispheric transimission time in the human brain. *Neuroreport*, 12(18), 4171-4175.

Nunan, D.(1997). Does learner strategy training make a difference? *Lenguas Modernas*, 24, 123-142.

Obler, L. (1981). Right hemisphere participation in second language acquisition. In: Diller K. (ed.), *Individual Differences and Universals in Language Learning Aptitude* (pp. 53-64). Newbury House: Rowley MA.

O´ Malley, J., Russo, R., Chamot, A., Stewnen- Manzanares, G. and Kupper, L.(1985). Learning strategy applications with students of English as a second language. *TESOL Quarterly*, 19(3), 557-584.

Orton, S.T.(1937). *Reading, Writing and Speech problems in children*. New York: Norton.

Oxford, R.L.(1990). *Language Learning Strategies: What every Teacher Should Know*. Boston: Heinle and Heinle.

Oxford, R., Ehrman, M. and Lavine, R. (1991).Style Wars: Teacher-Student Style Conflicts in the Language Classroom. In Magnan, S. (ed.) *Challenges in the 1990's for College Foreign Language Programs* (pp. 1-25). Boston: Heinle and Heinle.

Oxford, R. and Ehrman, M. (1993). Second Language Research on Individual Differences. *Annual Review of Applied Linguistics*, 13, 188-205.

Palmer, R. and Corballis, M. (1996). Predicting reading ability from handedness measures. *British Journal of Psychology*, 87, 609-620.

Paradis, M. (1994). Neurolinguistic aspects of implicit and explicit memory: Implications for bilingualism and SLA. In Ellis, N.C. (ed.), *Implicit and explicit learning of languages* (pp. 393-419). Academic Press: San Diego.

Park- Oh, Y. (1994). Self- regulated strategy training in second language reading. *Unpublished doctoral thesis*. University of Alabama.

Peacock, M. (2001). Match or mismatch? Learning styles and teaching styles in EFL. *International Journal of Applied Linguistics*, 11(1), 1-20.

Pompian, N., and Thun, C. (1988). Dyslexic/ Learning Disabled Students at Dartmouth College. *Annals of Dyslexia*, 38, 278-284.

Ramsden, P. and Entwistle, N. (1981). Effects of academic departments on students' approaches to studying. *British Journal of Educational Psychology*, 18, 3-13.

Reading- Brown, M. and Hayden, R. (1989). Learning styles- liberal arts and technical training: what' s the difference? *Psychological Reports*, 64, 507-518.

Reid, J. (1987). The learning style preferences of EFL students. *TESOL Quarterly*, 21, 87-111.

Resch, F., Haffner, J., Pfueller, U., Strehlow, U. and Zerahn- Hartung, C.(1997). Testing the hypothesis of relationships between laterality and ability according to Annett's right- left theory: findings in an epidemiological sample of young adults. *British Journal of Psychology*, 88, 621-635.

Rossi- Le, L.(1995). Learning styles and strategies in adult immigrant ESL students. In J. M. Reid, *Learning styles in the ESL/ EFL classroom*, (pp. 87-111). Boston: Heinle- Heinle.

Sadler- Smith, E.(1996). Approaches to studying: Age, gender and academic performance. *Educational Studies*, 22, 367-379.

Schmeck, R. (1988). *Learning strategies and learning styles.* New York: Plenum.

Smith, D., and Kolb, D. (1996).*User's Guide for the Learning-Style Inventory: A Manual for Teachers and Trainers.*Boston: McBer and Company.

Sparks, R., Ganschow, L. and Pohlman, J. (1989). Linguistic coding deficits in foreign language learners. *Annals of Dyslexia*, 39, 179-195.

Sparks, R. and Ganschow, L. (1993). The impact of native language learning problems on foreign language courses: Connections between native and foreign language learning: Case study illustrations of the linguistic coding deficit hypothesis. *Modern Language Journal*, 77, 58-74.

Sparks, R., Ganschow, L. and Patton, J. (1995). Prediction of performance in first- year foreign language learning. *Journal of Educational Psychology*, 87, 638-655.

Sparks, R. and Javorsky, J. (1999). Students classified as LD and the college foreign language requirement: replication and comparison studies. *Journal of Learning Disabilities,* 32 (4), 329-349.

Springer, S. and Deutsch, G. (1998). *Left brain right brain: Perspectives from cognitive neuroscience* (5th ed.). New York: W. H. Freeman and Company.

Stumpf, H. (1995). Gender differences in performance on tests of cognitive abilities: Experimental design issues and empirical results. Psychological and psychobiological perspectives on sex differences in cognition: I. Theory and research. *Learning and Individual Differences*, 7, 275-287.

Svensson, L. (1977). On qualitative differences in learning. III. Study skill and learning. *British Journal of Educational Psychology*, 47, 233-243.

Tait, H. and Entwistle, N. (1996). Identifying students at risk through ineffective study strategies. *Higher Education*, 31, 97-116.

Van Lancker, D. (1997). Rags to Riches: Our Increasing Appreciation of Cognitive and Communicative Abilities of the Human Right Cerebral Hemisphere. *Brain and Language*, 57, 1-11.

Wallace,B.and Oxford,R.L.(1992).Disparity in Learning Styles and Teaching Styles in the ESL Classroom :Does This Mean War? *AMTESOL Journal*, 1, 45-68.

Watkins, D.(1982). Identifying the study process dimensions of Australian university students. *The Australian Journal of Education*, 26(1), 76-85.

Willcoxson, L. and Prosser, M. (1996). Kolb's learning style inventory(1985): Review and further study of validity and reliability. *British Journal of Educational Psychology,* 66, 247-257.

Wilson, D. (1986). An investigation of the properties of Kolb's Learning Style Inventory. *Leadership and Organization Development Journal*, 7, 3-15.

Zangwill, O. (1960). *Cerebral dominance and its relation to psychological function.* Edinburgh: Oliver and Boyd.

In: Trends in Learning Reserch
Editor: Samuel N. Hogan, pp. 99-118

ISBN 1-59454-965-6
© 2006 Nova Science Publishers, Inc.

Chapter 5

NLP IN ACTION: THEORY AND TECHNIQUES IN TEACHING AND LEARNING

Kathryn Gow,[1,*] *Andrea Reupert*[2] *and Darryl Maybery*[2]
[1]Queensland University of Technology
[2]Charles Sturt University

ABSTRACT

In this chapter, the authors focus on describing and applying a range of NLP theory, strategies and techniques in school and tertiary settings. The authors outline the principles behind, and give examples of several NLP teaching tools that promote the learning of primary, secondary, tertiary and teacher training groups. While occasional reference will be made to therapy and business environments, the majority of the content will focus on teaching, training and school counselling.

Neuro-Linguistic Programming (NLP) techniques are based on an established set of theoretical principles that span the disciplines of psychology, linguistics, counselling, communication and hypnosis. However, while it is challenging to understand the basis on which these strategies and techniques rest, it is not essential to do so before trying out the techniques which have already been trialled successfully by others, as long as one stays within one's professional educational boundaries, and does not stray in to the field of therapy.

While many teachers already apply some of these principles to teaching, and there has been a concerted attempt to design and deliver educational input, in a way that accounts for the different ways that individual students learn, there is still much that can be done to make teaching and learning more stimulating, challenging, and satisfying processes than they currently are.

Key words: NLP, Neuro Linguistic Programming, Teaching, Learning, Education

---

[*] Corresponding author: Associate Professor Kathryn Gow,Queensland University of Technology,Beams Road, Carseldine, Brisbane,Queensland, 4034, Australia,Phone: 0412125301,Fax: 617 38644660, E-Mail: k.gow@qut.edu.au

INTRODUCTION

This chapter does not cover the history of NLP which originated in the early 1970's and readers are referred to McClendon's (1989) account of the meetings of the various actors in the early days of the birth of NLP. His book is really a series of stories, the type that both educationists and learners would enjoy.

In answering the question what is Neuro-Linguistic Programming, the founders (mathematician Richard Bandler and linguist John Grinder) and practitioners of NLP would say that it is a behavioural approach that is readily understood because it consists of models, skills and techniques, which were based on the work of famous communicators, psychologists, hypnotists, therapists and linguists (see Bandler and Grinder, 1975)

A large number of articles have been written about various aspects of the use of NLP in therapy (for a list, see Kammer, 2003). Some articles give testimonials that certain NLP tools have worked for them in the classroom and some of these are covered in the sections that follow.

The overarching components of NLP covered herein are dealt with in the sections on theories, strategies and techniques.

UNDERPINNING THEORIES

Metaprograms

Metaprograms (Robbins, 1992) are the key to the way individuals process information and as such are powerful internal patterns that help determine how they form their internal representations and direct their behaviors. Dilts (1994) defines them as "a level of mental programming that determines how we sort, orient to, and chunk our experiences" (p. 228). They are, however, more abstract than specific.

Values and Personality

These "sorts" (filters) help us to determine what to pay attention to and what to spend our time on during our lives. They include our values - in terms of the energy they release in moving towards or away from ideas and actions; our personality - whether we have an internal or external frame of reference (Rotter's (1966) Locus of Control refers) - whether we sort by self or others, the latter leading to teacher burnout in some cases; whether we are matchers or mismatchers (some students affirm or deny the statements of others constantly); what our convincer strategies are (e.g., the basis on which we convince ourselves to initiate a task); if we are into possibility or necessity (we could go on a picnic versus we must finish the assignment); and a range of personality variables some of which are discussed next.

Learning and thinking styles are aspects of personality that have been of ongoing interest in the NLP world. If there is one thing that seems to engage people's attention, it is to talk about themselves, and to have presented to them new and different ways of understanding other people. When they explore areas such as learning styles and thinking styles, it is challenging and entertaining for students and teachers, at all stages of development.

It is useful to mention here some of the research on personality that is important for teaching and learning outcomes. Zhang (2002), from the University of Hong Kong, has contributed to our knowledge of the relationship between creativity, generating and complex thinking styles, versus the analytic mode of thinking. He found that the former were significantly positively correlated (related) with the holistic mode of thinking, while the latter were significantly negatively correlated. This type of information is important for teachers to know in planning the ways they interact with students.

One of the more fascinating older pieces of research, that Paul Meehan (2005) reminds us about in education and training, is that of the concept of field dependence-field independence (Witkin, 1977a, b). Research, over many decades, has provided evidence that people may, or may not, be able to detect patterns, if they are embedded in competing fields. Those people who are able to determine that the pattern is separate from the overall field are called field independent, while those who more or less become lost in the immediate pattern/s are labelled field dependent. The ramifications for this in college trade education are as important as they are in professional engineering courses. Meehan (2005) reminds us that this research was applied in business environments to ascertain factors involved in decision making and information processing, as well as in strategy development.

Beliefs: Effects on Performance

Several decades ago, research by Rosenthal and Jacobsen (1968) demonstrated that a teacher's beliefs about the intelligence and future possibilities of a student were directly correlated to the educational outcomes for that student. Thus it is vitally important for teachers to know and to put into practice empowering attitudes and communications with students. This century, people like Galan and Maguire (2001) again continue to warn us about the influence of educators' beliefs to enable or disable their students.

Tauber (1998, ED426985) believes that "few educators understand exactly how to use the Pygmalion effect or self-fulfilling prophecy (SFP) as a purposeful pedagogical tool to convey positive expectations and, maybe even more importantly, to avoid conveying negative expectations." That is, Tauber is suggesting that we reframe the research findings to motivate students by being good coaches and implant positive expectations in students' minds about their immediate performance and their future potential (in a realistic manner).

In his book, "Strategies of Genius", Robert Dilts (1994) offers a framework which enables us to explore the way in which we construct beliefs. The model of organisation he proposes distinguishes six different logical levels: Environment - Behaviour - Capabilities – Beliefs/Values – Identity- Spiritual/Greater System. Blackerby (2005), who is known for his book *Rediscover the Joy of Learning* (1996), gives the theoretical background behind Dilts' model of the logical levels of experience, while Galan and Maguire (2001) apply it to education.

Blackerby (2005) clarifies the types of questions that can be asked under each logical level of experience; for example, under the level labelled *Spiritual/Greater System*, he suggests that by asking questions about higher purposes and visions and being part of the wider world system, we can understand our higher motives of operation. At the level of

Identity, we can ask who we are, whereas at the level of *Beliefs and Values*, more rational questions such as "Why do I do it?" may tell us how we are operating in terms of our everyday choices. In terms of the level of *Capabilities*, more technical questions about "How do I do it?" are more pertinent. Answering the question of "What do I do?" can alert us to our *Behavior* choices and change consequences, while on the level of how the *Environment* affects us, asking questions about "where and/or when and/or with whom do I do it?" can connect us to the wider environmental context in which we live and work.

In this chapter, one of the strategies we highlight is spelling and according to Blackerby (2005), spelling is an example of a learning strategy at the capability level, because in the English language, all words do not look like they sound. That is one of the reasons why non-English speaking people find it so difficult to learn English.

Here we give examples similar to that of Galan and Maguire (2001) to match the topics in the section on strategies. For instance, if a child is having problems with spelling, mathematics or history, the teacher might talk about the problem from any one of the five viewpoints. If the teacher is trying to empower the student, he/she might select from one of the original five logical levels as follows:

1. Environment: "You can do maths easily, because you know how to count money at the shop."
2. Behaviour: "Knowing how to focus your attention will assist your concentration."
3. Capabilities: "If you learn this simple strategy, you'll be able to spell more easily."
4. Beliefs: "Reading history can help you become a more creative writer."
5. Identity: "You come from a family of successful students and you're no different."

If beliefs can be changed, then so too can behavior. In several demonstrations by Anthony Robbins he uses the fire walk to change people's limiting beliefs about themselves, while Tad James uses board breaking, to demonstrate to people that they can change their beliefs, physiology and state and achieve performances they never thought possible. These performances, however, may follow hours or days of preparation and seeding of suggestion in training programs or coaching sessions.

Ways of changing students' emotional and mental states ought to be part of any teacher education curriculum, but one rarely hears about empowering changes of state. One such example is given in a later section of this chapter.

Motivation and Achievement

When a teacher takes into account individual learning styles, the student's attention is captured and his/her total thinking processes are brought to the task at hand.

If students block efforts to motivate them, then the teacher can attempt to get around their resistance, or to use it for the student's good (this is akin to Erickson's utilization principle, see Gilligan, 1987). The two main ideas on handling resistance (Robbins, 1992) are that firstly we can persuade better through agreement, than through conquest. Teachers may find this hard when they first begin to practise it, but at the tertiary level where adult learners are concerned, a failure to acknowledge the contribution of a student, whether one agrees with it or not, is an unwise policy.

The second main ideas on handling resistance is for everyone involved in educational settings to know that our behaviors are not indelibly carved into our brains as some people have said they are. It could be simply a matter of negotiation: the common ground is the concept of flexibility (Robbins, 1992). We have to be prepared to try new ways and new approaches; to use the creative side of our brains more, or to use one of Milton Erickson's favourite expressions, to "experiment with wanton curiosity". The more flexible we are, the more options we create. If teachers adopt this approach and discuss the approach with students, it tends to unlock doors to new and desired behaviors.

To help achieve those desired behaviours, sometimes reframing (Bandler and Grinder, 1979) is useful. While the term tends to be used more in school counselling than in teaching environments, teachers do utilise these techniques regularly without labelling them as reframing.

Reframing is about changing a negative statement into a positive statement, but it also has a wider application than that and becomes a frame of mind after a while; we just have to be careful that we use the information from the student for the reframe and not use our own meaning context, which may not work for that particular student's experience. There are two types of reframing that we mention here: content reframing and context reframing.

Changing the content could mean that a person, who thinks that they can not find a job in the supermarket, is being forced to think of themselves as being meant for higher things and that the job barriers may be a signal that they need to do some further study. Changing the context, so that being slow but meticulous and accurate, may mean that the student could be well suited for accounting work or code detection, where accuracy is more important than speed.

Another way of manoevering around resistance is to ask them to act "as if". Acting "as if" we are in a particular emotional and mental state helps to achieve that state. For example, in a tertiary psychology class, students were invited to act as if they were alert, refreshed and having an easy and enjoyable time in the night time class, as they feeling the after work energy drop and fatigue.

What the use of NLP does do in education is to motivate students and teachers alike; the strategies and techniques engage the students' attention; they stimulate interest and help students meet their goals. Behaviour changes have been reported as well by practitioners who use the techniques effectively and embed them in the relevant theory base, in a way that the students can understand, at their different developmental levels.

Dilts, Grinder, Bandler and DeLozier (1980, p. 7) present their model of achievement, based on decision making theory, as a flow chart of limitations, possibilities and goals. That is, there are a number of environmental variables (limitations – dimensions of experience *beyond* a person's control) that may get in the way of outcomes (teachers' and learners' goals) and it is the decision variables (that is the possibilities - the dimensions of experience *within* their control) that will mediate these outcomes.

Aims and Goals

Aims

Making a list of self motivating aims is useful when the aims are longer term and general. Thinking in terms of potential future positive outcomes, and imagining that one day they will be achieved, works well in energising many busy students and teachers.

Goals

Goals are more descriptive and are necessary for the immediate and short term. At the adult level, where people have little time to waste, it is important that they set goals and to do this, they need to know about the importance of setting specific goals in reaching desired outcomes. Robbins (1986) repeats the five NLP rules in formulating such outcomes:

1.   State your outcome in positive terms.
2.   Be as specific as possible.
3.   Have an evidence procedure.
4.   Be in control.
5.   Verify that your outcome is ecologically (holistically) sound and desirable.

Specific learning goals are important in reaching desired educational outcomes, because they draw the initiator to them like a powerful magnet. They need to be specific, concrete and detailed, and postgraduate students, for example in counseling or psychology, can be shown how to put them on their future timeline (see James and Woodsmall, 1988). The teacher elicits all the necessary submodalities (Andreas and Andreas, 1987) of the particular goal activity while the student is there, has them fully associate into how good it feels when the students is doing these actions, and then asks the student to dissociate out of the future time line and come back to now. The goals will then have a power and an energy that draws the person to them. Being dissociated from them in terms of the submodalities is very important, as sometimes being associated misleads the brain into thinking they have already been attained and thus there is no energy "pull" on the goal.

This process may sound very mysterious and complicated and it certainly requires skill and training. Often teachers do not have sufficient time to assist the students in this way, but school counsellors, trained in NLP, can help the student clarify their aims and set their goals.

Further information on modalities and submodalities can be found in Change Your Mind- And Keep the Chang: Advanced NLP Submodalities Interventions (Andreas and Andreas, 1987).

STRATEGIES FOR SCHOOL AND COLLEGE EDUCATION

Modeling (Dilts, Grinder, Bandler and DeLozier, 1980) allows us to "identify patterns in the interaction between human behaviour and the environment, sot that the behaviour of individual human beings can be systematized within the selected context to achieve desired and adaptive outcomes more efficiently, effectively and consistently (p. 3). In other words, it is the process of discovering exactly and specifically what people do in order to produce a specific result (Robbins, 1986). Dilts (1994) defines it positively as "the process of observing and mapping the successful behaviors of other people" (p. 228). We can determine for instance what someone's strategy is for spelling correctly or incorrectly; what their exam panic strategy or how to upgrade the output of a whole class of court reporters.

Eliciting Strategies

The key to eliciting strategies in a person is like the Locksmith Model described by Joseph Barber (1991). One must find the right key to the particular lock. In this case, people will tell you everything you need to know about their strategies (Robbins, 1986). Use their words, body and eye movements. Once you assist a person to fully experience what they are doing, then you can elicit the strategies and note the syntax. Then to make sure you have it right, go through it again with them using the notation – is this right ….you do …… and…… and……? Then you do it yourself using the notation and ask them if this is the correct way to do it.

Anthony Robbins, in his book *Unlimited Power* (p. 130), outlines the full strategy elicitation process and utilizes a series of specific questions which are geared at ascertaining what submodalities are involved and the sequence involved in that strategy. When the lead author was eliciting a student's strategy for an unwanted behavior in our advanced counseling class, the student quickly looked up to the right and was asked what picture she had just seen – this was part of eliciting exactly what she was imagining, but it could not be ascertained just from noting her words. While we are not going to include information on eye movements in this chapter, readers can consult a number of books on NLP, and Kammer's (2003) list is a good place to start in choosing from the vast range of books now available on NLP. Obviously going to the original texts will assist with learning the principles, while other texts may give applications that are additional to those conceived by the pioneers.

We have to understand the mental syntax, physiology and beliefs of the person to understand how they can, for example, become suggestible to behaving like a clown – the lead author experimented with this in an undergraduate hypnosis research class; one part of the class was the group who role played being clowns and the other was the group who role played being hypnotized to be clowns. Even though the latter group were only role playing being hypnotized, they really did take on the whole personae of clowns (and later reported that they had been fully associated into being a clown), while the role playing group reported that they did not fully associate into being a clown and this was consistent with the observance of a more forced and stilted style of clown behavior in the former group.

Firstly let us explore strategies for spelling at the primary and secondary levels and then court reporting at the tertiary level. The evidence for the court reporting is anecdotal, but evaluated by the lead author, while the data for the spelling strategies has been researched, as well as being anecdotal.

Installing Strategies

Spelling seems to have always been a problem for people in general and it really seems difficult to understand why this is a problem learning how to spell. Terry O'Brien's analysis

(1988) considers that it depends on your own theory of learning and language development, and he advocates for experimentation in spelling, such as inventing spelling. Bolstad (1995) has conducted his own reviews of research by Dilts and Epstein (1995) on NLP spelling visualisation strategies claims, and quotes research conducted at the university of Moncton in New Brunswick in Canada in 1985. The key finding here was that looking up to the left (visual recall mode) while learning nonsense words assisted learning, while looking down and to the right (kinaesthetic mode) did not. At the university of Utah, using actual words, researchers found that the same, but better, results occurred, using the visual recall mode. This outpaced other strategies.

So what are the practical tools that NLP claims it can bring to spelling woes? Blackerby (2005) suggests ways of analysing what happens with spelling problems, because the visual and phonetic methods can be in conflict. He gives the following five points of an NLP spelling strategy, which he has found to be effective. Firstly though, we would advise the student to look externally at the word on a page or board, and then to go through the following steps. Any words added in brackets have been added by the authors:

1. Get a clear internal image of the word broken down into syllables. (Keep checking with the original external word until you do.)
2. (Keeping the internal image in mind), spell the word backwards – from right to left.
3. While looking at the internal image of the word, pronounce it syllable by syllable.
4. Now spell the word (as seen in the internal image) from left to right.
5. To drop the spelling word into long term memory, practise step four 6-8 times over several days.

Blackerby advises that the student has to spell the word backwards in step two, so the teacher will know if the student has a good internal image, as no-one can spell a word backwards, unless they have an internal picture clearly outlined in their mind. According to Blackerby, step three sets up the retrieval system, so that the brain will bring up the image when the word is heard. The authors would suggest that the strategy and steps may vary depending on the preferences of each student and what works best for them.

In many books and training workshops on NLP, spelling is used as an example of what NLP techniques can do to change something that is a problem through what seems like a simple technique. However, the relationship of modeling to NLP is through this mechanism of understanding and enacting the precise sensory processing actions at the right time; for example in spelling, we must first understand the key steps in the strategy – and utilizing the NLP script (Grinder and Bandler, 1976) we have:

Ve/Vi – Aid – Vi/Ve – Vi – K+.

The shorthand notations used to represent various sensory modes is quite simple. There are the sensory modalities represented by V (visual), A (auditory), K (kinesthetic), O (olfactory) G (gustatory) and then Aid (internal dialogue). Access can be either via external (e) or internal (i) modes.

Then there are the arrows which represent the direction of the movement from one thought/action to the next. A line is placed underneath the formula when a feedback loop occurs at different phases of the strategy. That is, sometimes the person alters aspects of different strategies to achieve the desired result. Dilts (1994, p. 206) refers to this whole process as the T.O.T.E. model - the letters stand for Test-Operate-Test- Exit and came originally from the work of Miller, Galanter and Pribram (1960).

The T.O.T.E. model appears to be complex on first approach, but once demonstrated a couple of times, it holds potential keys to improving student learning strategies, firstly by determining how they are doing something (*eliciting*) that is not meeting their goals and those of the education system and then designing or transferring to a proven way of doing a task or action (*installing*) that will assist in meeting those goals.

Eliciting and Installing Best Practice Court Reporting Skills

NLP presupposes that we all share the same neurology (except in relation to handedness and then that is a different situation) and that if we can work out a strategy for one person, or a group of people, about a particular behavior, such as what the best court reporter does, then we can teach that best practice to other court reporter students.

In this example at a tertiary education level, an NLP consultant was brought in to improve the speed and accuracy of the graduates of court reporting stenographers. The expected outcome was to identify the court reporting strategy which represented best practice for that teaching institution and under the profession of court reporters.

After an hour of strategy elicitation, performed by a skilled NLP practitioner, and the installation of the most successful strategy for all students, we succeeded in having the students in one of our classes at a technical college all look horizontally to the left (for more information about eye movements, see Bandler and Grinder [1979] and Kammer's [2003] list) to remember the words the witnesses had said, where before they could not recall what the words on the dictaphone (used for practice sessions) had been and had had to continually stop the tape and rewind to listen again to the word. In the courtroom, however, there is only one chance to capture the testimony and then the words are gone forever, without access to other audio taping facilities. Thus installing effective court reporting strategies is critical for forensic settings. So let us analyse this process further.

After ascertaining from the class what several members did and what their normal output was, several strategies were proposed to the class and demonstrations given to show the outcome for the whole class of those chosen strategies. The best strategy was as follows:

The student places her fingers over the keys in a particular manner (Ke), listens to the tape recorder (Ae), points her eyes to the left (Ai) as she recalls what is said immediately after it has been said, and types (Ke). At this point, she registers fast internal feedback, if the spelling is correct by checking the external printed word with the internal visually generated word (Vi/Ve), and if it matches exactly, exits with an "okay" feeling (K+).

$$Ke \rightarrow Ae/Ai \rightarrow Ke \rightarrow Vi/Ve \rightarrow K+$$

This process is very fast and there can be no hesitation on the part of the typist. If there is a mistake (see notation with feedback loop below), the typist must change this later or make a note, but not while she is typing, or she will miss the next lot of information from the witness (in this case, on the tape for classroom purposes).

$$Ke \rightarrow Ae/Ai \rightarrow Ke \rightarrow Vi/Ve \rightarrow K\text{-}/\text{+}$$
$$\uparrow \downarrow$$
$$\leftarrow\leftarrow\leftarrow\leftarrow\leftarrow\leftarrow$$
Feedback

NLP TECHNIQUES FOR STUDENTS AND TEACHERS

This section will give a wide range of examples of how NLP can enhance the learning settings for both schools and teacher training environments.

Techniques for Primary and Secondary School Students

NLP is a tool that might successfully be applied by primary and secondary school personnel in three ways, (i) behaviour management, (ii) relationship building, and (iii) self esteem enhancement.

In schools, NLP techniques can effect behaviour change in students, build rapport, enhance children's self esteem and assist children with learning difficulties. In the section on schools we cover techniques such as: creating positive expectancy; using the principle of successive approximation; utilising the double bind principle, making use of contingency suggestions; incorporating truisms; creating yes sets; adopting the carrot principle; and focusing attention and repeating suggestions.

Starting a session in an interesting and captivating way is important for NLP communicators. Educators might also provide some initial statement to create a sense of curiosity as to what might happen at the end of the lesson or unit. This 'opening grabber or motivator' (Onosko and Jorgensen, 1998, p. 78) aims to motivate students and to sustain their interest throughout the lesson or unit. NLP therapists might also provide the same suggestion or instruction throughout a single session with a client, in a variety of ways, including direct verbal suggestions, the use of synonymous words and phrases, and through metaphors. Similarly, teachers might also provide the same instruction or message in a multitude of ways over the course of a lesson. Such strategies are useful for maintaining clearly defined and positive classrooms, as is behavior management.

Behaviour Management

While a whole school approach to discipline and welfare is generally advocated as the most effective way of ensuring a positive school environment, Conway (2002) points out that the interactions between students and teacher are the most stressful for teachers. The teacher's behaviour, his or her expectation of students and the type of language employed is critical in these interactions, and there are various instances in this area in which NLP techniques might be successfully applied.

An overarching principle of NLP is positive expectancy and this might be applied by school personnel in the way they convey directions. For example, rather than use words such as 'perhaps,' 'maybe,' 'can,' or 'might' such as 'perhaps, you could listen to your teachers and this might make your homework easier to understand' teachers could say instead, 'when you listen to your teachers, you will find that your homework is easier to understand'. Similarly, instructions need to be phrased as directives rather than requests, so rather than say to a child, 'Could you please put your bag away?' (which implies the student has a choice) a teacher needs to say 'Put your bag away, thanks'. The expectation that a desired and positive result will occur is an important principle in NLP, and one that can be readily and successfully employed in the classroom.

Similarly, NLP suggestions are usually directed towards enhancing the positive, rather than eliminating the negative. Taking advice from other professions, in this case, the counselling profession, rather than use the words 'heavy' or 'weight' when working with an overweight client, O'Leary (1985), for example, would instead focus on the attractiveness of being slim, or the benefits of exercise. Consequently, school personnel might focus on the positive outcomes of the child reaching his or her goal and clearly articulate this to the child, rather than the various obstacles he or she might encounter along the way (e.g., passing an important exam and gaining entry into university, rather than the problems the student might encounter while studying).

While NLP therapists convey confidence that a client will change, at the same time they will often express permissiveness concerning when such a change might occur. For example, when instructing a client to do something, a therapist might not expect this desired result immediately, but instead suggest that it will occur at an ambiguous time in the future, '... sooner or later...' or '...sometimes in the next week, I'm not sure exactly when...' thereby conveying confidence, but without being overly prescriptive. Similarly, school personnel might also imply that at some time (maybe now, maybe later) the student will achieve an established goal. 'First you will notice that you can do some of the four times table and you will notice that some of them, like two times four and ten times four, are easy, and then you will notice that others are also easy, like eleven times four, and one times four. And then, soon after, you will be able to do all of the four times table'.

The double bind (Gilligan, 1987) is another, albeit indirect, method employed by psychologists toward behaviour change. The double bind provides the client with a choice between two or more alternatives regarding the targeted behaviour, while at the same time creating a bind so that not changing in the desired direction is not an option. For example, a psychologist might ask a client who aims to lose weight: 'Are you going to lose weight quickly, or gradually?' In this example, it is assumed that the client will lose weight; it is only a question of how. Accordingly, a school counsellor might say to a child: 'You can make big changes in this problem, or medium changes, or little changes. There are so many kinds of changes.' A teacher might ask a student walking around the classroom: 'Are you going to sit on your chair, or on the floor?' Thus while providing the child with choice, the teacher nonetheless implies that walking around the classroom is not an option.

Another indirect strategy is the contingency suggestion, whereby the counseller connects a suggestion to an ongoing or inevitable behaviour (Hammond, 1990). For example, a counsellor might say to an anxious client, 'When you start talking, you will feel more relaxed'. Here, the client's expected verbal behaviour when meeting with a counsellor (that is, talking) is linked or chained to the desired behaviour, that is, feeling relaxed. In the same way, a teacher might say to a student, 'When you sit down at your desk, you will take out your book and start reading'. Here, the teacher identifies a behaviour the student currently engages in, and then chains this behaviour to the desired behaviour.

and indirect suggestions might both be made to great effect with clients (Hammond, 1984). An example of a direct suggestion that school personnel might apply are truisms, which consist of fact-orientated statements given to a client that cannot be denied or refuted. Truisms often start with 'Most people...' 'Everyone...' 'You already know...' 'Most of the us...' (Hammond, 1990, p. 29). Although true, truisms are effective because of what is not defined by the given facts (Otani, 1989). For instance, a therapist might say to a client, 'You don't want to lose weight suddenly.' The implicit message here is that the client does, however, want to lose weight, although slowly. Oldridge (1982) adds that truisms are more effective when made by an authority figure.

To create a truism, Otani (1989) suggests to first identify the definite facts relevant to the person and then to qualify the information in terms of time, extent and/or frequency. Applying this to the educational context, a teacher might say to a loud and boisterous student, 'Like everyone, you do need to be noisy sometimes', implying that there will be also be times when the student will not need to be noisy; subsequent discussions might also focus on when and how it might be appropriate for the student to be noisy.

Similar to truisms, another NLP technique routinely employed is the 'yes set'. This involves a series of comments made to the person that are factual, and serve to encourage the person's mind-set to accept subsequent suggestions. Teachers and school counsellors might also apply the yes-set procedure when attempting to effect behavioural change, for example, a teacher might ask the child a series of factual statements and other yes generating questions such as 'is it getting hot outside?' 'did your mother drop you off at school today?', 'are you sitting with Tom?' and so on. The series of 'yes' questions encourages the child to consider the next set of questions which focus directly on the target behaviour, such as 'do you need to work on how you manage your anger?', or 'do you think you need to be quieter when the teacher talks in class?'

The behavioural concept of providing a reward or positive reinforcement is extended in NLP language, by linking a person's goals with specific suggestions and instructions. For example, rather than use the word, 'if', which implies possible failure, a school counsellor might say, 'When ... (the desired behaviour) then (reward)'. This not only provides the client with an incentive towards specific goals, but also implies that the desired result will happen, it is just a matter of when. Accordingly, rather than say to a student 'If you work hard today, you will receive computer time', it is preferable for the teacher to say 'When you complete the worksheet, you will have some free time on the computer'.

Relationship Building

The importance of establishing warm and trusting relationships with children is widely acknowledged in therapeutic and teaching environments. Here again, various NLP strategies might be successfully applied to the educational context.

When talking to clients, effective NLP practitioners often pace their instructions to reflect what the client is currently doing. For instance, while the practitioner might ask a client to 'breathe in and out... in and out', his or her instructions will be matched to the actual breath of the client. While the instruction might initially be adjusted to the client's rate of response, suggestions might then be introduced to accelerate or slow down the speed of the response, according to the desired therapeutic aim, (what Hammond (1990) terms as 'leading' the client).

Similarly, many business communicators will reflect the idiosyncratic syntax and style of their clients' verbalisations, as well as his or her prominent processing channel, that is, visual, auditory and/or kinaesthetic; again these might be employed by teachers, in terms of the type of directions and the teaching processes employed. For example, kinaesthetic learners might be encouraged to hold a book, or move round while studying, while predominately visual learners are invited to organise their learning material into drawings, charts and symbols. Identifying and employing the way in which a child understands his or her world is an important way to 'work with', rather than 'on', the student and subsequently build a trusting, learning relationship.

Another important NLP technique, sourced from Milton Erickson's work (Zeig, 1985), is to listen carefully to what each client has to say, and to regard each client as an individual rather than a representative of a group (as some might stereotype certain groups of students or clients). To this end, Erickson (as cited in Zeig, 1985) strongly urged counsellors to listen to both explicit and implicit messages from clients, 'I listen to the meaningfulness of what [clients] describe... And too many people listen to the problem and they don't hear what the [client] *isn't* saying...' (Zeig 1985, pp.125-126, emphasis in the original).

Referring to Erickson, Otani (1989) suggests that there are three factors that need to be considered to understand a person's implicit and explicit messages: (1) content (what the client verbally expresses); (2) style of expression (how the client expresses him or herself, verbally and nonverbally); and (3) meaning (the underlying message). While explicit messages come from content, implicit messages are often conveyed in the style of expression and meaning (Zeig, 1980). This means that teachers and school counsellors need to listen to what children say, as well as what they don't say, and a child's non verbal and paralinguistic cues, for effective teaching relationships to be established.

Enhancing Self Esteem

As outlined in the earlier part of this chapter, the principle of positive expectancy encourages students to behave and achieve according to the expectations of others. Whilst important for all children, it is particularly important for children with learning difficulties. Such students may need to see themselves differently and believe that they have the potential to become competent readers or students, before effective change can occur. To this end, O'Leary (1985) advocates the use of creativity and play, as sourced from the general imagery and suggestion of NLP, with the aim of stimulating a child's optimism and resiliency. Pretending to be someone else, for instance, might help create this mindset. Describing a child with physical disabilities, O'Leary (1985, p. 32) writes:

As a princess, Gwen is not thinking about what she cannot or does not want to do. Freed from this conflict, her muscles are more responsive and hidden problems solving skills are stimulated. What the Princess learned is retained by the little girl.

O'Leary (1985) argues that such an approach does not constitute an attempt at 'positive thinking' or forced cheerfulness, but gives the possibly of self re-conceptualisation. The power of suggestion and role playing helped this student overcome her physical limitations and negativity, and instead enhanced her perception of her capabilities.

In one of the few research studies in this area, Oldridge (1982) investigated the use of hypnotic like instructions, without the process of inducing trance, for enhancing children's self esteem and reading ability. Three groups of remedial readers were compared; one group received hypnotic suggestions designed to reduce anxiety and build self confidence, another group received the same suggestions but without inducing trance (non-hypnosis group), and the last group received neither suggestion nor hypnosis (control). The study was conducted for six weeks during which time all children received a remedial reading course. Oldridge (1982) found both experimental groups scored significantly higher on several self esteem and reading achievement scores than the control group, demonstrating the efficacy of teachers using a variety of non-hypnotic like suggestions.

TECHNIQUES FOR TRAINING TEACHERS

Interestingly enough, these NLP techniques also seemed to translate across cultures. In teaching (via an interpreter) newly graduated technical teachers in Vietnam (from three different vocational colleges) how to engage the interest of their students more, Gow (2000) used certain aspects of what she had been taught in NLP training programs and that had proven effective at the tertiary level in Australia.

Together with a colleague from the oil industry and a registered nurse, she explained that it was important to make explicit why they, as new technical teachers, should engage the interest of their students and how they could better explain to the students why they should attend lectures and understand the content material.

Models of Learning

Utilising the 4MAT model (attributed to McCarthy, 1979) - why, what, how, what if - she explained why it was necessary for the teachers to outline first the content of the overall plan for that session, or for the whole of the program if it were the first session, and then to scale down to the content of the particular session, or the particular lecture on that day; that is, they had to give them a brief overview of what was to happen, in order of it happening. While Gow was training them in how to do this, she was also modelling the process during the training session with the technical teachers themselves.

This then led into discussion of the next parts of the 4MAT model (McCarthy, 1979), in terms of the 'what' and 'how'. As many people like to know what is to follow and in what particular order, it is also important to give an idea of how the teaching and learning process is going to proceed in that particular session. The newly graduated teachers were told that this process would assist the students in formulating and structuring in their minds how they might then categorise and store the information, as each person's learning style and preferred ways of storing and retrieving information was different. Reference was made to classifying information into the correct categories for correct semantic sense and recall purposes (Hirsch, 1988), and examples of categories of fish, rice and motorbikes were given, along with the classifications of food and transport. Classifying correctly the members of the class of fish, for instance, was explored in small group discussions.

[Later in the day again the role of the classification of information so that it could be stored in, and retrieved from, memory systems, was raised. It was emphasised in learning new information that sometimes people try to retrieve information from the wrong classification system in the memory banks; for instance, if they have misclassified the word power under the classification of energy, then it will be correct if the context is about electricity or gas, but not if it is about influence over other people or physical and personal power.] This example was given, as the province had just entered into experimenting with new forms of power and off shore gas operations had commenced with great sound and visual effects testifying to its emergence. The focus on theories of learning continued.

Bateson (1972; 1979), an anthropologist and scientist, said that every individual acts as a personal scientist, as they strive to make sense of their everyday world and we collect data/information to solve problems every day of our lives. Relevant theory was given along the way. Earlier George Kelly (1955) had expressed the view that each individual could be conceived as a scientist exploring and testing their world, and later Gordon (1978) also pointed out that every individual develops his or her own model of the world - it is the sum total of our experience in life and thus is unique and we are all different.
For example, we may all see the world quite differently, and particularly so across cultures. In the novel "The Ice Child", Elizabeth McGregor (1997) gives her readers a great amount of interesting information about snow and ice. It is said that the Eskimos have at least 18 different words for snow, leading to a great richness in the elaboration of an object or experience for the culture. If a person is Vietnamese, then one may use a personal pronoun depending on the relationships between the two people and that changes with each person you speak to - anh, ong, co, ba, chi, em. So cultures vary in their experiences and so do females and males, who understand the world differently – we need to observe and listen intently and to keep an open mind to be flexible to communicate successfully across cultures.

All of these teachers were learning English because they had realised its importance in the international markets and its role in the internet. An example of the importance of being culturally literate can be drawn from Hirsch (1988) who points to the fact that The Black Panther newspaper, which was radical in its causes, but conservative in its journalism, could never have campaigned for changes to legislation, if they had not learned, not just the formal language of English, but also the USA's linguistic expressions that are like a code to those born in other countries and to those whose native language is not English. (This is true of all languages within cultures). Hisrch gives the example of the cultural differences also within those who use English as their country's language (e.g., between the USA and Australia) and refers to the song Waltzing Matilda and says that while American could read the words, they would not understand what a billabong or a swagman was. This story leads into more discussion on nuances in language, especially where students in class were from different cultures.

A well known theory in education is that of Kolb's (1984) learning processes (action, observation, generalisation, change; or concrete experience, reflective observation, abstract conceptualization; active experimental). The 'how' of learning was thus enacted and underscored by the trainer at the end of the exercise.

The utilisation of the theory of the Kolb model of learning is an important one, as it demonstrates the various stages of learning, where one can commence with a discussion of theory, such as writing notes in chalk on the blackboard before the class moves into the electrical workshop. Then the student goes on to the practice and trialling of the ideas through action, such as assembling a switchboard over time, and after they have been given feedback, or indeed have used their own internal and external feedback mechanisms to tell them they are on the right track, they reflect on the process before they are able to take the correct action. Once again, then they are able to test that action and go back and obtain more feedback and then try again, that is, take more action until the process is fully learned with a positive outcome.

The 'what if' quadrant on the 4MAT model was investigated (and later modelled that afternoon with the teachers) so that at the end of the lecture, the teachers understood why it was important to generalise wider than the particular learned focus of their teaching session, in order for the students to generalise this specific learning to their own lives, to the world in which they work, socialise, and study, and to the international world at large in some cases.

Communication Models

Most often the communication model (Gray and Starke [1984, pp. 304-308] outline this in detail) comes up for discussion early in many training programs, as communication is always considered to be key problem in organisational issues. The basic communication model simply outlines the four components of the message transmission in terms of sender, message and receiver, via a selected medium. The role of encoding and decoding the message together with the ways in which interference can occur is always stimulating for class discussions as students and teachers alike understand this model. The feedback loop is explored and many examples from school, work, family, society and sport and television shows can be demonstrated and discussed. Where interpreters are involved, the diagramatic explanations are more complicated and the whole issue of beliefs, values, perceptions and stereotypes need to be explained in terms of communication across cultures, genders and age groups.

Sensory Information Channels

It is useful to explain to students and trainees that we are quite reliant on our five senses in terms of learning and that when we were first at school, we knew all about our senses – seeing, hearing, smelling, tasting and touching. It is important for teachers and trainers to understand this fact in terms of delivering content and programs in education and training. Generally once the trainees understand that the NLP term information processing channels (visual auditory kinaesthetic olfactory and gustatory) is simply about how they access and process information about the world both externally and internally, the training room becomes a hum of activity.

Examples are given of words and expressions, and it is explained that while many people do not talk about the olfactory and gustatory channels a great deal, it was explained that some people have jobs as wine tasters or perfume testers, where these two senses are critical to the success of the industry. These senses are useful at work because technicians need to be able to detect burning smells, and nurses need to be able to smell putrification as do fishmongers. Some people do have very strong taste and smell channels that they use in communication and interactions with other people as a normal part of their conversations.

It was then reiterated that the important point here is that students prefer to receive information through their own preferred information processing channel, and this means that as teachers we need to use all three main channels while teaching, even though you personally may have a preference for just one or two of these channels yourselves. Examples in English and Vietnamese were given.

The role of nonverbal communication and body language in teaching was also presented to the teachers in the form of a series of basic communication model flowcharts, and examples pertinent to Vietnamese culture were demonstrated. The feedback loop made sense to the technical teachers whose education had been in engineering. Because of modern technology, the interpretation of digital communication brings with it a whole new language, and examples from computing, engineering and tourism and hospitality were discussed in small groups. Thus the role of the secondary information processing mechanism, known in NLP as auditory digital, was raised and its pre-eminence in computer and internet technology use explored.

Trial and Error: Real Practice

A banner with Robert Allen's famous quote: 'There is no failure, only feedback' was unfurled for discussion next. This approach, advocated by Robbins (1992) is advisable when working with trainee technical students, but the dangers of uninformed and unsupervised experiments was stressed as electrical and mechanical accidents could occur. It is also important to be able to support that statement and to make sure that not only yourself, but the wider education system and also the working environment in which the graduate may operate, will actually honour that premise and not punish people as they make mistakes. Thus it is desirable to explain to the learner that not everyone may have this view and it wise to take a commonsense approach as to when to experiment and to try new things, and to obtain permission in the world of work, when they are not certain.

Typical examples of how we learned to do things as children and were enthusiastic about trying to learn most new skills, unless someone was ridiculing us, were given: riding a bike, kicking a ball, climbing a tree, tying shoelaces, or using chopsticks. The group was able to explore what happens to children and adults when parents, teachers and others, instil in the child a fear of making mistakes, as there are consequences to making mistakes. The example of the Japanese and Americans learning to play golf was given as an example of an adult learning to hit the ball. You must hit the ball and see where it lands, and hit again and see where it lands and putt it on the green and see if it goes into the hole or not. So you have to deliberately experiment to make errors in order to know how do it correctly -- there is no other way! So this is how most of the new skills that students need to learn in vocational education and in the workplace are learned. If we are fortunate, a skilled worker demonstrates what to do, then we try to do it the same way. We experiment, we try to do something, it fails; we try again, it fails; and we keep exploring other ways to solve the problem in our lives, in our families, in our jobs, and in our universe.

Whilst teaching the vocational teachers in the Long Dat Technical College, the technique made famous by Milton Erickson (Rosen, 1982): "My friend John "which was actually "My friend Ahn" in the Vietnamese culture was introduced to assist them with their lack of experience and thus credibility. It was explained to the young teachers that they could tell the students about the vocational experiences of their father, brothers, uncles, neighbours and friends, if they, themselves, did not have that life experience yet. They could also draw on stories and examples about famous people in the literature, or folklore, the live theatre, movies or television.

By the end of the day, about 30 charts decorated every wall in the hall, and had been colourfully translated into Vietnamese. Later feedback on the course suggested that the whole approach had been empowering for both new and experienced teachers, and that they became motivated to trial new ways of teaching and learning processes, even though they had few resources and little, if any educational materials to assist them in their endeavours. The program led to the Principal and then several teachers coming to Queensland and consulting with several Technical and Further Education colleges and engineering departments in universities.

SUMMARY AND CONCLUSION

Although limited research has been undertaken in the use of NLP principles in educational settings, it has been argued here that a range of NLP theory, strategies and techniques might be useful in improving the outcomes of teaching and learning and specifically with behaviour management, when building relationships with students, and for enhancing children's self esteem and confidence. While research is required to support the efficacy of such techniques, teachers and school and university counsellors might nonetheless find these techniques useful when working with students in educational settings. Additionally, the use of NLP theory and its tools serve as excellent motivating strategies for teachers whose energy and commitment is low and is in need of a recharge.

REFERENCES

Andreas, S. and Andreas, C. (1987). *Change Your Mind-And Keep the Change: Advanced NLP Submodalities Interventions.* Moab, Utah: Real People Press.
Bandler, R. and Grinder, J. (1975). *Patterns of the Hypnotic Techniques of Milton H. Erickson, M.D.,* Vol. I. Cupertino, California: Meta Publications.
Bandler, R. and Grinder, J. (1979). *Frogs into princes.* Moab, Utah: Real People Press.

Barber, J. (1991). The Locksmith Model: Accessing Hypnotic Responsiveness. In S.J. Lynn and J.W. Rhue, (Eds.) *Theories of Hypnosis: Current models and perspectives* (pp. 241-274). London: Guilford Press.

Bateson, G. (1972). *Steps to an ecology of mind.* NY: Ballantine Books.

Bateson, G. (1979). *Mind and Nature.* Valentine Books.

Blackerby, D.A. (1996). Rediscover the Joy of Learning. Oklahoma City, OK: Success Skills.

Blackerby, D.A. (2005). NLP in Education – A Magnificent Opportunity. *http://www.positivehealth.com/permit/Articles/NLP/black39.htm accessed 14.03.05*

Bolstad, R. (1995). Research on Neuro Linguistic Programming: A summary. *http://www.nlpschedule.com/random/research-summary.html*

Conway, R. (2002). Behaviour in and out of the classroom, In A. Ashman and J. Elkins (Eds.) *Educating children with diverse abilities* (pp. 172-236). Frenchs Forest: Prentice Hall.

Dilts, R., and Epstein, T. (1995). *Dynamic Learning.* Capitola, CA: Meta Publications.

Dilts, R.B. (1983). *Roots of Neuro-linguistic programming.* Cupertino, CA: Meta Publications.

Dilts, R.B. (1994). *Strategies of Genius.* Vol II: Albert Einstein. Capitola, California: Meta Publications.

Dilts, R., Grinder, J., Bandler, R., and DeLozier, J. (1980). *Neuro-Linguistic Programming: Vol 1.* Cupertino, CA: Meta Publications.

Galan, M. and Maguire, T. (2001). Education and Beliefs, The weekly column. November Article 79. *www.eltnewsletter.com/back/November2001/art792001.htm*

Gilligan, S.G. (1987). *Therapeutic Trances: The cooperation principle in Ericksonian hypnotherapy.* NY: Brunner Mazel.

Gordon, D. (1978). *Therapeutic metaphors: Helping others through the looking glass.* Cupertino, CA: Meta Publications.

Gow, K. (2000). The Science of Effective Teaching with Adult Learners. Paper presented at the *TEDI Conference: Effective Teaching and Learning at University*, 10th November. Brisbane: University of Queensland.

Gray, J.L., and Starke, F.A. (1984). *Organizational Behavior: Concepts and applications.* (3d ed.) Columbus, Ohio: Charles E. Merrill.

Grinder, M. (1991). *Righting the Educational Conveyor Belt.* Portland, OR: Metamorphous Press.

Grinder, J. and Bandler, R. (1975). *The Structure of Magic:* Volume II. Palo Alto, CA: Science and Behavior Books.

Hammond, D.C. (1984). Myths about Erickson and Ericksonian hypnosis. *American Journal of Clinical Hypnosis*, 26, 236-245.

Hammond, D.C. (Ed.) (1990). *Handbook of hypnotic suggestions and metaphors.* New York: W.W. Norton.

Hirsh, E.D. (Jr.) (1988). *Cultural Literacy; what every American needs to know.* NY: Random House.

James, T., and Woodsmall, W. (1988). *Time line therapy and the basis of personality.* Cupertino, California: Meta Publications.

Kammer, D. (2003). Neuro-Linguistic Programming Research Data Base. Accessed 14.04.05. *http://www.nlp.de/cgi-bin/reseach/nlp-rdb.cgi*

Kelly, G. (1955). *The psychology of personal constructs.* NY: Norton and Co.

Kolb, D. A. (1984). *Experiential Learning,* Englewood Cliffs, NJ.: Prentice Hall.

McCarthy, B. (1979). *4MAT in Action: Creative Lesson Plans for Teaching to Learning Styles with Right/Left Mode Techniques*

McClendon, T. (1989). *The wild days.* Cupertino, California: Meta Publications.

McGregor, E. (1997). *The Ice Child.* USA: Penguin.

Meehan, P. (2005). Accounting For Style. How an understanding of individual learning styles can pay dividends in class. *http://www.tefl.net/esl-articles/learning-styles.htm*

Miller, G.A., Galanter, E., and Pribram, K.H. (1960). *Plans and the Structure of Behavior.* New York: Holt, Rinehart and Winston.

O'Brien, T. (1988). Spelling analysis: it all depends upon your theory of learning and language development. In D. Plumber, (Ed.) *Planning for thinkers and learner: the early years* (pp. 70 – 80). Melbourne: Australian Reading Association.

O'Leary, C. J. (1985). Thinking like a hypnotist. *The Exceptional Parent,* 31-33.

Oldridge, O.A. (1982). Positive suggestion: It helps LD students learn. *Academic therapy* 17(3), 279-287.

Onosko, J.J., and Jorgensen, C.M. (1998). Unit and lesson planning in the inclusive classroom: Maximizing learning opportunities for all students. In C.M. Jorgensen, (Ed.), *Restructuring high schools for all students. Taking inclusion to the next level* (pp. 71-105). Baltimore: Paul H. Brooks.

Ontani, A. (1989). Integrating Milton H. Erikson's hypnotherapeutic techniques into general counseling and psychotherapy. *Journal of Counseling and Development*, 68, 203-207.

Robbins, A. (1986). *Unlimited Power.* NY: Simon and Schuster.

Robbins, A. (1992). *Awaken the giant within.* NY: Simon and Schuster.

Rosen, S. (Ed.). (1982). *My voice will go with you: The teaching tales of Milton H. Erickson.* NY: Norton.

Rosenthal, R., and Jacobsen, L. (1968). *Pygmalion in the classroom: Teacher expectation and pupil's intellectual development.* New York: Holt, Rinehart and Winston.

Rotter, J.B. (1966). Generalized expectancies for internal versus external control of reinforcement. *Psychological Monographs*, 80, (Whole No. 509).

Tauber, R. (1998). Good or bad, what teachers expect from students they generally get! *ERIC Digest.* Washington, DC: ERIC Clearinghouse on Teaching and Teacher Education, ED426985.

Witkin, H.A., Moore, C., Goodenough, D. and Cox, P. (1977a). Field Dependent and Field Independent Cognitive Styles and their Educational Implications. *Review of Educational Research*, 47, 1-64.

Witkin, H.A., Oltman, P., Goodenough, D., Friedman, F., Owen, D. and Raskin, E. (1977b). Role of Field Dependent and Field Independent Cognitive Styles in Academic Evolution: a longitudinal study. *Journal of Educational Psychology*, 69, 197-211.

Zeig, J.K. (Ed.) (1980). *A teaching seminar with Milton H. Erickson.* New York: Brunner/Mazel.

Zeig, J.K. (1985). *Experiencing Erickson: An introduction to the man and his work.* New York: Brunner/Mazel.

Zhang, L. F. (2002). Thinking styles and modes of thinking: implications for education and research. *J Psychol.,* 136(3), 245-61.

In: Trends in Learning Reserch
Editor: Samuel N. Hogan, pp. 119-138

ISBN 1-59454-965-6
© 2006 Nova Science Publishers, Inc.

Chapter 6

COLLABORATIVE LEARNING THROUGH ARGUMENT VISUALISATION IN SECONDARY SCHOOL[*]

Miika Marttunen and Leena Laurinen
Department of Education, University of Jyväskylä
Finland

ABSTRACT

The solving of ill-structured problems, commonly related to societal and educational questions, can be facilitated by a visual depiction of the variety of viewpoints relevant to the problem in hand, and the arguments used to support different solutions. Constructing argument diagrams is one way to visualise argumentation. Argument visualisation refers to graphical or other non-verbal means of making reasoning chains and conclusions explicit.

In this study 7 male and 10 female Finnish secondary school students were assigned the task of constructing and elaborating an argument diagram on the issue of genetically modified organisms (GMO). The task proceeded in three successive phases using a network-based diagram tool. The students constructed their first diagram on the basis of their previous knowledge of GMO, modified it after having read three articles on the theme, and finalised the diagram after they had engaged in a dyadic chat debate on the same theme. The diagrams were analysed for shape and content.

The students' final diagrams showed the largest number of argument boxes, the broadest and longest chains of argument, and the greatest number of topics relevant to the theme. The most evident change was observed after the students had read three articles on the topic. Thus the students deepened and broadened their knowledge on the theme during the course. It was concluded that by means of alternate phases of reading, discussion and reflection secondary school students' knowledge and thinking can be elaborated, thereby fostering their learning.

---

[*] The research reported here was carried out within the SCALE project (Internet-based intelligent tool to Support Collaborative Argumentation-based LEarning in secondary schools, March 2001 - February 2004) funded by the European Community.

INTRODUCTION

Argumentation means the putting forward of relevant and sufficient arguments in favour of one's views and opinions. Argumentation can be considered sufficient when the claims made have been adequately supported from several perspectives. Argumentation is relevant when the arguments presented are related to a claim in a meaningful way. Thus, relevance refers to the relation between a claim and an argument, not to their respective quality (Hitchcock, 1992).

A person skilled in argumentation is able to put forward relevant and sufficient arguments in support of his/her claims. Furthermore, s/he is able to warrant arguments and to refute counterarguments presented by other people. An argument is warranted when one has explained why the argument in question should be regarded as appropriate and as a good support for the claim (Toulmin et al., 1984). Counterarguments and refutations of counterarguments are of particular importance in argumentative discussions (van Eemeren, 2001). Counterarguments are used in order to oppose arguments presented by other people. When a person defends his/her arguments against others' counterarguments his/her aim is to show that those counterarguments are invalid and inappropriate.

Argumentation skills play an important role in getting one's voice heard in society. People today are increasingly expected to be able to participate actively in public discussions and to have an influence on political decisions on many, often global, societal issues, such as pollution and the distribution of welfare. Due to the rapid development of information and communication technology today's citizens have available to them many sources of information which can be utilized in modelling their opinions. Experience of argumentative discussion facilitates critical evaluation of information sources in general and the strengths and weaknesses of different items of information in particular.

Argumentation could be a useful means for learning collaboratively with other people. When different viewpoints, arguments and counterarguments are put forward in the course of discussion on particular issues, people may be able to learn about and understand those issues more thoroughly. The aim of collaborative argumentation is not to try to prove that our own thoughts and arguments are right and others' false but, jointly, to deepen and expand knowledge by critically examining issues from various perspectives (see Andriessen, Baker and Suthers, 2003).

One important task of secondary school education is to teach students the knowledge and skills they need to participate successfully in debates around societal questions and to engage in collaborative learning situations. Argumentation should thus play an important role in future school curricula and teaching practices. In a number of countries the teaching of argumentation is commonly included in the mother tongue curriculum (Marttunen, Laurinen, Litosseliti and Lund, 2005), and the teaching methods commonly used relate to reading and writing argumentative texts and to oral argumentative discussions and debates. However, visualising techniques, such as argument diagrams, may also be useful in practising argumentation, particularly in helping students to perceive and make explicit chains and structures of argumentation, and understand how different elements of argumentation relate to each other. This study concerns argumentation visualisation as a method of teaching argumentation in secondary school.

VISUALISATION OF ARGUMENTATION

Visualisation of argumentation refers to making chains of reasoning and arguments relating to claims and conclusions explicit using graphical or other non-verbal techniques (van Gelder, 2003). Visualising arguments can be regarded as an additional way of presenting opinions, and arguments in support of them, along with argumentative writing and argumentative discussions.

One way to visualise argumentation is to construct argument diagrams. By the aid of diagrams a person can effectively illustrate his/her viewpoint on some particular issue, and the arguments s/he wants to use in support of it. Diagrams are also helpful in showing how supporting arguments can be questioned and criticized, and in illustrating the interrelationships between claims, arguments and counterarguments. Making the arguments and counterarguments of different parties visible in a diagram is also useful during argumentative discussions. Argument diagrams have, for example, been found to improve university students' critical thinking (Twardy, 2004), and to help university students (van Boxtel and Veerman, 2001) and secondary school students (van Drie, van Boxtel, Jaspers and Kanselaar, 2005) to balance positively and negatively oriented arguments during discussions. Carr (2003), in turn, investigated computer supported argument visualization in legal education and found that the visualisation tool facilitated student discussion of those aspects in which they particularly disagreed with each other.

People engaging in argument together are not always sure about the factual reason for their disagreement or do not properly recognise the issue that they should, in fact, be discussing in order to reach agreement. Baker and Bielaczyc (1995) state that lack of common focus often hinders people from utilising the great potential argumentative discussions offer, for example, for learning. The use of argument diagrams could assist debaters to focus their discussion and help them collaborate and learn from each other. Fisher, Bruhn, Gräsel and Mandl (2002), for example, found that content-specific visualization based on mapping techniques encouraged university students to focus on the task-relevant content and increased the quality of their collaborative knowledge construction. Respectively, the use of concept maps among high school students has been found to lead to sustained discourse on the topic (Roth and Roychoudhury, 1993) and to elicit elaboration of the issues under discussion (Van Boxtel and Veerman, 2001).

According to van Gelder (2003), the difficulty in interpreting the relations between argumentative elements of a text often results in misunderstanding the writer. When reading argumentative texts the reader has, first, to identify the writer's claims and arguments and, second, to interpret the meaning of those arguments and their interconnections. The reader may, for example, find it difficult to understand unambiguously whether a specific argument is meant to support the main claim or whether it is merely an argument in support of some other argument relating to the main claim. A major benefit of argument diagrams compared to argumentative texts is that diagrams make it easier for the reader to form a general view of the opinions and arguments of the writer (van Gelder, 2003). This also reduces the risk for misunderstandings. Suthers (2003) found that representational guidance, like the use of argument diagrams, helped students to consider argumentative relations. When claims, arguments, and their interrelationships are depicted with the help of a diagram, the reader may also find it easier to focus his/her cognitive resources more appropriately. This means that the reader no longer has to struggle to find relevant information in the text and organise it into a more understandable form, but can concentrate directly on its argumentative content (c.f. van Bruggen and Kirschner, 2003).

ARGUMENTATION IN SOLVING ILL-STRUCTURED PROBLEMS

It is characteristic of ill-structured problems that they are often ambiguous and loosely defined, and that there is no single path to a valid solution. Examples of ill-structured problems are musical composition, design tasks, planning tasks and management tasks (van Bruggen, Boshuizen and Kirschner, 2003). Educational ill-structured problems are, for example, *How does one write a good argumentative text* and *How does one broaden and deepen one's knowledge by means of argumentative debate?* There are several ways of solving both of these problems. These solutions depend on the argumentative skills of persons, their manner and way of putting forward arguments, as well as their knowledge of the issues in question. However, a valid solution to both problems will include similar argumentative elements. A good argumentative text will indicate to the reader the opinion of the writer and the most important arguments the writer adduces in support of his/her opinion. A good text also includes counterarguments and criticism of the writer's own viewpoint. Similarly, during a high level argumentative debate one interlocutor puts forward arguments for his/her own opinions, criticises the other's arguments and defends his/her own opinions by refuting the other's counterarguments.

Cohen (1994) states that problems that do not have any fully predetermined answers, like ill-structured problems, are the most suitable kind for collaborative learning. Solving such problems necessitates negotiation and discussion on different points of view and arguments. Negotiations help participants to understand the issue at hand from different perspectives and promote the attainment of shared understanding of it. Argumentation is needed in negotiations on ill-structured problems: the relevance of the problem as well as the criteria for different optional solutions need to be justified. As van Bruggen and Kirschner (2003) put it, there are no true or false solutions to ill-structured problems, only good or bad ones. Good solutions are also often those that are well justified.

Forming a general view of the different types of arguments relevant to the issue under consideration is helpful in solving ill-structured problems (van Bruggen et al., 2003). This statement is also supported by empirical results. van Gelder (2003) investigated the use of argument visualisation in a company where the employer and staff together searched for the best way to organise their work. In the study visualisation of all the different reasons for and objections to different proposed solutions made it easier for the different parties to find a common solution to the problem. Diagrams have also been found useful in studies of subjects that include structured problem-solving tasks. Larkin and Simon (1987) investigated students' problem-solving in physics and maths and found that information contained in diagrams was easier to interpret than written texts. This also made problem-solving easier.

In spite of the many encouraging results on the pedagogical use of argument diagrams little research has been done on the use of diagrams within carefully designed sequences of pedagogical tasks. One example of this use of argument diagrams is a study by Munneke, van Amelsvoort and Andriessen (2003) in which diagrams were used during collaborative learning tasks where students discussed ill-defined topics. They found that students used diagrams in very different ways, ranging from a means of generating talk to just a notebook. The students also found the construction of diagrams rather difficult, which may also partially explain why their diagrams were not of very high quality. In spite of their low quality the researchers found the diagrams to support students' argumentative discourse. In another study, by Baker, Quignard, Lund and van Amelsvoort (2003), argument graphs were used simultaneously with chat debates to help students to organise and focus their argumentative discussion on the topic of genetically modified organisms. Students who used chat and graph facilities simultaneously were compared with students who used only the chat facility for their discussion. The students wrote an individual argumentative text before the debate, and then modified their text after the debate. The results indicated improvement in the students' quality of argumentation between the first and modified versions of their texts. However, the study did not reveal clear pedagogical benefits from the use of argument graphs together with the chat discussions. More research is needed on the pedagogical support students should be given when they construct argument diagrams during their studies, and on the pedagogical tasks that can best support their collaboration and learning.

This study focuses on constructing and elaborating argument diagrams in a virtual environment in secondary school during three successive tasks. The students were asked a) to design an argument diagram on the basis of their previous knowledge on a particular topic, b) to elaborate the diagram after having read topic-related texts, and c) to finalise the diagram after having discussed the topic together. The development of the students' successive diagrams and their opinions on the use of the diagrams were investigated with the help of the following research questions: (1) How many arguments did the diagrams include? (2) How deep and how broad were the students' diagrams? (3) How many viewpoints on the topic did the diagrams contain? (4) How well did the students differentiate arguments from counterarguments? (5) How clearly was the main claim presented in the diagrams? (6) What were the students' opinions on the use of argument diagrams as a part of their studies?

METHOD

Subjects

The subjects were 7 male and 10 female Finnish secondary school students aged from 16 to 17 years. During the fall term 2003, the students took a six-week course, *The power of language,* which is included in the national curriculum on the mother tongue in Finland. Among the topics covered on this obligatory 30-hour course is the study of argumentation. The argumentation-related course content covered such themes as the use of rhetoric in speech and writing, composition of argumentative texts on the basis of given source materials, and pictorial and textual ways of trying to influence people. Furthermore, during the course, the students practised argumentation with the CABLE (Collaborative Argumentation-Based Learning) internet tools. These tools form a network learning environment in which students can construct argument diagrams individually or collaboratively, engage in chat with each other, and write text together (more information on the tools can be found at: http://www.euroscale.net/). For eight class hours (four double lessons) the students practised argument visualisation by constructing argumentation diagrams with the help of CABLE tools. These lessons are described in more detail below.

Teaching Arrangements

Teaching argumentation with CABLE tools was divided into the following three phases: (1) Learning the basic concepts of argumentation, and training in the use of the tools; (2) Constructing and modifying argument diagrams; and (3) Debate and consolidation of learning.

Learning the Basic Concepts of Argumentation, and Training in the Use of CABLE Tools

The first double lesson (90 minutes) was spent on the theory of argumentation in order to prepare the students for subsequent exercises with the CABLE tools. The students and the teacher discussed together the essence and characteristics of argumentation, the purposes and aims of argumentation, and the difference between argumentation and merely presenting opinions. In addition, the following concepts were defined: thesis, secondary thesis, argument, counterargument, chain of arguments, and the elaboration of arguments. The students were also taught the basic rules for constructing argument diagrams. At the end of the session the students analysed the argumentative structure of a short passage of dialogue and constructed a diagram on the basis of their analysis.

During the second double lesson the students learned how to use the CABLE tools. They were given a self-study pack which advised them how to use the chat area, how to make argument boxes (claims, arguments and counterarguments) and fill them in with meaningful content, and how to add comments and elaborations to arguments by means of commentary boxes. The students also practised how argumentative links between the boxes could be created and labelled with either a plus (argument in favour) or minus (counterargument) sign.

Constructing and Modifying Argument Diagrams

At the beginning of the third double lesson the students constructed an individual argument diagram on the topic *Genetically Modified Organisms* (henceforth GMO). They were given 25 minutes to do the diagram according to the following instructions:

> Think about your own opinion on GMO. Think about the advantages and disadvantages of GMO, and the arguments for and counterarguments against it. Then construct an argument diagram in order to respond to the following question: Should the production of GMO be allowed?

After the students had completed the diagram they were given three articles on GMO. One of the articles was anti GMO (written by Greenpeace), another represented a permissive approach to GMO (on a food biotechnology company, Monsanto), and in the third article the approach (a report on the French ministry of research) was neutral. The students were asked to scan the articles, and to make notes and underline text if they so wished. The task was as follows:

> The following articles deal with GMO from three viewpoints: against, for, and neutral. Through the articles you can obtain a comprehensive understanding of the arguments and counterarguments commonly used to support or oppose the production of GMO. Familiarize yourselves with the articles for 30 minutes. The idea is not to read the articles in close detail but selectively. You will certainly find much in the articles which will help you improve your diagram. While reading the material you may make notes or mark text where issues are touched on that you find important.

After the students had read the articles they were given 35 minutes to further elaborate their individual diagrams. They were allowed to read and screen the articles while modifying their diagrams. The task was the following:

> After you have familiarized yourselves with the articles, improve your diagram on the basis of the information in them and in your notes. You can scan the articles and make use of them when improving your diagram. When modifying your diagram remember to connect the different boxes with argumentative links. Remember also to develop and supplement your arguments and counterarguments with help of the commentary boxes. The purpose of your diagram is to present your answer to the following question: Should the production of GMO be allowed?

Debate and Consolidation of Learning

In the fourth double lesson the students were given paper copies of the diagrams they had prepared in the previous lesson. With reference to their diagrams they were asked to recall their thoughts on GMO before engaging in chat debates. After 10 minutes the diagrams were collected in.

Next, the students engaged in dyadic debates on GMO for 30 minutes. The teacher formed seven dyads and one trio from the students. The teacher tried to form as many mixed gender pairs as possible. She also tried to form pairs with students she knew could work collaboratively. During the session the students discussed freely whether the production of GMO should be allowed or not.

After the debate the students were given 10 minutes to construct an argument diagram in collaboration with their partner. In their diagram the students depicted the most essential claims, arguments, and counterarguments their dyadic debate contained. They were also allowed to add new arguments and counterarguments to their diagram if they wished. After finishing the diagram the students recapitulated their discussion for five minutes. The students talked about what they had learned from the debate and from the co-construction of the diagram, and assessed how well their diagram presented the pros and cons of GMO.

During the next 25 minutes of the lesson the students completed their individual diagrams on GMO. The task was set as follows:

> "Your task is to modify and complete your argument diagram presenting your answer to the question: *Should the production of GMO be allowed?* In completing your diagram

you may utilise the viewpoints and arguments you discussed with your partner. In improving your diagram you may make use of the following suggestions: (1) Improve your diagram with new arguments which either support or criticize the ones that already exist in your diagram; (2) Read through each of your arguments once more and improve and specify their content if needed; (3) Check the argumentative links between different arguments. Check also the points at which you have elaborated your arguments (commentary boxes).

During the last 10 minutes of the lesson the students answered a short questionnaire on the course.

DATA AND ANALYSES

The data in this study consist of 16 diagrams the students constructed individually before reading the articles on GMO, 15 diagrams they elaborated after having read the texts, and 16 diagrams that the students finished after their dyadic debate (not all the 17 students were present in all lessons). The data also includes feedback questionnaires collected from 16 students who were present in the last lesson.

Argument Diagrams

The diagrams were analysed for shape and content (see Séjourné, Baker, Lund and Molinari, 2004). The analyses of shape focussed on the size, breadth, and depth of the diagram, as well as how branched the argumentation was.

The *size* of the diagram was assessed by counting the number of argument boxes and commentary boxes, and *breadth* was assessed by counting the arguments and counterarguments directly linked to the main thesis (e.g. a score of 3 was given for breadth in the diagram shown in Figure 1, 5 in Figure 2, and 6 in Figure 3). In addition to the size and breath of the diagram, another indicator of argumentation quality is the length of argument chains inside the diagram. Chains of arguments are formed by successive arguments and counterarguments. The *depth* of the argument chains inside the diagram was assessed by counting the number of arguments and counterarguments successively linked to each other. For example, the diagram in Figure 2 shows three argument chains. The depth of the two shorter chains was scored 2, and the longest chain was scored 4.

Furthermore, when arguments and counterarguments branch out from the main thesis so that they too form argument chains, they have the status of a secondary thesis. A secondary thesis thus refers to all the new arguments and counterarguments that are supported by one or more arguments or opposed by one or more counterarguments. The *branches* of the diagram were assessed by counting the number of secondary theses linked to more than one argument or counterargument. Figure 2, for example, shows two secondary theses linked to more than one argument or counterargument (Through genetic modification...; According to research...). Thus, the diagram scored 2 for the variable "Branches of arguments".

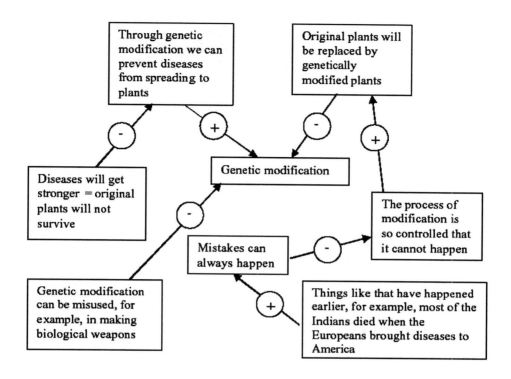

Figure 1. An argument diagram constructed before the texts were read (Matti)

Figures 1, 2 and 3 do not show any commentary boxes as these became visible only when the cursor was moved onto the argument box. The student was thus able to see only one commentary box at any one time. The content of the commentary boxes of diagrams 2 and 3 are presented in Table 2 in the results section (the diagram in Figure 1 did not contain any commentary boxes).

The content of the diagrams was analysed, first, by focussing on the *topics of the arguments and counterarguments* for and against GMO. Figure 1, for example, shows two topics: protection of plants, and biological warfare. In Figure 2 the number of topics has increased up to five: protection of plants, environmental diversity (Original plants will be replaced...), economic profit (Gene companies...), the world's food problem, and health. One topic, biological warfare, has been removed. Second, the content of the diagram was analysed by checking whether the students had *correctly linked* their supporting arguments to other arguments with plus (+) signs, and counterarguments with minus (-) signs. The third content criterion of the diagrams was the *clarity of the main thesis*.

STUDENTS' FEEDBACK ON ARGUMENTATION STUDIES WITH HELP OF DIAGRAMS

At the end of the course the students filled in a short feedback questionnaire on the course. The questionnaire included six structured Likert-scale (totally agree, agree, neutral, disagree, totally disagree) items concerning the use of argument diagrams, and three open-ended questions concerning the students' opinions on the argument diagrams and on argumentation as a topic of study more generally. The Likert-scale items were the following:

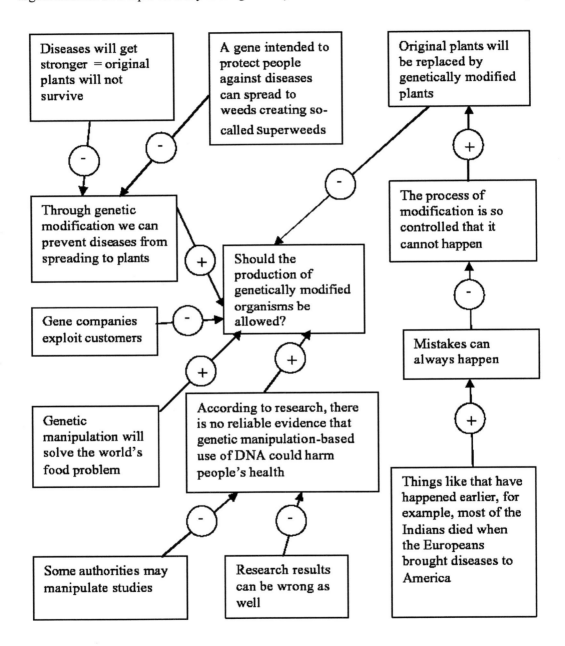

Figure 2. An argument diagram constructed after the texts were read (Matti)

1. It was easy to construct argument diagrams.
2. Construction of argument diagrams helps one to achieve a diversified understanding of the discussion topic.

3. Construction of argument diagrams was useful in learning argumentation skills.
4. Argumentation diagrams helped one to understand how an argumentative discussion is organised.
5. An argument diagram constructed collaboratively is of better quality than an individually constructed one.
6. It is easier to construct an argument diagram individually than collaboratively with a classmate.

In the analyses the categories "totally agree" and "agree" were merged to form the category "agree", and the categories "totally disagree" and "disagree" were merged to form the category "disagree". The students' answers to the open-ended questions were listed. The open-ended questions were the following:

1. What, to your mind, is the benefit of studying argumentation?
2. What do you think about training argumentation with help of computers?
3. What do you think about the idea of constructing argument diagrams (pros and cons)?

RESULTS

Development of the Students' Diagrams

As expected, the students' argumentation diagrams both deepened and broadened during the three successive elaborations. The interesting questions, however, are how and to what extent the diagrams improved. Table 1 shows that the diagrams grew considerably in extent: the students' first diagrams contained 5.8 argument boxes on average, while the mean number of boxes in the last diagram was 14.1. Correspondingly, the mean number of commentary boxes (see Table 2) increased from 0.3 in the first diagram to 5.3 in the third diagram. The students' diagrams also became broader and chains of argument longer: the mean number of arguments and counterarguments directly linked to the main thesis (breadth) increased from 2.6 to 5.9, and the chains of argument lengthened from 2.3 to 3.8. The increase in length was greatest after the texts had been read: from 2.3 to 3.7. The secondary theses did not branch out very often, but nevertheless the mean number of branches increased from 0.2 to 0.7.

The diagrams also improved in content (Table 1). In the first diagram only a few topics were presented (3.1 topics on average), but along with the successive modifications the number of topics increased up to 4.5. Reading the texts on GMO, in particular, increased the number of topics: from 3.1 to 4.3 on average. The organization of argumentation in the diagrams also become better: although the number of argument boxes increased considerably, the proportion of correctly marked argument links increased from 66 % to 74 %. The development of the content of the diagrams is also demonstrated by the improved clarity of the students' main theses. At first 69 % of the diagrams contained a thesis that did not clearly indicate the writer's stand on the topic. Finally, only 25 % of completed diagrams contained such vague theses. The development of the students' main theses is clearly illustrated in Matti's (pseudonym, male) three successive diagrams. In his first diagram (Figure 1) he presents his main thesis in only two words (Genetic modification), in the second diagram (Figure 2) his thesis has taken the form of a question (Should the production of genetically modified organisms be allowed?), and the thesis in his final diagram (Figure 3) is clear and unambiguous (The production of genetically modified organisms should be allowed).

Table 1. Shape and content of the students' argument diagrams

	Variable	Before the texts	Diagrams After the texts	After the debate
	Mean number of argument boxes	5.8	12.1	14.1
Shape	Mean number of commentary boxes	0.3	2.9	5.3
	Mean breadth of argumentation	2.6	4.9	5.9
	Mean depth of argumentation	2.3	3.7	3.8
	Mean branches of arguments	0.2	0.6	0.7
	Mean number of topics	3.1	4.3	4.5
Content	Correct argument links (%)	66	75	74
	Unclear main thesis (%)	69	47	25

The comments produced by Matti in his successive diagrams (Table 2) also exemplify the way the students used the opportunity to elaborate their arguments in more detail. In his first diagram Matti did not insert any comments on his arguments. After reading the articles he added four commentary boxes in his diagram and after the debate with his classmate Pia (pseudonym, female) he added one box more but did not make any changes in his earlier comments. The first comment in Table 2 concerns the possibility of creating strong dependencies between certain kinds of seeds and pesticides so that farmers are forced to use the same supplier during the whole production process. The next two comments in Table 2 are illustrative examples to support the arguments. In the fourth comment the word "over-enthusiasm" refers to an argumentation fallacy called hasty generalisation. The fifth comment in Table 2 has been created by moving the clarification (= original plants will not survive) from the argument box in Figure 2 to the commentary box. Here Matti is, however, doing more than mere copying as the verbal expression of the comment is more sophisticated than the original clarification.

When constructing the third argumentation graph Matti has revised his arguments in 7 argument boxes out of 13. In four cases he has removed some words from the box in order to make his arguments more succinct. This can be seen by looking at the following revisions in which the removed words are included in brackets:

- A gene [intended to protect people against disease] can spread to weeds creating, so-called super-weeds
- According to research [there is no reliable evidence that], genetic manipulation-based use of DNA does not harm people's health
- Things like that have happened earlier [for example, most of the Indians died when the Europeans brought diseases to America]
- Diseases will get stronger [= original plans will not survive]

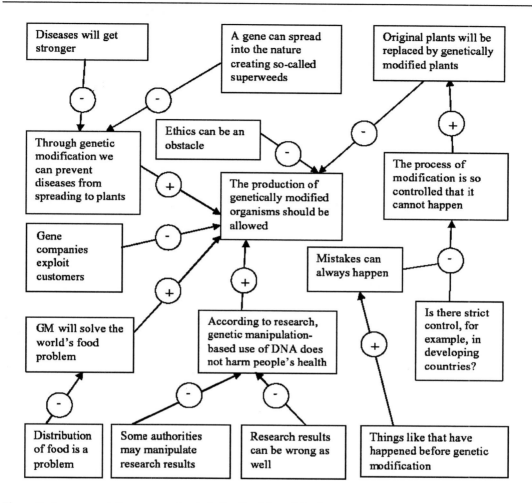

Figure 3. An argument diagram constructed after the debate (Matti)

Table 2. Comments on arguments in the diagrams shown in Figures 2 and 3

Argument in box	Comment in commentary box
Gene companies exploit customers	A company produces a genetically modified product which is resistant only to poisons produced by the same company (included in the 2nd and 3rd diagrams).
Some authorities may manipulate research	For example, according to some studies, smoking does not increase lung cancer risk (included in the 2nd and 3rd diagrams).
Research can be wrong as well	For example, in laboratory research genetically manipulated soy was not found to contain any properties causing allergies. When the research was repeated substances causing allergies were found (included in the 2nd and 3rd diagrams).
Mistakes can always happen	Or over-enthusiasm when modifications have not been studied enough (included in the 2nd and 3rd diagrams).
Diseases will get stronger	Original plants are not resistant to diseases (included only in the 3rd diagram).

Furthermore, Matti has replaced the word "studies" with the words "research results" in the sentence: "Some authorities may manipulate studies." This indicates that Matti is very sensitive to the exact meanings of his verbal expressions. The sixth revision was the use the abbreviation GM instead of the words "Genetic manipulation", and the seventh revision was the reformulation of the main thesis presented earlier in this paper.

In addition to the verbal revisions, the changes in the successive argumentation diagrams indicate that Matti is both deepening and broadening his argumentation. One example of the *deepening* argumentation is the inserted box "distribution of food is a problem" which is a counterargument to the box "GM will solve the world's food problem". This counterargument rejects the original argument by saying that the problem is not the amount of food but the uneven distribution of food in the world.

Matti's diagrams *broadened* mostly after he had read the articles. When developing his second diagram Matti inserted three new argument boxes and removed one box. The removed argument was: "Genetic modification can be misused, for example, in making biological weapons." This indicates a critical attitude because the thesis concerns whether the production of genetically modified organisms is justified, and in this context biological weapons is rather beside the point. Into his third diagram Matti inserted one new counterargument (Ethics can be an obstacle) against the main thesis. Ethical questions relating to genetic manipulation were dealt with four times during the debate between Matti and Pia, although they did not explicitly use the words ethics" or "ethical" during their discussion. The following four excerpts from their debate can, however, be interpreted as ethical concerns.

Excerpt 1
Pia: And the company wants to get products onto the market fast ONLY IN ORDER TO MAKE money! They are not interested in the state of the environment in the long term. So long as they line their own pockets the life of future generations doesn't matter. People are really stupid.

Excerpt 2
Pia: I think that it is wrong to tamper with something natural. Genetically manipulated products are unnatural.
Matti: That's true, let nature function according to its own laws.

Excerpt 3
Pia: I just wonder why the new gene technology could not be exploited for certain needs only, like medicine. Why is everybody living with the attitude: I want everything right now.
Matti: That's a new point. Companies that win out at the very beginning will succeed in the future, too.

Excerpt 4
Pia: I am only frightened about what kind of world awaits my own children. Gene technology does of course have many good sides as well but the problem is how to control it.
Matti:I have thought about the future as well, it frightens me a bit, too.
Pia: It is not a good thing is it that big companies can exploit small farms? They hold the fate of farmers in the palms of their hands....

STUDENTS' EXPERIENCES OF THE COURSE IN ARGUMENTATION AND THE USE OF ARGUMENT DIAGRAMS

The students' answers to the Likert-scale items reflected very positive experiences regarding the use of argument diagrams, since most (12 out of 17) of the students reported that it was easy for them to construct diagrams. In addition, the majority (10/17) of the students thought that constructing the diagrams enabled them to achieve a more diversified understanding of the discussion topic, that argument diagrams were useful in learning argumentation skills (11/17), and that diagrams helped them to understand how an argumentative discussion is organised (14/17). However, although most (13/17) of the students found a diagram constructed collaboratively with a classmate to be of better quality than an individually constructed one, almost a half (8/17) of the students agreed with the assertion that it is easier to do the diagram alone than with a classmate. Only about a third (5/17) of the students disagreed with this item, and about every fifth (3/17) presented a neutral viewpoint.

The students' answers to the open-ended question on the benefits of studying argumentation revealed that most (11/17) of them thought that it teaches one to put forward arguments for his/her opinions. This is indicated by the following answers:

- I can give reasons for my opinions better (student 2, female)
- You learn to state and justify your opinions (student 8, male)

Furthermore, many (6/17) students stated that argumentation is an important and useful skill, as indicated in the following:

- A lot of use in terms of life in the future (student 1, male)
- Certainly a useful thing that is worth mastering (student 5, female)

The students' answers to the question on training argumentation with help of computers showed that 6 students out of 17 found computer-based argumentation training to be a good idea as such:

- The computer is a good aid (student 15, male)
- Practising with computers works well (student 12, female)

In addition, 5 students said that training argumentation with computers clarified discussion and their thinking, as shown by the following examples:

- It made my thoughts clearer (student 5, female)
- It clarified discussion (student 8, male)

Finally, 3 students mentioned face-to-face discussion as a very important thing as well. The students' answers to the question on the pros and cons of constructing argument diagrams indicated that many (6/17) of the students found diagram construction to clarify their thinking,

- Things become clear better (student 13, male)
- You get the discussion clearly in front of your eyes (student 11, female)

a useful and interesting exercise (5/17),

- *A nice exercise* (student 2, female)
- *It is useful* (student 12, female)

and a helpful tool in organising and summarising a discussion (4/17):

- With their help (diagrams) you can construct an extended and useful summary of the topic (student 12, female)
- It is easy to summarise the debate with help of a diagram (student 15, male)

However, some (5/17) students found the construction of argument diagrams time-consuming and laborious:

- Time-consuming, maybe boring (student 3, male)
- Exhausting and hard (student 1, male)

CONCLUSION

The results indicated that the students' diagrams improved when they were able to elaborate them on the basis of successive periods of reading, discussion, reflection and thinking, The students' last diagrams, compared to their first ones, contained more arguments, longer and deeper chains of argumentation and more topics relating to the theme. This result suggests that the students deepened and broadened their knowledge of the topic during the intervention.

The results indicated that the clearest improvement in the quality of the diagrams occurred after the students had read the texts on the topic, i.e. from diagram 1 to diagram 2. Quite often, while still at the secondary level of education, students are not well-motivated to read texts and find reading hard work. One explanation for the low motivation to read may be that it is not clear to students how they can utilise their knowledge after reading. In this study, it is possible that, as the students knew that they were expected to make immediate use of the reading material in modifying their own diagrams, their reading motivation also improved. Thus, the improvement in the students' diagrams after the reading the articles may be due to their increased motivation to utilize what they just had read. On the other hand, the result can also be regarded as predictable since the students were directly asked to improve their diagrams on the basis of the articles and they also had access to the latter when they elaborated their diagrams.

It is important to notice that the students' diagrams also improved after they had engaged in the collaborative dyadic debate and a short period of reflection when they co-constructed an argument diagram on the basis of their previous debate. Although the improvement was not as clear as it was after the students had read the articles, the students' performance in seven out of the eight variables improved from diagram 2 to diagram 3, after the debate and period of reflection. Furthermore, it is worth noticing that the students did not have access to any supplementary material when they modified their final diagrams, which means that all the modifications they made were based on what they remembered from their earlier reading and discussion on the topic, the preceding debate with their classmate probably the freshest of these in their minds. The pedagogical importance of having the dyadic debate with a classmate is illustrated by Matti's use of the debate in modifying his diagram. This indicates that the debate helped Matti to broaden his knowledge and understanding of the issue at stake. Similar results have been achieved in previous studies in which collaborative dyadic discussions have been found to promote co-construction and extension (Storch, 2001), social transmission (Kuhn, Shawn and Felton, 1997), and deep processing of knowledge (van Boxtel, van der Linden and Kanselaar, 2000).

Argumentation is a difficult cognitive skill that has to been practised. High level argumentation consists of clearly expressed claims, relevant and sufficient arguments put forward to support those claims, and counterarguments against other's claims and arguments. If the participants' opinions on the discussion topic are unclear, the discussion can easily become unfocussed and a high level of argumentation cannot then be expected. In this study most (69 %) of the students held an unclear opinion on the discussion topic (GMO) at the beginning of the course. The reading of topic-related texts, collaborative argumentative discussions, and elaboration of their own thinking visualised by the construction of three successive argument diagrams helped students to clarify their personal opinion and thinking on the topic. At the end of the course the proportion of students still holding an unclear opinion on the topic had decreased to 25 %. Furthermore, most of the students reported that practising argumentation and constructing argument diagrams was a useful exercise. According to the students, they learned to present well-justified opinions by the aid of the diagrams. These results are in accordance with the observations of van Gelder (2003), who emphasises that the use of argument diagrams in summarising the argumentative structure of texts helps the reader to form a general view on opinions and arguments included in the text.

During the debate the students were freely allowed to express their own opinions about genetically manipulated products. Most of the students were not willing to take any strong stand on the issue and the few students who were against GMO when they commenced the task did not revise their opinion. Pia's aforementioned ethical arguments against the production of GMO are very typical among young persons in Finland, according to newspaper interviews and opinion polls. However, Pia was not certain whether opposing the production of genetically manipulated organisms is wise. She indicated her uncertainty by saying: *"I don't want to condemn anything out of hand because I'm not an expert, I just don't have any final opinion, I'm just afraid."*

Pia's unwillingness to oppose the production of GMO reflects the prevalent consensus-oriented Finnish discussion culture. For example, Mauranen (1993) found in a Finnish university seminar that disagreements are avoided since criticism is easily experienced as insulting. Finnish people, it seems, prefer to obtain a diversified picture of issues through exploring them from many different angles. This openness to different viewpoints can be seen as an advantage in learning because it prevents hasty generalisations and biased intake of information. The other side of the coin is, however, that long deliberation easily prevents active participation in international decision-making situations.

When analysing the results we did not assign different weights to the size, depth and breadth of the argumentation diagrams because the goal of the course was both learning to argue and arguing to learn. If learning new knowledge about GMO had been the main emphasis of the course, depth of argumentation would not have necessarily been an advantage. That is to say, long chains of arguments can easily lead discussion too far from the main claim. In this study, however, the argument chains were not very long and the students adhered well to the topic. In future studies the possibility of weighting certain properties of argument diagrams could be a useful way of directing students' attention towards specific learning goals. The content of single arguments and counterarguments could also be analysed more deeply.

Practising the elaboration of one's thinking about issues on the basis of different sources of information, and discussing ideas with other people is an important skill in today's working life where continuous education is of increasing importance. In the contemporary workplace the need to constantly update one's knowledge and skills is important in being able to cope with the increasing demands of working life. Successive periods of theoretical and practical work, during which theoretically acquired knowledge and skills are reflected on through concrete work assignments, will be increasingly common in the future. For this reason, it is important that students, already during their secondary school years, practise their knowledge-building skills on the basis of alternate periods of reading, discussion and reflection.

ACKNOWLEDGMENTS

The authors gratefully acknowledge Timo Salminen (M.Ed.) for his help in the data analysis.

REFERENCES

Andriessen, J., Baker, M., and Suthers, D. (2003). Argumentation, computer support, and the educational context of confronting cognitions. In J. Andriessen, M. Baker, and D. Suthers (Eds.), *Arguing to learn. Confronting cognitions in computer-supported collaborative learning environments* (pp. 1–25). Dordrecht: Kluwer.

Baker, M., and Bielaczyc, K. (1995). Missed opportunities for learning in collaborative problem solving interactions. In J. Greer (Ed.), *Proceedings of AI-ED 95. 7th World Conference on Artificial Intelligence in Education* (pp. 210–218). Charlottesville: Association for the Advancement of Computing in Education (AACE).

Baker, M., Quignard, M., Lund, K., and van Amelsvoort, M. (2003). Designing a computer-supported collaborative learning situation for broadening and deepening understanding of the space of debate. In F. H. van Eemeren, J. A. Blair, C. A. Willard, and A. F. Snoeck Henkemans (Eds.), *Proceedings of the fifth conference of the international society for the study of argumentation* (pp. 55–61). Sic Sat. International center for the study of argumentation.

Carr, C. S. (2003). Using computer supported argument visualisation to teach legal argumentation. In P. A. Kirschner, S. J. Buckingham Shum, and C. S. Carr (Eds.), *Visualizing argumentation. Software tools for collaborative and educational sense-making* (pp. 75–96). London: Springer.

Cohen, E. G. (1994). Restructuring the classroom: Conditions for productive small groups. *Review of Educational Research*, 64 (1), 1–35.

Fisher, F., Bruhn, J., Gräsel, C., and Mandl, H. (2002). Fostering collaborative knowledge construction with visualization tools. *Learning and Instruction*, 12 (2), 213–232.

Hitchcock, D. 1992. Relevance. *Argumentation*, 6 (2), 251–270.

Kuhn, D., Shaw, V., and Felton, M. (1997). Effects of dyadic interaction on argumentative reasoning. *Cognition and Instruction*, 15 (3), 287–315.

Larkin, J. H., and Simon, H. A. (1987). Why a diagram is (sometimes) worth ten thousand words? *Cognitive Science*, 11 (1), 65–99.

Marttunen, M., Laurinen, L., Litosseliti, L., and Lund, K. (2005). Argumentation skills as prerequisites for collaborative learning among Finnish, French and English secondary school students. *Educational Research and Evaluation*, 11 (4), 365–384.

Mauranen, A. (1993). Opiskelijan diskurssimaailmat – vaihto-opiskelijoiden perspektiivi [The discourse worlds of students – the perspective of exchange students]. In H. Jalkanen, and L. Lestinen (Eds.), *Korkeakoulutuksen kriisi? [Higher Education in a crisis]* (pp. 169–188). Jyväskylä: University of Jyväskylä, Institute for Educational Research.

Munneke, L., van Amelsvoort, M., and Andriessen, J. (2003). The role of diagrams in collaborative argumentation-based learning. *International Journal of Educational Research*, 39 (1–2), 113–131.

Roth, W-F., and Roychoudhury, A. (1993). The concept map as a tool for the collaborative construction of knowledge: A microanalysis of high school physics students. *Journal of Research in Science Teaching*, (30) 5, 503–534.

Séjourné, A., Baker, M., Lund, K., and Molinari, G. (2004). *Schématisation argumentative et co-élaboration de connaissances: le cas des interactions médiatisées par ordinateur. Actes du colloque international "Faut-il parler pour apprendre ?"*. Arras, Mars, pp. 1–14.

Storch, N. (2001). How collaborative is pair work? ESL tertiary students composing in pairs. *Language Teaching Research*, 5 (1), 29–53.

Suthers, D, D. (2003). Representational guidance for collaborative inquiry. In J. Andriessen, M. Baker, and D. Suthers (Eds.), *Arguing to learn. Confronting cognitions in computer-supported collaborative learning environments* (pp. 27–46). Dordrecht: Kluwer.

Toulmin, S., Rieke, R., and Janik, A. (1984). *An introduction to reasoning*. New York: Macmillan.

Twardy, C. R. (2004). Argument maps improve critical thinking. *Teaching Philosophy*, 27 (2), 95–116.

van Boxtel, C., van der Linden, J., and Kanselaar, G. (2000). Deep processing in a collaborative learning environment. In H. Cowie, and G. van der Aalsvoort (Eds.), *Social interaction in learning and instruction. The meaning of discourse for the construction of knowledge* (pp. 61–178). Amsterdam: Pergamon.

van Boxtel, C., and Veerman, A. (2001). Diagram-mediated collaborative learning. Diagrams as tools to provoke and support elaboration and argumentation. Teoksessa P. Dillenbourg, A. Eurelings, and K. Hakkarainen (Eds.), *European perspective on computer-supported collaborative learning. Proceedings of the First European conference on computer-supported collaborative learning* (pp. 131–138). Universiteit Maastricht, the Netherlands.

van Bruggen, J. M., Boshuizen, H. P. A., and Kirschner, P. A. (2003). A cognitive framework for cooperative problem solving with argument visualization. In P. A. Kirschner, S. J. Buckingham Shum, and C. S. Carr (Eds.), *Visualizing argumentation. Software tools for collaborative and educational sense-making* (pp. 25–47). London: Springer.

van Bruggen, J. M., and Kirschner, P. A. (2003). Designing external representations to support solving wicked problems. In J. Andriessen, M. Baker, and D. Suthers (Eds.), *Arguing to learn. Confronting cognitions in computer-supported collaborative learning environments* (pp. 177–203). Dordrecht: Kluwer.

van Drie, J., van Boxtel, C., Jaspers, J., and Kanselaar, G. (2005). Effects of representational guidance on domain specific reasoning in CSCL. *Computers in Human Behavior*, 21 (4), 575–602.

van Eemeren F. H. (2001). The state of the art in argumentation theory. In F. H. van Eemeren (Ed.), *Crucial concepts in argumentation theory* (pp. 11–21). Amsterdam University Press.

van Gelder, T. (2003). Enhancing deliberation through computer supported argument visualization. In P. A. Kirschner, S. J. Buckingham Shum, and C. S. Carr (Eds.), *Visualizing argumentation. Software tools for collaborative and educational sense-making* (pp. 97–115). London: Springer.

In: Trends in Learning Reserch
Editor: Samuel N. Hogan, pp. 139-170

ISBN 1-59454-965-6
© 2006 Nova Science Publishers, Inc.

Chapter 7

COGNITION AND EMERGENCE OF COORDINATION IN PERFORMING HITTING A TENNIS BALL IN NINE-YEAR-OLD CHILDREN

Jean Keller and Hubert Ripoll***
* UFR STAPS, Université René Descartes Paris5
1, Rue Lacretelle, F-75015 Paris
** Laboratoire des Sciences de l'Information et des Systèmes - UMR 6168.
Université de la Méditerranée, Marseille, France

ABSTRACT

Coordination in sport skills is presently described by both ecological and dynamical approaches. These approaches argue that coordination is an emergent property of constraints of an organism resulting from the interaction with environment. The constraints strain the movement, which is not the product of representation and computation to generate a motor program. Consequently, cognitive processes and human determinism are rejected, although learning of motor skills shows that the subject is active in his forming of change. Therefore, our concern is to show that coordination of a gross motor skill such as playing tennis is also a consequence of the achievement of cognitive processes.

The role of the cognitive style has been studied in coincidence-anticipation skills. The questioning of reflective–impulsive style indicated that style reflected a competence effect when the reflective children were the most efficient. As it has been shown through the results of a ball-hitting task and a ball-catching task, it raises the question about the coordination level of these motor skills and the effect of the experience of trained children. 35 nine-year-old boys were filmed and administered by the Matching Familiar Figures Test (MFFT). Children were classified into four groups using a double dichotomy of response latencies and errors on the MFFT (reflective, impulsive, fast-accurate and slow-inaccurate). Ethological categorization used to appraise the motor patterns of hitting a tennis ball with a mini racquet (split in two phases, one for orientating to the ball and the other for the stability during contact with the ball) and of catching a ball with a trajectory, which fell close to the feet.

Results showed that reflective boys are the most efficient and shaped more mature motor patterns. On the set of performance, the comparison between the cognitive task and the two motor tasks shows the correlation between response accuracy with the MFFT and the coordination levels on the two motor tasks. This finding is consistent with previous works showing that reflective–impulsive style reveals a competence skill particular to the reflective children, a very strong trend of these children that allows them to remain efficient whatever the situation by adjusting their response time to use the best solving strategy. The more efficient children in tennis show more mature motor patterns and score specifically on this task and are faster than novices according to the speed-accuracy tradeoff concept.

Among cognitive processes, we suggest that variation, selection, and activation-inhibition should be operative on motor pattern achievement. Coordination is not only an emergent process by mastering the degrees of freedom, as argued by the dynamical theories concerning Bernstein's work.

INTRODUCTION

Coordination is a recurring word for teachers who observe physical activity and the learning of motor skills throughout child development. Analysis of coordination refers to different theories, now renewed by the ecological approach that asserts motor patterns in sport skills emergent from the body environment relationships. The issue of the present contribution is to show that coordination is not limited to the emergent property of constraints, but also by the implication of cognition.

Coordination Models

The Precursors

Early, the coordination and the cognition have been linked in the psychomotor topic, which aligned motor motion and intellectual development. Basic motor development of locomotion and prehension generated first analysis of motor development of infants. Pérez (1878) described motor progress and various abilities of children with psychological development in a scientific view. In the same vein, Preyer (1882) studied developmental steps of motor action and intelligence with language. These steps constituted dated milestones of walk and prehension development. Gesell (1929) interpreted the motor development and the normal pattern of the motor behavior with the cephalo-caudal and proximo-distal laws of the orderly genetic sequence of development related to the posture transformation. The developmental steps of motor child development became more and more precise and illustrated with figures (McGraw, 1943).

Psychomotor Attitude

As the emphasis on motor development in regards to psychological development, authors explored the motor abilities. Ozeretsky (1936) suggested three kinds of coordination: static balance, gross body and fine movement of the hands, with upper limb speed, bimanual and disruptive motion. Since findings of Dupré and Tarrius (1911) about motor retardation, these associations with severe mental disorders, interdependence among intellectual, affective and motor functions, are recognized. Developmental psychologists highlighted sensory motor activity on the mental abilities throughout first developmental stages (Piaget, 1936; Wallon, 1925). The elicited features of motor acting enabled the study of behavioral and functional mode as reflexes, disabilities, muscle tone, posture, body schema, handedness, space, and so on, which entailed the pedagogical method and psychomotor upbringing. Psychomotor view gave birth to numerous methods.

The therapeutic rearing planned on physical activity, which is used for children who had learning disabilities in academic achievements were not studied enough. Ayres (1975) proposed to orient learning to the development of posture and balance and integration of vestibular system, motor planning, space perception and laterality. However, difficulty to obtain progress was explained by the role of attitude (Rarick, 1980; Tran-Thong, 1979). Ayres claimed that motor coordination was central to cognitive disabilities.

Psychomotor Abilities

Experimental psychology completed data on coordination with factorial analysis of anthropometrical, motor and cognitive data, which leaded to taxonomy (Harrow, 1972). They concerned cognitive-motor relationships and academic abilities during child development. Correlations were not always established between motor and intellectual abilities so investigators searched underlying factors. From the abilities of Ozeretsky's tests and the Bruininks – Ozeretsky scale, Krus, Bruininks and Robertson (1981) established two principal factors and noted that they are later differentiated. Differentiation influenced analysis because the relationships shown between intellectual and motor abilities at age of 5, 6 and 7, disappeared at 8 (Ismail, Kane and Kirkendall, 1969). Analysis of intellectual tests, vocabulary, calculating and perceptual motor tasks, showed variability due to learning and individual differences of children such as personality (Singer and Brunk, 1967). The perceptual motor tasks have links with intellectual tasks because they implied symbol analysis (Thomas and Chissom, 1972). Belka and Williams (1979) showed perceptual-motor tasks predicted well future achievements and batteries of child disabilities ought to include this kind of tasks. The psychometric studies showed links among perceptual-motor abilities, motor coordination and cognitive skills.

Ethological Coordination Form

Coordination and the description of the form of movement continued to be the object of studies. The locomotor development extended to child skill (Shirley, 1931). Ethological descriptions appeared with fundamental motor skills of children. Overarm throwing skill has been one of the first analyses of motor skill (Wild, 1938) with standing long jump (Hellebrandt, Rarick, Glassow, and Carns, 1961). Roberton (1977, 1978) tested validity of stages of development of Wild's work (1938) and refined the description of throwing skill. Seefeldt (1980) depicted figures of coordination based on a five-step development. The ethological approach described motor skill development according to the acquisition of coordination levels (Roberton and Halverson, 1984) where each level was neurobiological more efficient than the previous ones (Wickstrom, 1983). Stage theory predicts that movement develops in a fixed stage of sequences in accordance with a hierarchal view where a stage represents a given level of cognitive development (Piaget, 1936) or of maturation (Gesell, 1929). Each higher depicted stage was more efficient than the precedent according to three steps (Gallahue, 1982) or five steps (Wickstrom, 1983) and rules of development and of learning the coordination (Keller, 1992). From an ethological point of view, these coordination levels followed the improvement on skill and displayed throughout the development of fundamental motor patterns. They reflected the topological characteristics of the relative motion of trunk and limbs during the movement and we suggested other criterion of understanding within five mechanisms that contributed to the changes such as the joint span, the posture, the anticipation, the biomechanical work on the center of gravity and the orientation of the body in space (see Table 1).

Table 1: Changes of the mechanisms showing the improvement of the coordination. The different mechanisms have their own characteristic speed of development as in Roberton's and Langendorfer's (1980) assertions.

Join span	Posture	Anticipation	Biomechanics	Space
Restricted (to one joint)	Blocked	No	No action on the centre of gravity. backward movement	No movement
Locale (extended to near joins)	Passively differentiated at the end of the movement	Locale	Beginning of push-up	
Overall	Parallel girdles and broken hip	Locale and ample and ipsilateral step	Push-up insufficient	Oblique
	Differentiated at the end of the movement, flexion cross	Contralateral step broken / flexion cross	Push-up mostly vertically	
	Differentiated at the beginning of movement, stabilization pelvic body straight	Spatiotemporal synchronization leg – trunk - arm	Push-up effective, extension complete of the body horizontally	Sideways

The improvement of the motor skill is dependent on the joint span that implies the increase of the number of mobile joints. The posture contributed to the enhancement by the relative motion of the anatomical girdles, which are blocked first, the differentiated action of the scapular belt at the end of the movement, then the actively motion of the pelvic belt that rotated before the scapular one. The components of the body moved all together at the same time and some of them have a shift that triggers the following one, in a full range of motion, which performs the two proximo-distal and cephalo-caudal laws. The biomechanical action of the strength on the center of gravity, which does not work first, precedes the movement that is done by a backward motion of the body and strength action becomes effective by a push-up on it vertically followed a more horizontal action. First, the orientation of the body in the space does not operate, the body remains in front of the action, and is then moved by turning in the sideways space. Each mechanism change is consistent with three - five steps, which are not in a definite order like in the classical model of development, but on a differentiated speed in respect for the other (Figure 1).

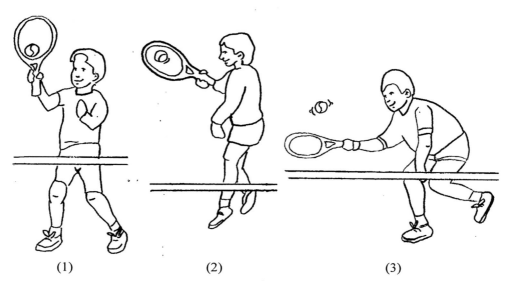

(1)   (2)   (3)

Figure 1. Sample of combination of cross mechanisms of span join, space orienting and posture without differentiation on a hitting tennis ball. (1) Restricted movement to elbow in front of the game and the ball. (2) As the child cannot differentiate the anatomical girdles, but can orientate and turn in space, he compensates it by a rotation and jump of the body at the hitting moment.

We have suggested the motor structure based on a logical relationship among components of the body, to another hypothetical mode of construction according to the Piagetian view. The first changes are in additive logic of the components of the body, when the number of joints implied on the movement increases. The improvement on the mobile components has some serial logic when the components activate one relative of the other according to a transitive mode, AB, BC, CD. The movement is smoother when it operates with orders differently from the components to achieve the same target: $a + (b + c) + d = a + b + (c + d)$ in an associative logic. This logic evolves into the inclusive logic, which implies that the posture as an operator basic to the movement.

However, the follow-up data of the motor patterns of the throwing skill of seven children throughout a continuous seventeen-year period showed that components had an instability of change sequences. Each component had a speed of change various with stabilization on a more or less long duration, skip step with possible regressive period on one or two steps (Roberton and Langendorfer, 1980). It suggested to more flexible stage model for motor development based on components of the movement rather than the gross motor skill. Although components showed continuity and variability of coordination changes, the development of the whole body coordination was discontinued. Therefore, Roberton and Halverson (1984) proposed a component model where each element of the body had its own developmental steps. Analysis of motor development by components allows methodological applications. Throughout the establishment of repertoires of coordination, the motor pattern lent support to process-oriented studies as claimed by Keogh (1977) and Rarick (1982).

In the vein of the first child psychologist, the development of the motor skill was viewed with regard to the biological changes of the Darwinian evolutionist theory. To explain jumping development, Hellebrandt et al. (1961) underscored the biological process of maturation and cephalo-caudal law. Later, as the maturation model lost its importance, cognitive processes became more prevalent in the developmental domain of motor skill (Connolly, 1970). Cognitive psychology studied the parameters of the motor program of motor skills.

As Kay (1969) denied the cognitive process of anticipation in catching a ball before five years of age, changes in the form of the movement occurred because of changes of the eye's gaze on the ball and later the attention processes. The learning of catching a ball and the increase of result was accompanied by change of the motor pattern regarding the attention strategies (Williams, 1992). The child did not need to integrate split sensory and motor systems, but to differentiate and coordinate motor action like in problem solving (Bruner and Koslowski, 1972). The integration of proactive and retroactive phases of the visuomotor coordination changed from 5 to 7 years of age (Hay, 1978). At the age of 5, there is no visual guidance and correction occurring late to a pointing movement. At the age of 7, the retroactive control appeared earliest and the guidance of the movement was effective at the age of 9. The harmonious integration of these systems were studied for a gross motor task. To hit a tennis ball, children had to move to the ball. From 5 to 9 years of age, children changed the shape for their displacement as a function of the mode of the motor control to be at an appropriate locus to the ball (Ripoll, Keller and Olivier, 1994). Increase of performance stemmed from the knowledge base and children have to generate cognitive rules (Chi and Ceci, 1987). Experts provide strategies as a function of declarative (factual information), procedural (how to do), and strategic (cognitive process) knowledge to be used for the learning of motor skills. Knowledge and action increased with the education of children on basketball (French and Thomas, 1987) and tennis (McPherson and Thomas, 1989).

Most of the studies of coordination have shown the integration of cognition with motor abilities whatever the importance of the maturation of innate schemas in relationship to the environment. Conversely to the psychomotor prospect, the cognitive approach affects the separation of the sensory (mind) and the motor (body) (Whitall, 1995) and viewed as a neo-behaviorism.

More recently, the ecological approach reintroduces the unity of the behavior. Among explanations of the changes of the motor patterns, the emergence for temporal invariance among limbs has been studied in reference to the dynamical approach (Kelso, Holt, Rubin and Kugler, 1981). The invariance could be calculated mathematically by a macroscopic value, which represents complexity. These findings on ecological and dynamical theories took into account coordination as an emergent property of constraints of the organism in interaction with the environment from the proposal of Kugler, Kelso and Turvey (1982). Application to the motor development of the children with the first works (Roberton and Halverson, 1988) labeled a developmental biodynamics (Turvey and Fitzpatrick, 1993) motor patterns emerged out of cognition.

Coordination and System Theories

Bernstein (1953/1996) showed the importance of studying the motor development of the human body in relationship to his environment and their mutual constraints. He noted that movement was not a repetition of identical form, only the process of a permanent cycle between perception and action generated variability. It changed and achieved according to a particular way of repetition without repetition and adjusted by feedback. Internal representations generated similar movements with each part of the body in a process, which displayed a motor equivalence. The control of the movement had a phylogenetic origin onto the brain, which built a multilayered structure. From each step of the brain emerged a kind of motor activity from reflex to complex coordination and learning. The more recent level controlled the more ancient and coupled the perception to action and generated synergies and assessed the mastering of the numerous degrees of freedom. The holistic analysis of movement joined other observations of human movement.

On the basic concepts of the Gestalt theory, Gibson (1986) argued for a whole analysis of perception and action in the ambient optic array. The array had an arrangement, which had a structure. When the observer moved, the environment changed only the structure of the array remained invariant. What remained invariant in the changing environment established an essential structure. The invariant combination of the object characteristics constituted an affordance that organisms perceived for acting. In his conception the perception is coupled to the action according to a temporal invariance. An opposing point of view of Sherrington (1906/1961) who devised central nervous system in exteroceptive, proprioceptive and interoceptive functions, questioned this assumption and claimed an unity when exteroceptive function was also the proprioceptive function. The exteroceptive and proprioceptive perception had common bases and mutual interaction. Perception-action systems accounted for the numerous degrees of freedom unified by attractors. Lee and Aronson (1974) showed that the balance of young infants did not have feedback control with the mechanoreceptors of proprioceptive system, only a visual proprioceptive control of the body sway. The invariance ensured stabilization of the perception-action within the world and can be considered as a macroscopic variable, the time-to-contact, which is determined by the tau. The tau was a variable optic directly available by the nervous system (Lee, 1976). It was mathematically calculated by the ratio of the displacement on the speed of this displacement, which was representative of the expansive variation of the image object on the retina. The visuo-motor coordination controlled by this optic variable triggered the adaptive movement to the approach of an object or an obstacle (Lee and Reddish, 1981).

Lee and Reddish (1981) computed the time-to-contact with the water and the diving time, of the plummeting gannet who had streamlined posture by folding its wings. Shapiro, Zernicke, Gregor and Diestel (1981) measured the relative timing of the joint motion during walking and running which showed invariance time of the knee among various speeds. In sports, the change of race during the run-up of the long jump was dependent on the optic flow. The athlete regulated the gait on the basis of perceptual information with regard to the takeoff board by changing the size of the stride six steps before it (Lee, Lishman and Thomson, 1982). The learning of the tennis table skill was more efficient when it took account of the time-to-contact to the ball (Bootsma, Houbiers, Whiting and van Wierengen, 1991). The invariance timing seemed essential to achieve a sport skill such as a forward somersault executed on a trampoline (Lee, Young and Rewt, 1992) or backward somersault (Bardy and Laurent, 1998) because it reduced body orientation variability and initiated limbs coordination before landing.

The coupling system and temporal invariance constituted attractors, which generated movement rhythm. An attractor reflects an equilibrium state (Thom, 1989), which stabilized the pattern of a movement. Muscles and bones were controlled by coordinative structures, which constituted organic constraints, which emerged from energetic functions and scale changes (Kugler, Kelso and Turvey, 1982). The qualitative changes of the motor patterns were viewed by the ecological theorists as the emergent property of biological, environmental and task constraints imposed on action, rather than the acquisition of prescriptions for action (Newell, 1986). All changes of motor patterns achieved by the freezing and the release of the degrees of freedom are in accordance to proximo-distal coordination. It revealed the torque work of the neuromuscular system and the stretch short cycle to constitute law of learning and the emergence of coordination from various constraints (Vereijken, van Emmerik, Whiting, and Newell, 1992). Studies tried to show the invariant timing of the motor skill by measured either the speed ratio, or the timing profile of space parameters or the relative timing of the joint motion (Sporns and Edelman, 1993). The learning effect was highlighted by the timing of the motor patterns and also the relative motion of the components of the body organized according to biodynamic principles of proximo-distal and cephalo-caudal laws of Gesell (1929). However, Newell, Kugler, van Emmerik, and Mc Donald (1989) rejected the maturationist explanation of these typical organizations because they sustained that they were the results of the relationships between mechanical and environmental constraints. The qualitative changes of the motor patterns of the throwing skill followed the proximo-distal law after two weeks of training for the dominant arm, which had an increased releasing motion of each joint (Mc Donald, van Emmerik and Newell, 1989). In volleyball, the expert novice comparison of the intra-limb coordination revealed that the novice froze the joints of the arm to process as sole dynamical unit where as the expert released the joints to generate proximo-distal motor patterns (Temprado, Della-Grasta, Farell and Laurent (1997).

Bernstein's ideas coupled with those of Gibson enriched psychological topics of perception, action and knowledge of human behavior in relationship with his environment contributing to the advancement of the ecological psychology. However, it is important to note that Bernstein, in the same report, suggested basic concepts presently used by dynamic and cognitive theories. They were respectively, the "mastering of the redundant degrees of freedom of the moving organ, in other words its conversion in a controllable system" (Bernstein, 1957/1986, p.355) and the cybernetic prospect of the "motor co-ordination as a system, which controlled" the motor acts (p.356). The organism was a servomechanism composed of subsystems, which worked as a whole relative to the environment. The motor act is an answer to a motor problem that incorporated a basis of some program. The program was in the "Sollwert" and the changes of the movement were not stable and durable because the information of the receptors and the transmission of corrections for the automatization concerned the lower subsystems of coordination rather than the representation and the attention. These two aspects of the Bernstein's view, the mastering of degrees of freedom and the hierarchical model of regulation will be the support of strong opposition among the tenets of cognitive and ecological theories.

Coordination, System Theories and Cognitive Approach

Bernstein's construct needed to be reintroduced with neuroscience advances to determine which level of the nervous system, as internal representations (*Gestalt*-type) acted to control movement, which includes numerous and redundant degrees of freedom (Ingen Schenau, Soest, Gabreëls, and Horstink, 1995). The internal anticipation loop and external intended loop of the movement induced correction and entailed new intention as a link between environment and action (Seiler, 2000; Semjen, 1994).

Whitall (1989) first studied the stability of galloping and running stride from infant to adulthood by an additional load on the ankle. The analysis of the rhythmical structure of the locomotor patterns established early at 2.5 - 4 years of age showed that changes concerned the amplitude of the step but not on the rhythm. Double tasks added to these two locomotor skills showed the motor control differentiated (Whitall, 1991). The neuromuscular control required few attentional cost and development changed with the control parameters amplitude, speed and force throughout development (Whitall, 1991).

Developmental Psychology

Piagetian Questioning

These works corresponded to the development of traditional course, in reference to the developmental stage models, particularly Piaget's structural model (1936) and developmental psychology also renewed concepts from criticisms of the Piagetian model. The Piagetian and the neo-Piagetian models were controversial because many studies showed that all children did not systematically follow the stages described and that many gaps exist (Wohlwill, 1973). The sequential change of the structures, which implied the universality (all the children), the stability (one structure for a stage) and the intransitivity (the same order and speed of change) of the stages, began with Fantz (1961). He showed scale lag for logical structure, e.g. representation, the developmental consequence of the sensory motor steps, which could be viewed early in the development. Conversely, some logical structure could have appeared later. Numerous abilities appeared early in the development, which could explain that the child has much capability, which can interact, compete and prepare for problem solving. Children think and act in many different ways during problem solving before selecting a strategy (Siegler, 1994). In this case, the structural units are not changed by substitution and coordination-activation because the child chooses among competing schemes by selecting the most efficient and by inhibiting misleading schemes that is selection-inhibition (Houdé, 1999). The child is thus an efficient rather than an inefficient inhibitor (Harnishfeger, 1995) and can sometimes resist interference among different processes. The mature process of inhibition appeared at ten – twelve years of age (Passler, Isaac, and Hynd, 1985).

Developmental Cognitive Process

As impulsivity and inhibition (Harnishfeger, 1995) are multidimensional and as there are links between impulsivity and motor skill (Visser, Das-Smaal and Kwakman, 1996), it seemed conceivable to determine whether inhibition occurs during the performance of gross motor task. Inhibition involves various processes that share common operating characteristics including a suppressive effect that defines the limit of information processing (Harnishfeger, 1995). Tipper (1985) suggested that suppressive process should occur to the perceptive or motor stages of the response. According to Treisman (1992) these processes involved the temporary perceptual memory according to spatio-temporal coordinates of a situation. In this case, failure of motor patterns may lack as a result of the inefficient inhibition of a motor scheme. The learning of gross motor skills such as running, jumping and catching skills, was dependent upon the previous trials (Jacklin, 1987). Inhibition of cognitive process was examined on a motor task of hitting a tennis ball with a mini racquet of the forehand drive using the retroactive interference procedure. The six- to ten-year-old children demonstrated that the motor pattern levels diminished after the interference task and the operating of inhibition for a forehand tennis shot was inefficient (Rosey and Keller, 2004). This finding showed that cognitive control as an inhibitory process can contribute to the generation of motor patterns and the coordination is not only an emergent property of the constraints imposed on actions by the environment. It appeared the inhibitor process began to be effective with the oldest children, suggesting the onset of their functionality from ten years (Passler, et al., 1985). Another aspect of the Piagetian questioning about transitivity of stages gave rise to the development, learning and individual differences.

Differential psychology identified cognitive styles, which referred to a way of information processing that a large group of children used over a large variety of tasks. In this case, there is no task specificity and individual consistency affects the performance. Impulsivity seemed a good candidate to allow this effect on the cognitive processes on coordination could be established particularly in developmental and individual differences to perform a motor skill (Keller and Ripoll, 2001). We employed the reflective and impulsive style, which reflected an analytic attitude to solve a perceptual motor task with high uncertainty (Kagan, Rosman, Day, Albert and Phillips, 1964). The reflective and impulsive style measured by the Matching Familiar Figures Test (MFFT) that when a child had to find a figure among six alternatives and the efficiency of the response depended on the conceptual tempo, e.g., the response time. The reflective children had a slower response but made few errors when the impulsive one did the converse. Although this construct is widely used, it has been questioned by long life span longitudinal studies (Block, Block, and Harrington, 1974; Gjerde, Block, and Block, 1985; Victor, Halverson and Montague, 1985) and intertask studies (Bush and Dweck, 1975) when the reliability of the response time of a category of children changed when the error number remained stable. They claimed that the MFFT reflected not a personality trait, as response time changed but the trend to do error remained permanent, revealing a competence skill to use strategies for solving a problem.

Impulsivity and inhibition are presently revisited by their multidimensional features and inhibition seems likely to occur in the performance of a gross motor task. The MFFT appeared relevant to the study of motor skill and inhibition because Kagan, et al., (1964) suggested that the test showed the tendency to inhibit the first and following appraisal before responding to solve a problem. Impulsivity established the tendency to fail the inhibition of movement in response to the demand for a task (Maccoby, Dowley, Hagen, and Degerman, 1965) and implied delay, motor abilities and social competence (Olson, 1989). It could be observed on the changes of the movement speed of the child displacement (Costantini, Corsini, and Davis, 1973). The inhibition effect was operative on the cognitive and motor learning and its role established when in the course of the development of the child an old pattern did not overwhelm and disturb the emergence of a new skill (Bruner, 1970). The reflective children remained the more efficient in two interceptive tasks, which had similar requirements, the hitting of tennis ball with a mini racquet and catching the ball (Keller and Ripoll, 2004). Results lent support to the hypothesis that MFFT was consistent with a competence skill to use the best strategy to solve problem whatever the context by fitting the response time. However, the non linear relationships, a quadratic (inverted-U-curve), between the latency response of the child to react to the starting ball and the score for the ball-hitting task was not for the ball-catching task. We suggested that the high temporal constraint, which reduced the window of response, should be unsuitable for the individual variability and the span of the results. The statistical regressions (quadratic versus linear) acknowledged the specificity of these tasks. Consequently, we questioned this difference and the examination of the motor response of the catching of the ball showed that the movement started preferentially with hands. It suggested it was a dynamical appraisal with the constraint of the task, but not a psychological situation where children expressed behavior with the variability of the starting parts of the body. Therefore we compared the two triggering movement, of the ball, the response latency on the hitting skill, which evoked attitude and the starting moment of the hand-racquet to touch the tennis ball, which reflected the temporal invariance of visuomotor coordination. Our observation showed that learning was concerned with different kinds of mechanisms on the life span.

Developmental psychology suggested the acquisition of a new skill was dependent on competing schemes and the organism has to select the more appropriate scheme and to inhibit the irrelevant one. The consequence of the competition and selection on the development is that there was no stage sequence in a similar order, so the behavior depended on the experience of the subject and on the context. The developmental model materialized as an overlapping wave of each level change from abilities and behaviors, which occurred according to their frequencies of occurrence (Siegler, 1994). Wohlwill (1973), Roberton (1982) set up qualitative studies of the developmental sequences, reciprocal action between action and function and the interference from processes. The development of coordination relative to each component and to age of children and their probability of changes established a prelongitudinal screening (Roberton, Williams and Langendorfer, 1980) of striking a tennis ball with a racquet (Langendorfer, 1988) and of hopping (Halverson and Williams, 1985).

Motor Development and Ecological Theories

The developmental discontinuity suggested an interaction of dynamical, relational and multilevel processes and eight subsystems having with their own speed of maturation. They were not specified programs and processes competed, inhibited and activated each of them to generate a movement (Thelen, 1995). The interaction between the neuromuscular system and context, of general and non-specific factors, contributes to the emergence for coordination that represents an attractor state of development and learning (Thelen, 1995). New motor patterns emerged from the development because of the child exploration and action of the spontaneous movements with respect to the environment (Gibson, 1988). The several processes and tasks interacted according to the dynamics of the intrinsic properties of the system to master the degrees of freedom of coordination. They changed because of searched strategies by the initiation and the annihilation from a dynamical attractor (Newell et al, 1989). A new coordination arose when synergies constituted and revealed a temporal invariance to link the components of the body. The physician Preyer (1882) studied on the cause of flexion and extension of the leg when the locomotion appeared. He ignored the existence of neuronal structure, which sustained the motor pattern. From ethological repertoires, Roberton and Halverson (1988) showed the qualitative changes from less advanced patterns to more advanced one by the invariant timing of the knee flexion at the landing of the hopping leg, between the controlateral limbs of the same anatomical belt and between lower and upper limbs. The temporal invariance worked early in infancy for the joints tightly coupled of baby kicking (Thelen and Fisher, 1982) the step cycle of the walking

(Clark, Phillips, and Petersen, 1989), running and galloping (Whitall, 1989) among the peak extension velocities of the lower extremity for a standing jump (Jensen, Phillips, and Clark, 1994) for arms and legs among intra and interlimb (Piek, Gasson, Barrett, Case, 2002).

In order to account for these assumptions, two kinds of conceptions stood to rationalize the emergence of a new coordination involved in the acquisition of a new gross motor skill. A later view regarded coordination generated by some central instance, which represents and controls the motor action through cognitive processes. A more recent one posits that action emerges and is self-organized in a dynamical way, which is construed on line. It is conceivable to acknowledge some kind of interaction between these two conceptions, which are complementary.

Hypothesis

Coordination of movement in sport skills is presently taken into account by ecological and dynamical approaches. They argued that coordination was an emergent property of constraints of the organism in interaction with the environment. Constraints strain movement, which is not the product of representation and motor program and movement emerged without higher cortical control (Thelen, 1986) although changes were effect of a control parameter. Cognitive processes and human determinism are rejected, although learning of motor skill shows that the subject is active as forming the change. Cognitive psychology emphasize the information process but does not take into account coordination and does not explain how information generates movement. Therefore our concern is to show that coordination is not only an emergent property of constraints, but is also related to cognition processes.

We hypothesize that cognitive processes reflected by individual differences affect the efficiency of the motor skill. Particularly, the reflective-impulsive style has an effect on behavior and motor performance (Keller and Ripoll, 2001, 2004) and could be considered as a competence skill. We suggested that the reflective children that used cognitive processes more involved in control of the coordination were more efficient. This hypothesis tested by studying two gross motor skills of ball interceptive tasks, one is hitting a tennis ball with a mini racquet, another one is catching a ball. Conversely, if coordination only results from the emergence of motor patterns and perception-action coupling, coordination ought to show a temporal invariance out of cognitive style.

In order to accomplish our analysis, an expert group of two or three years of practice in scholar tennis practice, with the same age, is compared to the first one. We postulate that practice improves cognitive capacities of the more advanced group and coordination level, out of temporal invariance.

Two independent variables were selected to illustrate these processes. Firstly, the duration between the releasing moment of the ball and the beginning moment of the body movement. Secondly, the starting moment of the arm movement as the ratio of the trajectory duration of the ball. If coordination emerges as a function of triggering the movement of motor response (or body movement) latency responses from the releasing moment ought to be invariant and adjusted according to a linear regression, if not it should reflect an attitude as we measured previously. In this case, overall coordination of the gross motor skill should not emerge as a function of a temporal invariance, but rather should be dependent on cognitive strategies and attitudes of children. The cognitive variability of the boys and the dynamical invariance of the arm movement have to be differentiated.

Moreover, the starting movement of the arm involves dynamical constraints, e.i. the temporal invariance of visuomotor coordination. It does not constitute the overall coordination, which is not independent of cognitive processes of preparatory step and selective mechanisms reflected by latency duration. The achievement of motor pattern is not only an emergent process but implies cognitive competence.

METHOD

Participants

35 nine-year-old boys included two groups, one of nine advanced, boys who practiced tennis in club two or three years ($M = 9$ years and 5 months, $SD = 5$ months) and twenty-six untrained in tennis ($M = 9$ years and 6 months, $SD = 6.4$ months) were filmed on the two motor skills and administered by the Matching Familiar Figures Test (MFFT).

Procedure

MFFT was administered after the hitting tennis ball task, with a mini racquet and the catching ball task, which were filmed with S VHS videotape. Films were analyzed frame by frame with a ± 20 ms precision and inter observer comparison was 0.86.

Matching Familiar Figures Test

The Matching Familiar Figures Test was administered in a quiet room close to the experimental place. It arranged of twelve sorts of figures presented, first alone on a board, which is the standard figure, then on another board, among six alternatives, i.e. five variants and the good one. It asked the child to find the standard figure. If his response was wrong, he invited the choice again until he had the correct answer. The response latency at the first response and the overall error numbers appraisal. From the average of response time and errors on the MFFT, children labeled impulsive took a shorter time to respond and preformed many errors, whereas reflective children took a longer time but had few errors. However, the double dichotomy between the two measures delineates four groups, whom the two other groups labeled "fast-accurate" with long response time and few errors and "slow-inaccurate" with short response time and many errors.

1st Motor Task: Hitting a Ball

Children had to hit back a tennis ball with a mini racquet in a square target, 2,50m x 2,50m, located behind a little net of 40 cm high. Six preparatory trials were carried out before the experiment. The same thrower tossed the tennis ball from the same spot, at 2,50m from the net either 20 forehands or 15 backhands at random rank. Additional trials were carried out to replace the failed trials in case of a missed ball. Score were evaluated by points: two points when the ball dropped in the squared zone behind the small net, one point when the ball was out of this area but touched by the racquet and zero when the child touched not it, even when it brushed past the racquet but continued its displacement.

Coordination level of hitting a tennis ball was estimated from three depicted figures of Haywood (1986) to which two figure levels from Keller (1992) were added, implying way of differentiated anatomical girdle of the posture (see Table 2) and utilized by Rosey and Keller (2004). Such types of motor pattern is the object of an analysis of the pirouette of expert ballerinas of Paris Opera (Keller, Bouillette, Mertz, and Golomer, revision).

Table 2: Appraisal of coordination levels related to the depicted motor patterns

Preparatory Step	
Points	
1	Legs and trunk do not move and child faces the ball. Only arm moves from high to down.
2	Legs and trunk do not move and child faces the ball. Only arm moves horizontally
3	Legs do not move but trunk turned by first differentiated motion of shoulders. Only arm moves (one leg could have displacement)
4	Sideways striking movement by back displacement of ipsilateral leg. Body has a half rotation.
5	Striker step by displacement of back leg then forehead leg with first differentiated trunk rotation of hips.
Hitting Stance and Stability at the ball contact	
1	The body moves during the striking action.
2	Backward rotation and/or back away (on one leg) or jump
3	Stable, static stance and the two feet on the ground.
4	Stable with step forward.

The coordination description of the hitting ball was divided into two phases, the first one, the motion and the adjustment to the ball, the preparatory step and the second one, the swing motion of the arm to the contact moment with the ball included in the hitting stance, which implied the stability of the interceptive phase (Figure 2).

The hitting skill included different periods (Figure 3). The starting of the arm movement measured at the acceleration moment of the racquet, which was best seen by the zooming effect of the racquet. The contact moment was obviously estimated at the coincidence point between the ball and the racquet, but if the child missed the ball, the vertical plan common to the two objects established this moment. The movement time of the arm was calculated from the acceleration moment to the contact moment. The variability of this movement calculated the standard deviation of the average of the whole movement times. The variability of the latency response of the hitting skill from the initiation of the ball displacement compared with the previous one.

Figure 2a. Example of a returning of a tennis ball. The level 2 for the adjustment phase when child stands in front of the ball and the level 2 for the instability at the hitting moment when he is not on two feet or jumps (drawn by Jean Bodin).

Figure 2b. The level 4 for the adjustment phase when child turns and the level 3 for the stability at the hitting moment when he remains on two feet (drawn by Jean Bodin).

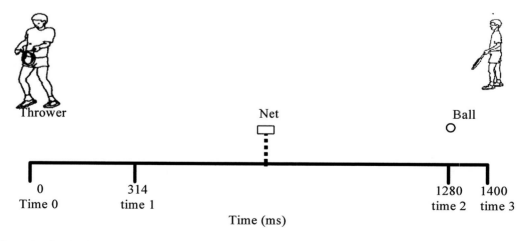

Figure 3. Distribution of the event periods and the calculated characteristics. The time 0 was the releasing moment of the ball and basic for the various calculations. The time 1 was the response latency time ($M = 314$ ms). The time 2 was the starting of the arm movement ($M = 1280$ ms) and the time 3 was the ball contact. The temporal invariance was the ratio of the times 2 on 3 and the time movement the time 3 less the time 2.

2nd Motor Task: Catching A Ball

The catching ball was executed with a screen to hide the thrower. The height of this screen was adjusted to the size of the child, ten centimeters more, who was waiting in front of it, 1.2 m further. The ball was tossed underhand by the same thrower. Human tossing avoided the noise of a ball machine, which would warn the beginning of the flight of the ball and would work like a preparatory signal. The camera was situated at the side. Coordination of the catching ball was appraised with a low forehead catching obtained by a running high down ball trajectory dropping near feet, which was encompassed with two other ball trajectories, a high one and lateral one to generate uncertainty. Type of catch was selected randomly and each child had the same order of presentation. Motor patterns were evaluated with a previous work on several types of trajectory on ball catching (Keller and Fleurance, 1987). The low forehead catching of a ball was portrayed with five levels, which constituted developmental sequences. Earlier, child does not move, then, an immature one appeared when child moves by a dropping, squatting movement on place (Figure 4).

Figure 4. Occurring of motion to catch a low ball by flexion of legs in place. A period of development appears when a motion triggered seemingly out of its target.

Following developmental level announced the motion by a back movement of one leg, but the body does not move forward. An intermediary one shows an initiation of advance movement by giving a bow of the trunk and the mature one by forward motion of the hips by keeping an upright trunk (see Table 3).

Table 3: Changes of the postural stabilization during the catching of the falling ball near the feet from the waiting position to the interceptive action.

Catching Ball	
0	No move.
1	Flexion on place.
2	Fencing by back movement of one leg.
3	Fencing by ahead movement of trunk within flexion of it (hip strategy or broken body).
4	Fencing posture with step forward and maintaining stable upright trunk (stretched body).

Each developmental sequence appraised: 1 point for the deficiency of movement, 2 points for the immature level, 3 points for the back movement of leg, 4 points for the intermediary one and 5 points for the mature one.

In summary, three scores, calculated by an average of twenty trials for each child, estimated the motor patterns of children, two for the striking ball, added to appraise in one score to estimate his broad level and another one for the catching ball. As two previous publications showed the competence effect of the MFFT cognitive style, only coordination was taken in account but not the response times neither the latency response of the motor skill to the ball initiation of the displacement.

RESULTS

ANOVA Among Cognitive Styles of Novice Groups

Children were analyzed in a 26 (subjects) x 4 (style) analysis of variance. The one-way multivariate analysis of variance showed a significant effect of cognitive style in the hitting task on the score, $F(3, 22) = 5.14$, $p < .01$, on the preparatory step, $F(3, 22) = 3.53$, $p < .05$, on the coordination, $F(3, 22) = 3.22$, $p < .05$ and the variability of the latency response $F(3, 19) = 3.58$, $p < .05$. No other significant effect was found (see Table 4).

In the catching task, the style showed differences on the score, $F(3, 22) = 3.31$, $p < .05$ and the motor patterns, $F(3, 22) = 6.61$, $p < .01$ only.

Table 4 Analysis of Variance among Cognitive Styles of Novice Groups

Task characteristics	Means				Standard Deviation				F	p
	I	F-A	R	S-I	I	F-A	R	S-I		
MMFT Time	11.5	13.8	28.5	27.1	1.9	2.7	1.7	5.5	1.9	.08
MMFT Errors	12.4	3.8	3.3	7	1.0	1.7	1.0	3.4	13.8	.001*
Tennis Latency	320	268	317	410	15	26	16	51	2.30	.11
Tennis Score	23.8	31.6	30.6	16	1.6	2.6	1.7	5.3	5.14	.01*
Preparatory Step	3.1	3.7	3.5	2.5	0.13	0.22	0.14	0.45	3.53	.05*
Hitting Stance	2.5	2.9	2.7	2.7	0.10	0.17	0.11	0.34	1.68	.20
Tennis Coordination	5.6	6.6	6.2	5.1	0.20	0.34	0.21	0.68	3.22	.05*
Catching Latency	311	324	308	354	13.1	21.7	13.7	43.5	0.44	.73
Catching Score	9.2	13.5	14.8	6	1.4	2.3	1.46	4.6	3.31	.05*
Catching Coordination	2.9	3.3	3.6	2	0.13	0.22	0.14	0.44	6.6	.01*
Starting Arm	1261	1316	1279	1316	44	62	39	124	0.2	.90
Movement Time	113	116	118	80	7	9	6	19	1.27	.31
Variability Tennis Latency	81	72	72	149	8	11	7	23	3.58	.05*
Variability MT	23	24	23	16	3	5	3	9	0.19	.90

Note. For the I, N = 11, except for the three last characteristics N = 8, the F-A, N = 4, the R, N = 10 and the S-I, N = 1.

The analysis of variance showed that reflective boys were the most efficient on the scores and they had a more mature coordination of the motor skills (except the hitting stance) and had less variability on the latency response time. They had the same activity on the two latency times, the movement time and its variability and the starting moment of the arm.

Correlation Among MFFT Error Numbers, Score Skills and Motor Patterns

The analysis of MFFT errors showed a significant negative correlation within tennis score, $r(23) = -.59$, $p < .05$ and catching score, $r(23) = -.57$, $p < .05$ and between the two scores of motor skills $r(23) = .63$, $p < .05$. The MFFT errors showed a significant negative correlation within the hitting skill coordination, $r(23) = -.42$, $p < .05$ and the catching coordination, $r(23) = -.46$, $p < .05$. Coordination comparison showed a significant correlation between the preparatory step of hitting and the catching skills, $r(23) = .44$, $p < .05$. Scores of each skill were correlated with coordination levels, for the tennis skill, $r(23) = .60$, $p < .05$ and the preparatory steps, $r(23) = .63$, $p < .05$. Errors in the MFFT viewed as a competence criterion of the reflective-impulsive style, were correlated with the score of interceptive skills and most of the motor control of coordination. However, the latency time of the hitting skill was correlated with the preparatory step, $r(23) = -.48$, $p < .05$, the overall hitting coordination, $r(23) = -.42$, $p < .05$, the latency time of the catching skill, $r(23) = .46$, $p < .05$, the catching coordination, $r(23) = -.51$, $p < .05$ and its own variability. The attitude defined here by the time to respond was linked with coordination of the two motor skills. Moreover, this analysis of variance showed correlation among the variability of the latency response with the latency response of the hitting skill, $r(23) = .73$, $p < .05$ and negative one with the motor patterns, the preparatory step, $r(23) = -.59$, $p < .05$, the gross hitting coordination, $r(23) = -.49$, $p < .05$ and the catching coordination, $r(23) = -.52$, $p < .05$. The variability of the movement time of the arm correlated with the movement time of the arm, $r(23) = .80$, $p < .05$ and the flight of the ball, $r(23) = .63$, $p < .05$. No other significant correlation was found (see Table 5).

Table 5 Correlation among the Variables of the Cognitive and Motor Tasks

Task characteristics	1	2	3	4	5	6	7	8	9	10	11	12
1. MMFT Errors		.19	-.59*	-.35	-.40	-.42*	.18	-.57*	-.46*	-.29	-.33	.07
2. Tennis Latency	.19		-.28	-.48*	-.25	-.42*	.46*	-.44*	-.51*	.24	-.05	.73*
3. Tennis Score	-.59*	-.28		.63*	.40	.60	-.10	.63*	.62*	.29	.21	-.25
4. Preparatory Step	-.35	-.48*	.63*		.58*	.91*	.09	.40	.44*	.12	.05	-.59*
5. Hitting Stance	-.40	-.25	.40	.58*		.86*	.24	.08	.02	.33	-.11	-.26
6. Tennis Skill	-.42	-.42*	.60	.91*	.86*		.18	.28	.26	.24	-.03	-.49*
7. Catching Latency	.18	.46*	-.10	.09	.24	.18		-.41	-.30	.03	-.09	.29
8. Catching Score	-.57*	-.44*	.63*	.40	.08	.28	-.41		.66*	.02	.12	-.38
9. Catching Skill	-.46*	-.51*	.62*	.44*	.02	.26	-.30	.66*		-.19	.46*	-.52*
10. Starting Arm Movement	-.29	.24	.29	.12	.33	.24	.03	.02	-.19		.31	.19
11. Movement Time	-.33	-.05	.21	.05	-.11	-.03	-.09	.12	.46*	.31		.13
12. Variability Tennis Latency	.07	.73*	-.25	-.59*	-.26	-.49*	.29	-.38	-.52*	.19	.13	
13. Variability MT	.19	.13	-.15	-.18	-.35	-.29	-.13	.01	.13	.35	.80*	.04

The correlation supported the relationships established by the differentiation based on the categories of the cognitive style.

ANOVA Between Advanced and Novice Groups

Matching Familiar Figures Test

Children were analyzed in a 35 (subjects) x 2 (practiced) analysis of variance. The one-way univariate analysis of variance showed no significant effect on the two variables of the MMFT.

Hitting of the Tennis Ball Task

The analysis of the hitting of the tennis ball showed a significant effect on the latency time, $F(1, 33) = 4.24$, $p < .05$, respectively novice vs. advanced group ($M = 314$ ms vs. 274 ms), the score, $F(1, 33) = 51.75$, $p < .001$ ($M = 27$ vs. 36 points), the preparatory step, $F(1, 33) = 11.36$, $p < .01$ ($M = 3.31$ vs. 3.93 points), the hitting stance, $F(1, 33) = 15.3$, $p < .001$ ($M = 2.6$ vs. 3.1 points) and the hitting coordination, $F(1, 33) = 17.2$, $p < .001$ ($M = 5.9$ vs. 7.1 points). No other significant effect was found (see Table 6).

Catching Ball Task

The analysis effect of the catching ball showed a significant effect the score ($M = 14$ vs. 18 points) $F(1, 33) = 7.66$, $p < .01$, only.

Table 6 Means, Standard Deviation and Analysis of Variance between Advanced and Novice Groups

Task	Means		Standard deviation		F	p
characteristics	Advanced	Novices	Advanced	Novices		
MFFT Time	18.6 s	19.5 s	3.1	1.8	0.07	.80
MFFT errors	4.1	7.3	1.6	0.9	2.94	.10
Tennis Latency	273 ms	314 ms	16.9	9.9	4.2	.05*
Tennis Score	36	27	1.9	1.1	15.7	.001*
Preparatory Step	3.9	3.3	0.16	0.09	11.4	.01*
Hitting Stance	3.1	2.6	0.1	0.06	15.3	.001*
Hitting Coordination	7.1	5.9	0.23	0.14	17.2	.001*
Catching Latency	283 ms	313 ms	13.5	7.9	3.7	.06
Catching Score	17.3	11.9	1.7	1.0	7.7	.01*
Catching Coordination	3.4	3.2	0.17	0.10	1.4	.23
Starting Arm	1236 ms	1281 ms	39.5	23.3	0.94	.34
Movement Time	112 ms	114 ms	6.3	3.7	0.05	.83
Variability Tennis Latency	60 ms	78 ms	8.4	4.9	3.4	.07
Variability MT	23 ms	22 ms	3.0	1.8	0.02	.90

Note. N = 35 and 31.

The effect of learning to hit a tennis ball with mini racquet was specific to the score, the latency response and the motor patterns of this task and the score of the catching task, but the starting moment and the movement time of the arm and the variability of the latency and of the movement time were stable.

ANOVA Between the Reflective and Fast-Accurate Advanced Boys and the Reflective and Fast-Accurate Novice Boys

ANOVA executed about the reflective boys between advanced and novice groups showed no effect on response time on MFFT, $F(1, 21) = 1.82$, $p > .05$, MFFT errors, $F(1, 21) = 1.02$, $p > .05$, the latency response time, $F(1, 21) = 2.06$, $p > .05$, the starting of the arm movement, $F(1, 20) = 1.25$, $p > .05$, the movement time $F(1, 20) = 0.47$, $p > .05$, the variability of the latency response $F(1, 20) = 2.02$, $p > .05$ and the variability of movement time of the arm $F(1, 20) = 2.02$, $p > .05$, $F(1, 20) = 0.0004$, $p > .05$, but an effect of practice on tennis score, $F(1, 21) = 10.06$, $p < .05$, the preparatory step, $F(1, 21) = 6.22$, $p < .05$, the hitting stance, $F(1, 21) = 7.22$, $p < .05$, and the tennis skill coordination, $F(1, 21) = 9.39$, $p < .01$. For the catching skill, there was no effect on the latency, $F(1, 21) = 2.89$, $p > .05$, the score, $F(1, 21) = 2.63$, $p > .05$ and the coordination, $F(1, 21) = 0.14$, $p > .05$. As Advanced boys were mainly reflective and fast – accurate boys, and as the basic categorization of MFFT is the reflective children, these results showed that significant results derived not from a secondary effect of the cognitive style with the reflective boys, but an effect of advanced boys because they had no better performance on the MFFT and the main effect was on the practice of the tennis skill, the score and the motor patterns.

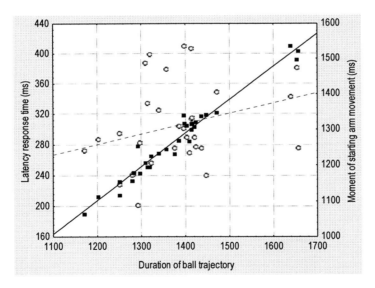

Figure 5. Distribution and relationships between latency response time and the starting arm movement with the duration of the flight ball. Linear regression of latency response time ---O--- and starting arm movement —■—.

Pearson Correlation Between Ball Trajectory Duration and Starting Movement of Body and Arm

Analysis of the ball trajectory duration and the starting movement of the arm showed a correlation, $r(31) = .98$, $p < .001$ and a linear relationship with the regression coefficient and the standard error (SE) (b = -26.7 (SE = 0.03) and a = 0.94). There was no correlation between the ball trajectory duration and the latency response time of the body, $r(31) = .28$, $p > .05$ (b = 117.7 (SE = 0.08) and a = 0.14). Figure 5 illustrated the dispersion of each moment of triggering movement, strongest for the latency time and weakest for the starting movement time.

Student T Between Variability

Analysis of the variability showed the variability of the response latency to the release of the tossed ball was higher than the movement time of the arm. The results from t tests showed the difference between the two variables was significant for all the boys ($M = 73.65$, $SD = 24.64$, $M = 22.68$, $SD = 8.34$), $t(31) = 10.95$, $p < .001$, whatever the group, for the novices, ($M = 78.3$, $SD = 26.54$, $M = 22.57$, $SD = 8.68$), $t(23) = 9.70$, $p < .001$ and the advanced, ($M = 60.25$, $SD = 10.65$, ($M = 23$, $SD = 7.8$), $t(8) = 7.42$, $p < .001$.

CONCLUSION

Our results show the reflective (i.e. having the best performance at the MFFT) have the best scores and the more advanced motor patterns. In comparison with the novice, the practiced boys have a better score with the two motor skills, only a quicker response time and more advanced motor patterns than the other boys on the hitting skill. These findings confirm the behavior changes in respect to the criteria of speed and precision as they have been defined by Pachella and Pew (1968). These authors showed the parameters of speed and precision of movement are interdependent, evolve in opposition and reflect the efficiency of the response. In this way, when speed of response increases, it conflicts with accuracy, which decreases and conversely. Throughout learning of a skill, the learner increases the two factors of performance together. So, in our experimentation, although these two gross motor tasks of ball interception are time stressing, the practiced group responds quicker and is more accurate than the novice group on tennis task.

From the average of speed and precision criteria of response, child categories have defined as a function of their efficiency to solve problem in terms of reflective versus impulsive by the MFFT. Because of this double dichotomy, some children are eliminated (Ault, Mitchell and Hartmann, 1976). They are the fast-accurate and the slow-inaccurate, thirty percent of the children, a relatively large number of children, which could distort the interpretation of the results (Mitchell and Ault, 1979). Our work does not show this inconvenience when the comparison between categories and correlation does not affect the issue of statistical analyses. However, the bipolar taxonomy depends on the assumption of an only function. The impulsivity implies that the personality trait has the characteristic opposite of the reflection. As Reuchlin (1990) has shown, this relationship is not relevant and we found that the motor patterns evolve in a different way according to the two interceptive tasks.

So, taking into account the specificity of the cognitive style shows that a child category adopts an ability more adapted with the task characteristics, this one entailing a more efficient response. Various authors showed a relationship between the psychological type of child and his adaptation to the task characteristics (Yando and Kagan, 1970), to the information quantity (Barratt, 1967), to the speed of information processing (Zelniker, Cochavi, and Yered, 1974) and to the detail (advantageous for the reflective) versus global (helpful for the impulsive) processing (Zelniker and Oppenheimer, 1973; Zelniker and Jeffrey, 1976). The specificity could also concern motor skill and Sugden and Connell (1979) suggested that the best children during lessons of physical education would be the quickest on MFFT. However, when a test is administered, which emphasizes the response speed, impulsive children are just as effective as the reflective children (Brown, Singer, Cauraugh, and Lucariello, 1985; Dickman and Meyer, 1988). The impulsive children were not the most efficient for the holistic information processing (Smith and Kemler Nelson, 1988). The reflective children are not more efficient for gymnastic complex motor skills and perceptive tests of learning (Swinnen, Vandenberghe, and Van Assche, 1986). Lee, Landin, Greenockle, Hill, and Edwards (1987) do not see a difference between the two styles by the execution of a set of motor tasks (walking, running and hopping) evaluated by speed, but the reflective are more efficient for learning with a motor model of a set of complex motor skills of jumps, dribbles and throwing (DeVard Brown and Lee, 1988). Our results confirm these findings and we show the motor patterns of the impulsive children are not more advanced than these of the reflective children. The event that a personality trait is not more efficient as a function of the task specificity has not verified that the reflective impulsive style confirms the reinterpretation of this cognitive style as a competence criterion (Block, Block, and Harrington, 1974) and already proven by our previous findings (Keller and Ripoll, 2001, 2004).

This effect of cognitive style as a competence factor enables the analysis the results of the children on the two tasks. In our experimentation, although the cognitive style generates a similar effect on the performance of the two motor skills, it is different from the coordination. However, the effect of practice on tennis skill improves the catching, what can be interpreted as a transfer, without yet increasing the coordination, whereas these two skills require common processes, we would expect to view an inter-task transfer.

Behaviorists explained the transfer of shared elements among various responses. So the interception of a ball should imply similar activation for the two motor skills (Adams, 1987). However, some variations are present, as the view of the thrower posture, the temporal stress, the context, the orientation in the space, the kind of interception, the nature of motor patterns and the ball size. Regarding this last factor, Burton, Greer, and Wiese (1992) showed that the increase of the ball size plays a role on the coordination, when it is greater than the hand size. In our study (a tennis ball vs. a volleyball ball on the catching) should be a good candidate to explain the difference of coordination. As well as the different size of the targets on the two tasks should be able, as showed Roberton (1988), to change the coordination. So, this set of features could hinder the transfer, which requires, as showed Langendorfer (1983) that inter-task co-ordinations have to be near.

As the behaviorist analyzes the transfer due to common stimuli, gestaltists questioned elementary aspect to argue the whole aspect of the situation whose their setting arrangement is the base to the learning (Köhler, 1959). The perception of the situation as a totality and the perception of the structure of a form or the relation among objects establish insight learning. The transpositional phenomenon works when the learner responds to the relational structure of the situation and transfers it to another situation. The context can act in an interference process for learning, which organize the structure of the movement and is a basis for the transfer (Shea and Morgan, 1979; Lee, Magill, and Weeks, 1985). On our experimentation, another aspect should explain the lack of transfer for the coordination, the task context of catching, which is very different, because it is performed in front of a screen, which hides the thrower posture, whereas the tennis area is opened. The proposed factors, to explain the lack of transfer of the coordination, suggests the increase of the coordination should depend on the determination of cognitive factors. Analysis of how reflective children are efficient should allow determining the cognitive processes of motor skill.

However, we noticed the more advanced group concerned only the reflective and the fast-accurate boys. As our results show, the best performers to the MFFT are the highest scorer and shaped the more mature motor patterns. As the reflective advanced children are more efficient, we verified whether or not the learning effect was due to the competence effect of this cognitive style. The two groups of reflective and fast-accurate children practicing tennis are more efficient than the two novice groups. This selection of the reflected children suggested that the more efficient children on their initiation improve better than the less efficient. This confirms a finding of Dusenberry (1952) who already observed that during learning of a throwing skill, the better children at the beginning of the experience, improved more during learning sessions than the lesser. The relative selection of reflective-impulsive style confirms its role as a competence factor that questioned the reflection and the impulsivity concept as a personality trait. The studies on the reflective-impulsive style evolved to the analysis of the construct of impulsivity by itself.

The impulsivity concept was dependent on tasks to execute or tests that the MFFT defined as the ability to inhibit the first response to solve a problem (Kagan et al., 1964). The impulsivity is also appraisal of the ability to wait for a desired object or to delay the response (Mischel and Patterson, 1978), the resistance to act (Paulsen and Johnson, 1980). The impulsivity implies a strong factor relate to inhibition and cannot be defined as an unidimensional concept (Bentler and McClain, 1976; Paulsen and Johnson, 1980). Olson (1989) searched for a consistent construct among various components of impulsivity in the self-control, which is a mode inhibiting the impulsive responses.

The inhibition renewed the behavioral studies based on numerous theories (Dempster, 1995). It includes in the frame of the criticism of the Piagetian model and Houdé et al. (2000) argues that it is a basic process of development and learning. So, the inhibition is a mechanism of cognitive suppression by keeping the non relevant information on working memory (Harnishfeger, 1995). However, like impulsivity, it is not an unidimentional construct and Dempster (1995) suggested three types of inhibition, a motor, a perceptive and a linguistic one. The motion study (Maccoby, Dowley, Hagen, and Degerman, 1965) is limited to the ability to inhibit the speed of movement on three tasks of displacement. After the execution of a motion without constraint of drawing a line on a paper, walking on a line on the ground and tracking a toy on a rail, the child has to do the same as slow as he can (Maccoby, Dowley, Hagen, and Degerman, 1965). Costantini, Corsini, and Davis (1973) used these tasks and found that the impulsive children had difficulties to inhibit their attitude, but the inhibitory control improved with age (Bucky, Banta, and Gross, 1972). Studies on inhibition are often related to motor impulsivity (Harrison and Nadelman, 1972; Visser, Das-Smaal, and Kwakman, 1996). As the reflection-impulsivity mode of problem solving affects the interceptive tasks, inhibition as a cognitive process for performing a gross motor skill, we tested inhibition on an interceptive task.

The assumption verified throughout the study of a forehand hit of a tennis ball of 145 six-to ten-year-old children by using the retroactive interference paradigm (Rosey and Keller, 2004). After performing a forehand drive, which requires the body to rotate towards the ball (Table 2 and Figure 2b) and the interference established by the return of a ball flying frontally and directly results in disturbance of the previous one. After the interference task, children still performed the first task of forehands and we observed that the level of the motor patterns decreased. These results show six- to ten-year-old children do not have enough developed inhibitory processes to suppress the effects of an unelaborated motor pattern (frontal motion). It means that the activation – inhibition process contributes to generate coordination. Moreover, the interference effect affects the preparatory step, when the position of the body in the space adjusted according to the position of the ball, but does not affect the hitting stance. We suggest that the coordination level and the first stage of the hitting ball should involve the perception of space and should be affected by cognitive processes and individual variability.

The variability is a stability index of the sensorimotor system (Newell and Corcos, 1993) and we demonstrated that it changes according to the periods of the task of hitting a tennis ball. At the contact of the ball its decrease reveals the perception-action coupling (Savelsbergh and Bootsma, 1994). Coordination defined and restrained to the visuomotor coordination as a function of the temporal invariance, implied biological mechanisms (Mc Leod, Mc Laughlin, and Nimmo-Smith, 1985) but does not indicate the whole motor pattern. All the children have the same temporal invariance, but they have various scores and motor patterns. Numerous types of motor patterns do not correspond to the single event of the emergence of the coordination between hand movement and ball flight (even when the ball is not touched).

A current assumption, influenced by dynamical approach, is to conceive coordination as only an emergent process, which does not imply a cognitive process. However, the emergence of coordination does not only involve the mastering of degrees of freedom, as exposed by dynamical theories concerning Bernstein's work, which involved nevertheless a higher control. In fact, in the same issue, Bernstein (1957/1986, p.355) postulated that movement regulated by feed back in a permanent cycle of perception and action corrected by a comparator. Ecological (Gibsonian) and activity (Bernsteinian) approaches are limited and reintroduced psychological concepts. Newell (1986) reintroduced the account of the task in the model as a third constraint, this one acting like an organism. However, the task also implied the environment and the goal of the individual variability with experience and cognition. Although, task constraints evolved specific constraints versus ambient conditions of environmental constraints, the task highlights mainly the goal of action. Finally, the task reveals the human dimension of intentionality. In one of the prime studies of Kelso, Scholz and Schöner (1986) the change of rhythm of the wrist or finger movements was not caused by environmental and organism constraints that remained the same, only from the goal to change the frequency.

Paradoxically, the ecological approach whose purpose was to have a global view as the Gestalttheorie (Gibson, 1986) affects a reductionism appraisal of a macroscopic and mathematical measure of the temporal invariance. The end point measure is a methodological bias and in the case of the interceptive object the window of the contact is so tight that it compelled the temporal invariance. If the subject is not in this period, he cannot touch a ball or an object. However the organism shows its ability to achieve this complex function. All of children have temporal invariance, but their results have different results and motor pattern levels. Perception-action coupling is not sufficient to reflect the whole coordination. The motor invariance reveals as the physical working of the coordination between organism and environment, but only limited to the contact phase. The overall motor pattern indicates more functional settings for cognitive processes with respect to the neuromotor system.

REFERENCES

Adams, J. A. (1987). Historical review and appraisal of research on the learning, retention, and transfer of human motor skills. *Psychological Bulletin, 101*, 41-74.

Ault, R. L., Mitchell, C., and Hartmann, D. P. (1976). Some methodological problems in reflection-impulsivity research. *Child Development, 47*, 227-231.

Ayres, A. J. (1975). Sensorimotor foundations of academic ability. In W. M. Cruickshank and D. P. Hallahan (Eds.), *Perceptual and learning disabilities in children* (Vol. 2). New York: Syracuse University Press.

Bardy, B. G., and Laurent, M. (1998). How is body orientation controlled during somersaulting? *Journal of Experimental Psychology: Human Perception and Performance, 24*(3), 963-977.

Barratt, E. S. (1967). Perceptual-motor performance related to impulsiveness and anxiety. *Perceptual and Motor Skills, 25*, 485-492.

Belka, D. E., and Williams, H. G. (1979). Predictions of later cognitive behavior from early school perceptual-motor, perceptual, and cognitive performances. *Perceptual and Motor Skills, 49*, 131-141.

Bentler, P. M., and McClain, J. (1976). A multitrait-multimethod analysis of reflection-impulsivity. *Child Development, 47*, 218-226.

Bernstein, N. (1986). Some emergent problems of the regulation of motor acts. In H. T. A. Whiting (Ed.), *Human motor actions (Bernstein reassessed): Vol. 17. Advances in psychology* (pp. 343-371). Amsterdam: New-Holland. Published in journal, *Questions of Psychology* (1957), 6.

Bernstein, N. A. (1996). *On dexterity and its development*, translated from the Russian by M. L., Latash. In M. L., Latash and M. T. Turvey, (Eds.), Dexterity and its Development. Hahwah, NJ: LEA (Original work published 1953).

Block, J., Block, J. H., and Harrington, D. M. (1974). Some misgivings about the Matching Familiar Figures Test as a measure of Reflection-Impulsivity. *Developmental Psychology, 10*(5), 611-632.

Bootsma, R. J., Houbiers, M. H. J., Whiting, H. T. A., and Wierengen, van P. C. W. (1991) Acquiring and attacking forehand drive: the effects of static and dynamic environmental conditions. *Research Quarterly for Exercise and Sport, 62*(3), 276-284.

Brown, H. J., Singer, R. N., Cauraugh, J. H., and Lucariello, G. (1985). Cognitive style and learner strategy interaction in the performance of primary and related Maze tasks. *Research Quarterly, 56*(1), 10-14.

Bruner, J. S. (1970). The growth and structure of skill. In K. Connolly, *Mechanisms of motor skill development* (pp. 63-94). London: Academic Press.

Bruner, J. S., and Koslowski, B. (1972). Visually preadapted constituents of manipulatory action. *Perception, 1*, 3-14.

Bucky, S. F., Banta, T. J., and Gross, R. B. (1972). Development of motor impulse control and reflectivity. *Perceptual and Motor Skills, 34*, 813-814.

Burton, A. W., Greer, N. L., and Wiese, D. M. (1992). Changes in overhand throwing patterns as a function of ball size. *Pediatric Exercise Science, 4*(1), 50-67.

Bush, E. S., and Dweck, C. S. (1975). Reflexions on conceptual tempo: relationship between cognitive style and performance as a function of task characteristics. *Developmental Psychology, 11*, 567-574.

Chi, M. T. H., and Ceci, S. J. (1987). Content knowledge: its role, representation, and restructuring in memory development. *Advances in Child Developmental and Behavior, 20*, 91-142.

Clark, J. E., Phillips, S. J., and Petersen, R. (1989). Developmental stability in jumping. *Developmental Psychology, 5*(6), 929-935.

Connolly, K. (1970). Skill development: problems and plans. In K. Connolly (Ed.), *Mechanisms of motor skill development* (pp. 3-21). London: Academic Press.

Costantini, A. F., Corsini, D. A., and Davis, J. E. (1973). Conceptual tempo, inhibition of movement, and acceleration of movement in 4-, 7-, and 9-yr.-old children. *Perceptual and Motor Skills, 37*, 779-784.

Dempster, F. N. (1995). Interference and inhibition in cognition. An historical perspective. In F. N. Dempster and C. J. Brainerd (Eds.), *Interference and inhibition in cognition* (pp. 3-26). San Diego, CA: Academic Press.

DeVard Brown, S., and Lee, A. M. (1988). The interaction of conceptual tempo and modeling on the motor performance of 10- and 11-year-old children. In J. E. Clark and J. H. Humphrey (Eds.), *Advances in motor development research 2* (pp. 103-114). New York: A.M.S. Press.

Dickman, S. J., and Meyer, D. E. (1988) Impulsivity and speed-accuracy tradeoffs in information processing. *Journal of Personality and Social Psychology, 54*(2), 274-290.

Dupré, E., and Tarrius, J. (1911). Puérilisme mental chez une maniaque. Rapports du puérilisme avec le délire d'imagination. Paris : Delarue.

Dusenberry, L. (1952). A study of the effects of training in ball throwing by children ages 3 to 7. *Research Quarterly, 23*, 9-14.

Fantz, R. L. (1961). The origin of form perception. *Scientific American, 204*, 66-72.

French, K. E. and Thomas, J. R. (1987). The Relation of knowledge development to children's basket-ball performance. *Journal of Sport Psychology, 9*, 15-32.

Gallahue, D. L. (1982). *Understanding motor development in children.* New York: Wiley and Sons.

Gesell, A. (1929). Maturation and infant behavior pattern. *Psychological Review, 36*, 307-319.

Gibson, E. J. (1988). Exploratory behavior in the development of perceiving, acting, and the acquiring of knowledge. *Annual Reviews of Psychology, 39*, 1-41.

Gibson, J. J. (1986). *The ecological approach to visual perception.* Hillsdale, NJ: Erlbaum.

Gjerde, F. P., Block, J., and Block, J. H. (1985). Longitudinal consistency of Matching Familiar Figures Test from early childhood to preadolescence. *Developmental Psychology, 21*(2), 262-271.

Halverson, L. E., and Williams, K. (1985). Developmental sequences for hopping over distance: a prelongitudinal screening. *Research Quarterly for Exercise and Sport, 56*, 37-44.

Harnishfeger, K. K. (1995). The development of cognitive inhibition: theories, definitions, and research evidence. In F. N. Dempster and C. J. Brainerd (Eds.), *Interference and inhibition in cognition* (pp. 175-204). San Diego, CA: Academic Press.

Harrison, A. and Nadelman, L. (1972). Conceptual tempo and inhibition of movement in black preschool children. *Child Development, 43*, 657-668.

Harrow, A. (1972). A taxonomy of the psychomotor domain. New York: McKay Company.

Hay, L. (1978). Accuracy of children on an open-loop pointing task. *Perceptual and Motor Skills, 47*, 1079-1082.

Haywood, K. M. (1986) *Life span motor development.* Champaign, IL: Human Kinetics.

Hellebrandt, F. A., Rarick, G. L., Glassow, R., and Carns, M. L. (1961). Physiological analysis of basic motor skills. *American Journal of Physical Medicine, 40*, 14-25.

Houdé, O. (1999). Executive performance/competence, and inhibition in cognitive development. Object, number, categorization and reasoning. *Developmental Science, 2*, 273-275.

Houdé, O., Zago, L., Mellet, E., Moutier, S., Pineau, A., Mazoyer, B., and Tzourio-Mazoyer, N. (2000). Shifting from the perceptual brain to the logical brain: the neural impact of cognitive inhibition training. *Journal of cognitive Neuroscience, 12*(5), 721-728.

Ingen Schenau, G., van Soest, A. J., Gabreëls, F. J. M., and Horstink, M. W. I. M. (1995). The control of multi-joint movements relies on detailed internal representations. *Human Movement Science, 14*, 511-538.

Ismail, A. H., Kane, J., and Kirkendall, D. R. (1969). Relationships among intellectual and non intellectual variables. *The Research Quarterly, 40*(1), 83-92.

Jacklin, S. M. (1987). Gross motor coincidence timing by children with learning difficulties and children matched on mean chronological and mental age. *Research Quarterly for Exercise and Sport, 58*(1), 30-35.

Jensen, J. L., Phillips, S. J., and Clark, J. E. (1994). For young jumpers, differences are in the movement's control, not its coordination. *Research Quarterly for Exercise and Sport, 65*(3), 258-268.

Kagan, J., Rosman, B. L., Day, D., Albert, J., and Phillips, W. (1964) Information processing in the child: significance of analytic and reflective attitudes. *Psychological Monographs: General and applied, 78*(1, Whole No. 578), 1-37.

Kay, H. (1969). The development of motor skills from birth to adolescence. In E. A. Bilodeau (Ed.), *Principles of skills acquisition* (pp. 133-157). New York: Academic Press.

Keller, J. (1992). *L'activité physique et sportive et la motricité de l'enfant.* Paris: Vigot.

Keller, J., Bouillette, A., Mertz C., and Golomer, E. (revision). Pelvic and scapular girdles differentiation in whole body rotations in female expert dancers and untrained participants.

Keller, J., Fleurance, P. (1987). Adaptation fonctionnelle à l'espace déterminé par les trajectoires de balle chez l'enfant de 3 à 9 ans. In M. Laurent and P. Therme (Eds.). *Recherches en activités physiques et sportives 2* (pp. 111-122). Marseille: Centre de recherche en APS.

Keller, J., and Ripoll, H. (2001). Reflective–impulsive style and conceptual tempo in a gross motor task. *Perceptual and Motor Skills, 92*, 739-749.

Keller, J., and Ripoll, H. (2004). Stability of reflective-impulsive style in coincidence-anticipation motor tasks. *Learning and Individual Differences, 14*, 209-218.

Kelso, J. A. S., Holt, K. G., Rubin, P., and Kugler, P. N. (1981). Patterns of human interlimb coordination emerge from the properties of non-linear, limit cycle oscillatory processes: theory and data. *Journal of Motor Behavior, 13*(4), 226-261.

Kelso, J. A. S., Scholz, J. P., and Schöner, G. (1986). Nonequilibrium phase transitions in coordinated biological motion: critical fluctuations. *Physical Letters A, 118*(6), 279-284.

Keogh, J. F. (1977). The study of movement skill development. *Quest, 28,* 76-88.

Köhler, W. (1959). Gestalt psychology today. *American Psychologist, 14,* 727-734.

Kotchoubey, B. (1988). What do event-related brain potentials tell us about the organization of action? In J. S. Jordan (Ed.), *Advances in Psychology: No 126. Systems theories and a priori aspects of perception* (chapt.9, pp. 209-256). North Holland: Elsevier.

Krus, P. H., Bruininks, R. H., and Robertson, G. (1981). Structure of motor abilities in children. *Perceptual and Motor Skills, 3,* 119-129.

Kugler, P. N., Kelso, J. A. S., and Turvey, M. T. (1982). On the control and co-ordination of naturally developing systems. In J. A. S. Kelso and J. E. Clark (Eds.), *The development of movement control and co-ordination* (pp. 5-78). New York: Wiley.

Langendorfer, S. (1983). Developmental relationships between throwing and striking: a prelongitudinal test of motor stage theory. *Dissertation Abstracts International, 43A*(8), 2595A-2596A.

Langendorfer, S. (1988). Prelongitudinal screening of overarm striking development performed under two environmental conditions. In J. E. Clark and J. H. Humphrey, *Advances in motor development research 1* (pp. 17-47). New York: A.M.S. Press.

Latash, M. L., and Gutman, S. R. (1993). Variability of Fast Single-Joint Movements and the Equilibrium-Point Hypothesis. In K. M. Newell and D. M. Corcos (Eds.), *Variability and motor control* (pp. 157-182). Champaign, IL: Human Kinetics.

Lee, A., Landin, D., Greenockle, K. M., Hill, K., and Edwards, R. V. (1987). Role of reflection-impulsivity in time to learn a sequential movement task. *Perceptual and Motor Skills, 64,* 1144-1146.

Lee, D. N. (1976). A theory of visual control of braking based on information about time-to-collision. *Perception, 5,* 437-459.

Lee, D. N., and Aronson, E. (1974). Visual proprioceptive control of standing in human infants. *Perception and Psychophysics, 15*(3), 529-539.

Lee, D. N., Lishman, J. R., and Thomson, J. A. (1982). Regulation of gait in long jumping. *Journal of Experimental Psychology: Human Perception and Performance, 8*(3), 448-459.

Lee, D. N., and Reddish, P. E. (1981). Plummeting gannets: a paradigm of ecological optics. *Nature, 293,* 293-294.

Lee, D. N., Young, D. S., and Rewt, D. (1992). How do somersaulters land on their feet? *Journal of Experimental Psychology: Human Perception and Performance,* 18(4), 1195-1202.

Lee, T. D., Magill, R. A., and Weeks, D. J. (1985). Influence of practice schedule on testing schema. Theory predictions in adults. *Journal of Motor Behavior, 17*(3), 283-299.

Maccoby, E. E., Dowley, E. M., Hagen, J. W., and Degerman, E. (1965). Activity level and intellectual functioning in normal preschool children. *Child Development, 36,* 761-770.

McDonald, P. V., Emmerik, R. E. A. van, and Newell, K. M. (1989). The effects of practice on limb kinematics in a throwing task. *Journal of Motor Behavior, 21*(3), 245-264.

McLeod, P., Mc Laughlin, C., and Nimmo-Smith, I. (1985). Information encapsulation and automaticity: evidence from the visual control of finally timed actions. In M. I. Posner and O. S. M. Marin (Eds.), *Attention and performance: Vol. XI* (pp.391-406). NJ, Hillsdale: Erlbaum.

McGraw, M. B. (1943). *The neuromuscular maturation of the human infant.* NY: Columbia Univ. Press.

McPherson, S. L., and Thomas, J. R. (1989). Relation of knowledge and performance in boys' tennis: age and expertise. *Journal of Experimental Child Psychology, 48,* 190-211.

Mischel, W., Shoda, Y., and Rodriguez, M. L. (1989). Delay of gratification in children. *Science, 244,* 933-938.

Mitchell, C., and Ault, R. L. (1979). Reflection-impulsivity and the evaluation process. *Child Development, 50,* 1043-1049.

Newell, K. M. (1986). Constraints on the development of coordination. In M. G. Wade and H. T. A. Whiting (Eds.), *Motor development in children: Aspects of coordination and control* (pp. 341-360). Dordrecht: Martinus Nijhoff.

Newell, K. M., and Corcos, D. M. (1993). Issues in variability and motor control. In K. M. Newell and D. M. Corcos (Eds.), *Variability and motor control* (pp. 1-12). Champaign, IL: Human Kinetics.

Newell, K. M., Kugler, P. N., van Emmerik, R. E. A., and Mc Donald, M. V. (1989). Search strategies and the acquisition of coordination. In S. A. Wallace (Ed.), *Advances in Psychology: No 61. Perspectives on the coordination of movement* (pp. 85-122). North Holland: Elsevier.

Nicholls, J. G. (1984). Achievement motivation: conceptions of ability, subjective experience, task choice, and performance. *Psychological Review, 91*(3), 328-346.

Olson, S. L. (1989). Assessment of impulsivity in preschoolers: cross-measure convergences, longitudinal stability, and relevance to social competence. *Journal of Clinical Child Psychology, 18*(2), 176-183.

Ozeretsky, N. (1936). Échelle métrique du développement de la motricité chez l'enfant et chez l'adolescent. *Revue belge de pédagogie, XXXIème année*(3), 63-75.

Pachella, R. G., and Pew, R. W. (1968). Speed-accuracy tradeoff in reaction time: effect of discrete criterion times. *Journal of Experimental Psychology, 76,* 19-24.

Passler, M. A., Isaac, W., and Hynd, G.W. (1985). Neuropsychological development of behavior attributed to frontal lobe functioning in children. *Developmental Neuropsychology, 4*(1), 349-370.

Pérez, B. (1878). *Les trois premières années de l'enfant* [The three first years of child]. Paris : Félix Alcan.

Piaget, J. (1977). *La naissance de l'intelligence chez l'enfant.* Neuchâtel: Delachaux et Niestlé. (9ème éd., original work published 1936).

Piek, J. P., Gasson, N., Barrett, N., and Case, I. (2002). Limb and gender differences in the development of coordination in early infancy. *Human Movement Science, 21,* 621-639.

Preyer, W. (1882). *Die Seele des Kindes* [The feeling of children]. Leipzig: Verlag.

Rarick, G. L. (1980). Cognitive-motor relationships in the growing years. *Research Quarterly for Exercise and Sport, 51*(1), 174-192.

Rarick, G. L. (1982). Descriptive research and process-oriented explanations of the motor development of children. In J. A. S. Kelso and J. E. Clark (Eds.), *The development of movement control and co-ordination* (pp. 275-291). New York: Wiley.

Reuchlin, M. (1990). *Les différences individuelles dans le développement conatif de l'enfant.* Paris: PUF, Psychologie d'aujourd'hui.

Ripoll, H., Keller, J., and Olivier, I. (1994). Le développement du comportement moteur de l'enfant: l'exemple des saisies et des interceptions de balle. *Enfance, L'enfant et le sport*, N° Spécial, 265-284.

Roberton, M.A. (1977) Stability of stage categorization across trials: Implications for the stage theory of overarm throw development. *Journal of Human Movement Studies*, 3, 49-59.

Roberton, M. A. (1978). Longitudinal evidence for developmental stages in the forceful overarm throw. *Journal of Human Movement Studies, 4*(2), 167-175.

Roberton, M. A. (1982). Describing "stage" within and across motor tasks. In J. A. S. Kelso, and J. E. Clark (Eds.), *The development of movement control and co-ordination* (pp. 293-307). New-York: Wiley.

Roberton, M. A. (1988). Developmental level as a function of the immediate environment. In J. E. Clark and J. H. Humphrey (Eds.), *Advances in Motor Development Research 1* (pp. 1-15). New-York: A.M.S. Press.

Roberton, M. A., and Halverson, L. E. (1984). *Developing children: their changing movement.* Philadelphia: Lea and Febiger.

Roberton, M. A., and Halverson, L. E. (1988). The development of locomotor coordination: longitudinal change and invariance. *Journal of Motor Behavior, 20*, 197-241.

Roberton, M. A., Halverson, L. E., Langendorfer, S., and Williams, K. (1979). Longitudinal changes in children's overam throw ball velocities. *Research Quarterly, 50*(2), 256-264.

Roberton, M. A., and Langendorfer, S. (1980). Testing motor development sequences across 9-14 years. In C.H. Nadeau, R. Halliwel, M. Newell, and C. Roberts (Eds.), *Psychology of motor behavior and sport* (pp. 268-279). Champaign, IL: Human Kinetics.

Roberton, M. A., Williams, K., and Langendorfer, S. (1980). Pre-longitudinal screening of motor development sequences. *Research Quarterly for Exercise and Sport, 51*(4), 724-731.

Rosey, F., and Keller, J. (2004). Effect of an Interference Task on a Ball Hitting Skill in 6- to 10-Year-Old Children. *Perceptual and Motor Skills, 99*, 547-544.

Savelsbergh, G. J. P., and Bootsma, R. J. (1994). Perception-action coupling in hitting and catching. *International Journal of Sport Psychology, 25*, 331-343.

Seefeldt, V. (1980) Testing motor development sequences across 9-14 years. In C. H. Nadeau, R. Halliwel, M. Newell, and C. Roberts (Eds.), *Psychology of Motor Behavior and Sport* (pp. 314-323.). Champaign, IL: Human Kinetics.

Seiler, R. (2000). The intentional link between environment and action in the acquisition of skill. *International Journal of Sport Psychology, 31*(4), 496-514.

Semjen, A. (1994).Qu'y a-t-il de programmé dans les activités motrices ? Les avatars du programme moteur. *Science et Motricité*, (23), 48-57.

Shapiro, D. C., Zernicke, R. F., Gregor, R. J., and Diestel, I. D. (1981). Evidence for generalized motor programs using gait pattern analysis. *Journal of Motor Behavior, 13*, 33-47.

Shea, J. B., and Morgan, R. L. (1979). Contextual interference effects on the acquisition, retention, and transfer or a motor skill. *Journal of Experimental Psychology: Human Learning and Memory, 5*(2), 179-187.

Sherrington, C. (1961). *The integrative action of the nervous system* (2nd ed.). New Haven: Yale University Press. (Original published 1906).

Shirley, M. (1931). *The first two years: a study of twenty-five babies 1: postural and locomotor development*. Minneapolis: University of Minneapolis Press.

Siegler R. S. (1994) Cognitive variability: a key to understanding cognitive development. *Current Directions in Psychological Science, 3*(1), 1-5.

Singer, R. N., and Brunk, J. W. (1967). Relation of perceptual-motor ability and intellectual ability variables in elementary school children. *Perceptual and Motor Skills, 24*, 967-970.

Smith, J. D., and Kemler Nelson, D. G. (1988). Is the more impulsive child a more holistic processor? A reconsideration. *Child Development, 59*, 719-727.

Sporns, O., and Edelman, G. M. (1993). Solving Bernstein's problem: a proposal for the development of coordinated movement by selection. *Child Development, 64*, 960-981.

Sugden, D. A. (1980). Movement speed in children. *Journal of Motor Behavior, 12*(2), 125-132.

Sugden, D. A., and Connell, R. A. (1979). Information processing in children's motor skills. *Physical Education Review, 2*(2), 123-140.

Swinnen, S., Vandenberg, J., and Van Assche, E. (1986). Role of cognitive style constructs, field dependence-independence and reflection-impulsivity in skill acquisition. *Journal of Sport Psychology, 8*, 51-69.

Temprado, J.-J., Della-Grasta, M., Farell, M., and Laurent, M. (1997). A novice-expert comparison of (intra-limb) coordination subserving the volley-ball serve. *Human Movement Sciences, 16*, 653-676.

Thelen, E. (1986). Development of coordinated movement: implications for early human development. In M. G. Wade and H. T. A. Whiting (Eds.), *Motor development in children: Aspects of coordination and control* (pp. 107-124). Dordrecht: Martinus Nijhoff.

Thelen, E. (1995). Motor development. *American Psychologist, 50*(2), 79-95.

Thelen, E., and Fisher, D. M. (1982). Newborn stepping: an explanation for a "disappearing" reflex. *Developmental Psychology, 18*(5), 760-775.

Thom, R. (1989). *Théorie des systèmes et théorie des catastrophes. René Thom expliqué par lui-même*. PISTES.

Thomas, J. R., and Chissom, B. S. (1972). Relationships as assessed by canonical correlation between perceptual-motor and intellectual abilities for pre-school and early elementary age children. *Journal of Motor Behavior, 4*(1), 23-29.

Tipper, S. P. (1985). The negative priming effect: inhibitory priming by ignored objects. *Quarterly Journal of Experimental Psychology, 37A*, 571-590.

Tran-Thong (1969). *La pensée pédagogique d'Henri Wallon*. Paris: P.U.F.

Treisman, A. M. (1992). Perceiving and re-perceiving objects. *American Psychologist, 47*, 862-875.

Turvey, M. T., and Fitzpatrick, P. (1993). Commentary: Development of perception-action system and general principles of pattern formation. *Child Development, 64*, 1175-1190.

Vereijken, B., van Emmerik, R. E. A., Whiting, H. T. A., and Newell, K. M. (1992). Free(z)ing degrees of freedom in skill acquisition. *Journal of Motor Behavior, 24*(1), 133-142.

Victor, J. B., Halverson, C. F., and Montague, R. B. (1985). Relations between reflexion-impulsivity and behavioral impulsivity in preschool children. *Developmental Psychology*, *21*(1), 141-148.

Visser M., Das-Smaal, E., and Kwakman, H. (1996) Impulsivity and negative priming: evidence for dished cognitive inhibition in impulsive children. *British Journal of Psychology*, 97, 131-140.

Wallon, H. (1925). *L'enfant turbulent*. Paris: Alban, Ière et IIème partie.

Whitall, J. (1989). A developmental study of the interlimb coordination in running and galloping. *Journal of Motor Behavior*, *21*, 409-428.

Whitall, J. (1991). The developmental effects of concurrent cognitive and locomotor skills: time-sharing from a dynamical perspective. *Journal of Experimental Child Psychology*, *51*, 245-266.

Whitall, J. (1995). The evolution of research on motor development: new approaches bringing new insights. *Exercise and Sport Science Review*, *23*, 243-273.

Wickstrom, R. L. (1983). *Fundamental motor patterns* (3rd ed.). Philadelphia: Lea and Febiger.

Wild, M. (1938). The behavior patterns of throwing and some observations concerning its course of development in children. *Research Quarterly*, *9*, 20-24.

Williams, J. G. (1992). Catching action: visuomotor adaptations in children. *Perceptual and Motor Skills*, *75*(1), 211-219.

Wohlwill, J. (1973). *The study of behavioural development*. New York: Academic Press.

Yando, R., and Kagan, J. (1970). The effect of task complexity on reflection-impulsivity. *Cognitive Psychology*, *1*, 192-200.

Zelniker, T., Cochavi, D., and Yered, J. (1974). The relationship between speed of performance and conceptual style: the effect of imposed modification of response latency. *Child Development*, *45*, 779-784.

Zelniker, T., and Jeffrey, W. (1976). Reflective and impulsive children: strategies of information processing underlying differences in problem solving. *Monographs of the Society for Research in Child Development, 41*, No. 5 (Serial No. 168) 1-59.

Zelniker, T., and Oppenheimer, L. (1973). Modification of information processing of impulsive children. *Child Development*, *44*, 445-450.

INDEX

D

E

F

follow-up, 143
food, 12, 113, 124, 127, 132
forebrain, 15, 18, 19, 33
foreign language, ix, 82, 83, 85, 87, 92, 94, 95, 96, 98
forensic settings, 107
framework, 101, 138
freedom, x, 66, 140, 145, 146, 149, 162, 169
frequency, 110, 162
friends, 116
frontal lobe, 78, 167
frustration, 87
fulfillment, 93
functional, 5, 24, 31, 36, 77, 85, 94, 96, 141, 163
functional imaging, 77
functioning, vii, 22, 41, 47, 166, 167
funds, 23

G

gait, 145, 166, 168
gender, viii, 48, 81, 82, 84, 93, 98, 125, 167
gender differences, 84, 93, 167
gene, 2, 5, 8, 20, 29, 32, 34, 86, 130, 132
gene expression, 2, 20, 29
generalization, 44, 61, 114, 130
generation(s), viii, 42, 47, 56, 61, 69, 84, 96, 132
genes, 8, 20, 33
Gestalt psychology, 166
Gestalt theory, 145
gland, vii, 1, 3, 6
glial cells, 21
glioma, 28
glutamate, 35
goal setting, 47, 57
goals, 42, 45, 47, 89, 103, 104, 107, 110, 136
grades, 42
gradings, 13, 45, 47, 70, 83, 87, 100, 109, 113, 126, 147, 148
gravity, 142
group activities, 57
groups, vii, ix, x, 42, 43, 48, 50, 51, 53, 54, 55, 56, 60, 72, 75, 99, 111, 112, 114, 115, 137, 139, 151, 158, 161
growth, vii, 1, 3, 5, 8, 29, 55, 93, 163
growth factor, vii, 1, 8
guanine, 6, 25
gustatory, 106, 114, 115

H

habituation, 2, 24

handedness, viii, 81, 82, 84, 85, 90, 91, 93, 96, 97, 107, 141
hands, 78, 87, 132, 140, 149
health, 68, 80, 127, 130
heart failure, 4, 29, 31
heart rate, 4, 15
hemisphere, 78, 84, 85, 97
heterogenous, 85
high school, vii, viii, 42, 58, 63, 64, 118, 121, 137
higher education, 82, 85, 87, 88, 89, 93, 94
hippocampus, vii, 1, 2, 6, 7, 10, 11, 14, 15, 18, 19, 21, 24, 25, 28, 30, 31, 32, 33, 37
history, 16, 68, 70, 71, 100, 102
holistic, 54, 84, 101, 145, 160, 169
homeostasis, 27
homework, 109
hormones, vii, 1, 3, 96
hospitalization, 69
human behavior, 146
human brain, 85, 97
human development, 169
hypnosis, ix, 99, 105, 112, 117
hypnotherapy, 117
hypotensive, 34
hypothalamus, 6, 12, 14
hypothesis, 12, 19, 20, 24, 35, 49, 68, 70, 76, 82, 83, 91, 97, 98, 148, 150, 166

I

ideas, 45, 47, 49, 56, 59, 61, 62, 86, 88, 89, 92, 100, 102, 103, 114, 136, 146
identification, 26, 34, 35, 52
identity, 5, 70
ideology, 59
idiosyncratic, 111
imagination, 92
imbalances, 8
immigration, 59
immunoreactivity, 14, 33
implementation, 44
implicit and explicit memory, 97
impulsiveness, 163
impulsivity, 147, 148, 159, 161, 163, 164, 166, 167, 169, 170
in vitro, 15, 24, 26, 30
in vivo, 37
incentive, 110
independence, 101, 169
independent variable, 150
Indians, 130
individual differences, v, ix, 81, 82, 93, 94, 96, 97, 98, 141, 148, 150, 165

DATE DUE
